McJeffert 303
STANWYCK
Spring '82

(Rd.) purple, purple/red
red, red/brown

p320 —
Types of
Wine Glasses

WINE
AN INTRODUCTION

M. A. Amerine
and
V. L. Singleton

WINE

AN INTRODUCTION
Second Edition

University of California Press
Berkeley, Los Angeles, London

University of California Press
Berkeley and Los Angeles, California

University of California Press, Ltd.
London, England

Copyright © 1965, 1977 by
The Regents of the University of California
Second edition, completely revised 1976
ISBN 0-520-03187-3
Library of Congress Catalog Card Number: 75-46031
Printed in the United States of America

2 3 4 5 6 7 8 9 0

CONTENTS

LIST OF FIGURES

PREFACE
TO THE SECOND EDITION

Application of the scientific revolution to the grape and wine industry initiated by Louis Pasteur over 100 years ago continues at an accelerated pace. This is the basic reason a new edition is appropriate—to update the book. Changes in all aspects of wine's production and marketing have been relatively rapid. Furthermore, wine has become increasingly popular with an ever-wider segment of the population. Because of this increasing interest and knowledgeability among our readers, it is essential to be as currently factual and complete as possible.

From the viticultural point of view, there has been a worldwide expansion in grape production, much of it in finer varieties of grapes, especially those for table wines. The importance of climatic region, season, control of crop, and time of harvesting appears now to be of greater and greater significance to the composition and quality of the resulting wines. Appreciation of this significance is growing not only among viticulturists and enologists, but also among sellers and consumers of wine. Mechanical harvesting and associated changes in trellising, etc., have been introduced in many countries, with results that are not yet completely evaluated but appear to be the wave of the future.

From the enological point of view, the winery proper has been and is being truly revolutionized. New types of crushers, juice extractors, presses, fermentors, etc., are continually being introduced. In general, wineries are larger, with better temperature control, continued improvement in sanitation, sophisticated new equipment, and more detailed laboratory surveillance. Methods of clarification have changed, new types of wine have been developed, and more use is being made of careful sensory evaluation.

The standards of comparison for the world's wines are no longer the exclusive prerogative of a few European districts. Fine wines are, of course, still produced in Bordeaux, Burgundy, on the Rhine and Moselle, at Jerez de la Frontera, and on the Douro. But Madeira and Tokay have lost much of their former fame. The Rioja and Chianti districts have done relatively little to enhance their reputation. Meanwhile recognition and acceptance of the wines of Australia and South Africa, and particularly those of California and other U.S. areas, as truly high-quality products have greatly increased. A number of other countries have become conscious of possible export markets and the benefits of upgrading their wines, so that consumers today have the choice of a wider array of wines than ever before. For example, a recent tasting of locally available Cabernet Sauvignon wines included representatives from nine countries and five continents.

The first edition of this book was intended primarily for readers in the United States. This second edition continues to emphasize legal and statistical aspects of the U.S. market. However, the interrelationships of wine make "one world," and in this edition we have attempted to generalize more. The increased knowledgeability of the American wine drinker, as well as increased interest abroad in wines from "newer" but high-quality sources like the United States, have encouraged this generalization.

Davis, California   MAYNARD A. AMERINE
January 1976   VERNON L. SINGLETON

PREFACE
TO THE FIRST EDITION

Although there are many books on wine, each with particularly informative or pleasurable sections, none seem to be without deficiencies for the general reader. Those which dwell on the romantic aspects tend to entertain but not inform. Those which surround the subject with arbitrary admonitions and mysticism frighten and confuse. Those which discuss the technology of wine usually ignore the origins and uses of wine. Often one type of wine or one country is emphasized and others are ignored. Books on wine in English are often by Englishmen or expatriates, or are translations and reflect attitudes and descriptions which may not be pertinent or correct from an American viewpoint.

This book attempts to give a broad introduction to the whole subject of wine for Americans. It is intended to be factual where facts are available and give considered opinions where they are required. Sufficient detail is offered to explain the underlying principles and the nature of the world of wines. Since nearly 90 percent of the wine consumed in the United States is of American origin, a great majority of this from California, the production practices, commercial situation, and legal requirements in the United States market are emphasized. Key references and suggestions for further reading are given for those wishing verification, more detail, or different viewpoints. The authors wish to acknowledge that helpful suggestions and criticisms for various portions of the manuscript have been made by our colleagues. Our thanks are particularly offered to Professors William V. Cruess, Albert J. Winkler, and A. Dinsmoor Webb. We are also indebted to Miss Genevieve Rogers and Mr. Ernest Callenbach for editorial assistance.

The Wine Institute has kindly furnished many of the photographs presented here.

Davis, California   M. A. AMERINE
1965   V. L. SINGLETON

Good wine needs neither bush nor preface to make it welcome.
—SIR WALTER SCOTT

INTRODUCTION

There are many reasons and rewards for the study of wine. The grape has been said to be the only fruit that naturally preserves itself, and there is historical justification for the statement. At a time when our modern techniques of storing fresh food were undreamed of, and fresh vegetables and fruits were available only during the short local season, wine was indeed the gift of God. With only modest intervention by ancient man, the grape and its associated yeast produced wine. Here was a food with a flavor like the fresh fruit which could be stored and transported under the existing conditions. At least part of the time it survived in drinkable condition from season to season or occasionally for many seasons.

The fact that wine produced euphoria was not lost on ancient man, and it became not only a regular part of the diet but also a social beverage used for feasting, celebrating, and entertaining guests. The great variability possible in quality and type of wine naturally led to rating and selection: the best wine for auspicious occasions or esteemed guests, the poor or ordinary wine for everyday use. So wine early became an item of commerce, with appropriate quality judgments, records, and connoisseurship. As a result of all this, wine has deeply penetrated the social fabric and culture of times and countries from which we spring.

1

Wine still occupies a unique position among foods and beverages. In some areas wine is on the table in the poorest homes and is one of the least expensive comestibles. In other regions it may be served only on special occasions. Students of wines and wine lore, by hobby and avocation, abound. Those who make a profession of wine production and sale cannot escape the historical background of their product. Neither can the romanticist, connoisseur, and historian really know wine without a knowledge of the grape-growing and winemaking practices which result in the myriad kinds of wine.

Wine is not just another product, and its worthiness for study is further illustrated by the extent of literature available. When Thudichum and Dupré wrote their scientific treatise on wine in 1872, they stated that they had consulted 200 of the 600 extant works on enology. (Enology, the study or science of wine and winemaking, is derived from *oinos,* the Greek word for wine.) It is estimated that more than 20,000 books and pamphlets, in various languages, dealing specifically with wine or wine grapes have been published in this century. A limited sampling is listed at the end of this book, under Supplementary Reading. An untold number of additional publications deal with wine as an important aspect of more general topics. Knowledge of wine contributes to an understanding of Greek mythology, Egyptian and Oriental art, excavations at Pompeii, early agriculture and its spread, aesthetics and sensory appreciation, commerce, treaties, laws from Hammurabi to Prohibition to vehicle codes, and social interaction from ancient symposia through Shakespeare and Pepys to a modern diplomatic dinner. In spite of great interest in beer, cheeses, tea, perfumes, spices, etc., wine is unique in the length, diversity, and intensity of its fascination, and the publications thereon.

Social ills are also associated with alcoholic beverages, and understanding and control of these ills require study of the nature and effects of such beverages in general, and wines in particular, whether we seek to avoid such problems and still enjoy wine individually, or wish to control the social consequences of overindulgence by others.

Opinions and attitudes on wine may be frivolous or passionate, doting or deploring, but are seldom insipid. For example:

> There is evil in every berry of grape.
> —THE KORAN

> If penicillin can cure those who are ill,
> Spanish sherry can bring the dead back to life.
> —SIR ALEXANDER FLEMING (discoverer of penicillin)

> 'Tis pity wine should be so deleterious,
> For tea and coffee leave us much more serious.
> —LORD BYRON

> Come, come, good wine is a good familiar creature if it be well used; exclaim no more against it.
> —SHAKESPEARE

> Wine is the drink of the gods, milk the drink of babes, tea the drink of women, and water the drink of beasts.
> —JOHN STUART BLACKIE

> I wonder what the vintners buy
> One half so precious as the stuff they sell.
> —OMAR KHAYYAM

> Wine makes a man more pleased with himself;
> I do not say it makes him more pleasing to others.
> —SAMUEL JOHNSON

A subject about which there is so much history, romance, and dispute is surely fascinating and cannot be treated in a coldly technical manner—but this is intended to be a factual discussion. It is hoped that you will find it useful whether you are seeking to learn how wine is made and what types come from which countries, or just want to enjoy wine more by knowing more about it.

To define wine simply is not easy, for the definition would vary according to the context and the attitudes of the definer and his audience. Wine is even defined differently in the detailed laws of various countries, and in popular usage wine means different things to different people. In Chinese the unqualified word for wine also means "alcoholic beverage"; so beer becomes a "wine" and may be translated "appetite wine." Perhaps this accounts for the fact that we speak of "rice wine," a literal translation from Chinese. Even within the group of beverages which certainly are wine, as we use the term, there are many products with varied origins and uses. For our purposes, the most generally satisfying definition seems to be that wine is a beverage resulting from the fermentation by yeasts of the juice of the grape, with appropriate (and legal) processing and additions. Before devotees of blackberry wine and such take us to task, it should be pointed out that for both legal and commercial reasons a product labeled simply "wine" would be considered misleading if it obviously tasted like blackberries. Qualifying terms are necessary, such as "blackberry wine," "apricot wine," and so on.

Wine—that is, fermented grape juice—has had a long and varied history; and the many variations on this theme may bewilder the novice. An outline of the major types of wine may clear up the confusion. Wines can be assigned to one or the other of two major groups, with rare exceptions. The first group in point of historical origin includes the "natural wines" which result from a more or less complete fermentation. The fermentable sugar has been consumed, so further fermentation by yeasts is prevented by lack of "food," and spoilage organisms such as the vinegar bacterium do not develop if the wine is kept from contact with the air. Owing to the natural limit of sugar present in ripe grapes, the alcohol content of such wines is normally about 12 percent. The major subclass of these wines is the still (i.e., without noticeable carbon dioxide) wine group. Further subdivision of this class depends upon color and residual sugar. Although all the fermentable sugar is consumed as completely as possible in many of these wines, and historically they were all "dry" (without noticeable sweetness), various artful and scientific procedures have produced wines of this class today which have moderate or high amounts of residual sugar.

As a class, the natural still wines are traditionally what are called "table wines," intended to be part of a meal. The other major subclass of natural wines is the opposite of still—these are the sparkling wines. They have undergone not one but two complete fermentations, and the carbon dioxide of the

ONE SYSTEM OF BROADLY CLASSIFYING WINES

A. "Natural" wines, 9 to 14 percent alcohol (nature and keeping qualities depend heavily on a "complete" yeast fermentation and protection from air)
  I. *Still wines* (no evident carbon dioxide)
     a. *Dry* (no noticeable sweetness) *table wines,* intended for use during meals
        1. White
        2. Rosé (pink)
        3. Red
        (Further subclasses are based primarily on grape variety or region of origin)
     b. *Slightly sweet table wines* ("mellow," "vino" types)
        1. White
        2. Rosé (pink)
        3. Red
     c. *Sweet table wines*
        1. White
        2. Rosé (pink)
     d. *Specialty types*
        1. Slightly carbonated types, red, rosé (pink), and white
        2. Flavored table wines, red, rosé (pink), and white
  II. *Sparkling wines* (appreciable carbon dioxide under pressure)
     a. White (champagne, sparkling muscat)
     b. Rosé (pink champagne)
     c. Red (sparkling burgundy, cold duck)
B. Dessert and appetizer wines, "generous" wines, 15 to 21 percent alcohol (nature and keeping qualities depend heavily on the addition of wine spirits)
  I. *Sweet wines*
     a. White (muscatel, white port, angelica)
     b. Pink (California tokay, tawny port)
     c. Red (port, black muscat)
  II. *Sherries* (white sweet or dry wines with oxidized flavors)
     a. Aged types
     b. Flor sherry types (secondary aerobic yeast fermentation)
     c. Baked types
  III. *Flavored, specialty wines* (usually white port base)
     a. Vermouth (pale dry, French; Italian, sweet types)
     b. Proprietary products
        1. Special natural wines
        2. Other "brand name" specialty wines

second has been retained as the "sparkle." For reasons that will become clear later (Chapter 9) they should not be called "carbonated," but the effect is superficially similar. The sparkling wines belong in the class of natural wines, since they are derived from table wines and have similar alcohol content. They may be served with meals, but are often served on other occasions as well.

The second major group includes the dessert and appetizer wines. As their name implies, they are usually served before or at the end of a meal but not during the main courses. These wines are of higher alcohol content. The nature and keeping qualities of these wines depend heavily on the addition of spirits distilled from wine. The consumer often presumes that this addition is intended merely to raise the alcohol content for his benefit, but this is not so. The amount of extra alcohol added to these wines is just about the minimum at which one can be certain that the wine will resist spoilage by further growth of yeasts or other organisms. In sweet wines, a major subclass of these wines, the addition of wine spirits serves to arrest the yeast fermentation with part of the sugar unfermented, stabilizing the wine in this condition. The alcohol level is too high to permit further yeast fermentation. Sherries, a second subclass, may be sweet or dry; sherries are characterized by flavors induced by various types and degrees of oxidation. The third major subclass is the flavored wines such as vermouths and trade-named specialty wines. The latter are ordinarily proprietary products, i.e., their owner or proprietor holds their formula secret and guards the name against infringement.

One might wonder why all the sparkling wines are in the natural class and most of the oxidized types and flavored wines are in the group fortified with wine spirits. There would seem to be no reason why carbonated port, or herb-flavored or oxidized table wine, could not be sold. Ignoring the fact that such products might not be palatable (and some have been marketed, inadvertently or otherwise), the difference lies in the manner of consumption. A natural wine, still or sparkling, is ordinarily consumed immediately after opening. Servings are usually fairly generous, and a few people dining together can easily consume a bottle without excessive alcohol intake.

Such wines store poorly in partly empty containers; if not entirely consumed in one meal, the remainder of a bottle is usually a disappointing remnant of its former self within hours, owing to aroma loss and other changes, especially if loss of "sparkle" is also involved. The fortified wines, however, owing partly to their alcohol content and partly to their richness in sugar and other flavors, are usually served in small portions and even several guests may not consume a whole bottle. They usually do keep fairly well after opening, and may still be very good after some time. But a carbonated port would be too rich for a few guests to consume the whole bottle after dinner, and the remainder of the wine would lose its identity. A vermouth-like wine or a sherry with a natural wine base might be too full-flavored for complete consumption of a bottle at a single sitting by a small dinner party. Moreover, a low alcohol content would allow spoilage organisms to grow, if a portion was left over.

The general classification of still and sparkling natural or table wines and of sweet, oxidized, or flavored dessert or fortified wines, modified to suit yourself as your acquaintance with wine increases, will enable you to categorize wines and, with a minimum of tasting, become credited with a broad, if not deep, knowledge of wine. It is surprising how many people confuse port with table wine, sherry with chablis, and so on. Even persons versed in the pleasant intricacies of one type of wine may be uninformed about others. They thus miss pleasures afforded the eclectic and denied to the parochial student of wine. More on this subject is presented in Chapter 6.

To place the basic categories of wines in perspective in relation to wine consumption, consider the year 1975, when 368 million gallons of wine and 15.4 million gallons of brandy were consumed in the United States. The per capita (all persons regardless of age) consumption was about 1.73 gallons of wine, compared to about 33 gallons of milk and 28 gallons of soft drinks. On the basis of population over age 21, wine consumption in the United States was 2.74 gallons per capita in 1975, compared to 3.2 gallons of distilled spirits, 34 gallons of beer, about 24 gallons of coffee, and 9 gallons of tea. Per capita annual consumption of wine is nearly 30 gallons in France and Italy and from 10 to 25 gallons in a number of other countries including Argentina, Austria, Chile, Greece, Hungary, Portugal, and Spain. If the total annual consumption of *alcohol* per adult is estimated, however, United States consumption approaches or exceeds that of other countries with five to ten times our wine usage. These figures emphasize that wine does not represent nearly so high a total intake nor a proportion of the alcohol consumed in the United States as it does in many other countries.

The wine consumed in the United States in 1975 consisted of about 214 million gallons of table wines, 67 million gallons of dessert wines (including sherry), 10 million gallons of vermouth, 57 million gallons of other flavored wines, and 20 million gallons of sparkling wines. For several years the trend of consumption in the United States has been strongly upward in table wines and low-alcohol flavored wines, and downward in dessert and other wines over 14-percent alcohol. Still table wines now represent about 70 percent and dessert and appetizer wines about one quarter of the total wine consumed; a decade ago the figures were almost reversed. Sparkling wines grew rapidly from under 4 percent of the total wine consumed in 1964 to over 8 percent in 1970, but dropped back to 5.5 percent by 1975. If we estimate an average *retail* cost of at least $2 per bottle or $10 per gallon of wine, current consumption represents about $3.7 billion spent by American consumers for wine. About $175 million in U.S. federal excise taxes were collected on wine and nearly $183 million on brandy in 1975. Many other countries also gain considerable revenue from direct or indirect taxes on wine and brandy.

Chapter 1

HISTORY OF THE GRAPE AND WINE INDUSTRY

In the eighth chapter of Genesis, Noah's Ark is said to have come to rest on Mount Ararat, which is in the Caucasus Mountains in Turkey. Later it is noted, in Genesis 9:20-21, "and Noah began to be a husbandman, and he planted a vineyard; and he drank of the wine and was drunken." Certain it is that a grape-growing Neolithic civilization developed first in a region which is now northern Iran, or possibly between the Black and Caspian seas. This is an area where the grape grows wild. It is quite possible that mead (honey wine) and beer are older alcoholic beverages than wine. Honey was available in the forests. Grains, from which beer is made, seem to have been cultivated at an earlier date than grapes. However, the cultivation of the grape is a very ancient industry, as is indicated by the remnants of grape seeds which have been found in villages dating from several thousand years B.C.

The wine industry certainly dates from at least 3000 B.C., probably in the area indicated above. Since yeasts are everywhere abundant, fermentation would be no problem. Some early housewife probably left crushed grapes in a jar and found, a few days later, that an alcoholic product had been formed. All these early wines must have been of very poor quality, just as the early beers were of poor quality. The wines

9

were probably drunk during or soon after the primary fermentation, before they "turned" to vinegar.

The antiquity of wine is indicated by the words which have been used for it. The Hittites, who were the dominant linguistic group in the Middle East in 1500 B.C., referred to wine as *uiian-* or as *uianas,* which in the Luwian language became *uin-*. The earliest Greek scripts speak of wine as *woinos,* but in the classical Greek the *w* was lost and the word became *oinos*. From this were derived the Latin and Etruscan *vinum* and later words such as *vino, vin, Wein,* and *wine*. Even the neighboring languages accepted the Hittite word: in Armenian it is *gini,* in Mingrelian *gvin-i,* and in Georgian *-gvino*. Even the Semitic languages used the word: *wayin* (later *yayin*) in Hebrew, *wayn* in Sabaean, Arabic, and Ethiopian.

Some of the best records of the early wine industry come from Egypt in the predynastic period. There is evidence of the production of red and white wines from the Delta area and in other areas to the south. Hieroglyphics reveal there was a small but rather well-developed grape industry, including arbors and pruning (Figure 1). They also had a form of wine press. However, wines were expensive and hence were used almost entirely by priests and royalty. Some medicinal use of wines is indicated. Beer was the usual beverage of workers and rulers.

In the "fertile crescent" area, where wine was especially common, it was taxed, and at a fairly early date both the common people and the rich drank wine. The problem of dilution of wine with water was already noted in the Code of Hammurabi, which dates from ca. 1792-1750 B.C. There is evidence that at this period the effect of temperature on wine was known, since many of the wines of Asia Minor and the Caucasus were stored in jars which had been sunk in the ground or in containers which were cut out of stone and plastered to prevent leakage. Such containers kept the wines at a cool and nearly constant temperature. They had evidently begun to learn the harmful effects of air on the wine, for the tops of the wine containers, later clay amphorae, were usually covered and often sealed with pitch or grease.

FIG. 1. Harvesting grapes and making wine in the Egyptian Eighteenth Dynasty (about 1500 B.C.). (Source: Bruckmann Photo.)

Even so, the wines of the pre-Hebrew and pre-Greek period must have been very poor indeed, and must have been drunk soon after their fermentation.

But as the Greek civilization began to develop, the wine industry reached a much higher degree of perfection. Homer's *Iliad* and *Odyssey* contain excellent descriptions of wines. The Greeks made wine one of their important articles of trade, and Greek wine containers have been found scattered throughout the Mediterranean, Egypt, and the Middle East. Wine was not only an important item of trade for the Greeks, but it was also a part of Greek religious ceremonies during the Homeric period. Wine was pictured as having been offered to comfort a weary man, as in the *Iliad,* when Hector returns to Troy and his mother Hecuba gives him wine. Most Greek doctors used wines medicinally. They may even have been used as aperitifs before meals, but more often wine was taken with meals, frequently diluted with water. Many of the Greek wines were blended with odorous materials, or grated goat's-milk cheese and white barley were added before consumption. This would not indicate high-quality wine, but does indicate that wine was an important contribution to the diet.

The practice of adding herbs or other materials suggests the intention of covering up undesirable odors associated with wine spoilage. And there can be no doubt that the wines contained alcohol. The cult of Dionysus (later Bacchus) indicates that a group devoted to wine and having wine-induced celebrations of an orgiastic character had developed in Greece, certainly no later than the seventh century B.C.

Archaeologists have shown that the Celtic leaders had acquired a taste for wine and imported Greek and Roman wines. Cups and flagons for drinking or serving wine indicate that wine reached Celtic Europe from the Mediterranean during the pre-Christian period. Wine was important to the Hebrews also. The Bible includes many reports, other than that of Noah, about grapes and wine. It is recorded that Moses sent spies into the Promised Land, and that one grape cluster was so heavy that it required two men to carry it back to the waiting Israelites. The good and bad effects of wine, including that on Noah himself, are reported, and there is considerable moralizing on both the good and bad effects of wine, particularly in Proverbs.

In the New Testament, wine is not only the beverage recommended for Timothy's stomach, but it became a part of the religious ceremonial of the Church. Two of the New Testament quotations deserve explanation. The first is that of the Feast of Cana, in John 2:3–10:

> And when they wanted wine, the mother of Jesus saith unto him, They have no wine.
>
> Jesus saith unto her, Woman, what have I to do with thee? mine hour is not yet come.
>
> His mother saith unto the servants, Whatsoever he saith unto you, do *it*.
>
> And there were set there six waterpots of stone, after the manner of the purifying of the Jews, containing two or three firkins apiece.
>
> Jesus saith unto them, Fill the waterpots with water. And they filled them up to the brim.
>
> And he saith unto them, Draw out now, and bear unto the governor of the feast. And they bare *it*.
>
> When the ruler of the feast had tasted the water that was made wine, and knew not whence it was: (but the servants which drew the water knew) the governor of the feast called the bridegroom,
>
> And saith unto him, Every man at the beginning doth set forth good wine; and when men have well drunk, then that which is worse: *but* thou hast kept the good wine until now.

This indicates that the wine which had been made from water was better than that which had preceded it. And the guests remarked that the host must be a very wealthy man to be able to serve a good wine after bad wine, which was not the usual procedure. Normally the host served the good wine first, and when the guests had become tipsy and less critical he served the bad wine. The implication is clear: there was very little good wine available, and the host gave his guests the good wine first and then pawned off on them whatever other wines could be found or afforded.

The other New Testament quotation is that of the parable of not putting new wine into old bottles, from Mark 2:22:

> And no man putteth new wine into old bottles; else the new wine doth burst the bottles, and the wine is spilled, and the bottles will be marred: but new wine must be put into new bottles.

This translation makes little sense unless we realize that instead of "bottles" the translators of the King James Bible should have written "goatskins." The explanation is that new wine, which is subject to fermentation from residual sugar, should not be placed in old goatskins, which are hard and will not stretch. Fermentation and the pressure of the carbon dioxide produced would then break the goatskin and the contents would be lost. New wine should be put into new goatskins. The new skins being pliable, the gas from the fermentation would stretch them and be less likely to cause them to burst. Actually, this has a symbolic significance; according to modern theologians, the parable is an admonition not to try to put the new religion in the forms of the old religion. Nevertheless, it indicates that in Hebrew times there was a recognition of the differences in quality of wine and the differences in characteristics of new and old wine, and that this knowledge was so widespread that it could be used to illustrate a theological idea to the common people.

Before the beginning of the Christian Era, grapes and wines had considerable significance for Middle Eastern and Mediterranean peoples. Fresh grapes had a high caloric value, being about 20 to 25 percent sugar—which is higher than that of most of our common fruits—and the caloric value of dried grapes was even higher, for they may contain 75 percent sugar.

Thus grapes constituted one of the few sources of sweet material and one of the few easily stored and transported food sources of high caloric value. Dried grapes were and still are very popular with nomadic peoples of the Middle East. They were used not only alone but in cooking, or were boiled as a source of a sweet syrup. The importance of such high-energy, easily transported foods in the diet of primitive peoples has not been adequately studied.

A number of favorable factors made wine important to ancient peoples. It was actually less likely to be contaminated than water, particularly in cities where public sanitation was difficult and water-borne diseases were common. The pleasant effects of wine were early noted, and seem to be an important basis for the use of wine as a beverage. Furthermore, the effects of wine were somewhat quicker and greater than those from beer, a beverage of lower alcohol content. This must have been a very important factor in the pre-Christian period, since life was not pleasant for either the rich or the poor. Winter was difficult, even in the southern regions, and the vicissitudes of life, with wars and slavery, made wine a welcome beverage, enabling people to forget their problems and ease their aches. This is, of course, basically an effect of alcohol.

Wines as well as beers were drunk soon after fermentation and were cloudy; consequently they were an important source of vitamins from the suspended yeast cells. Not until much later were methods for easy and early removal of suspended solids developed. Wines were valued for other reasons too. Homer, especially, seems to have been aware of the aesthetic pleasures of drinking old wines, but he is by no means unique. The many poetic connoisseurs in classical Greece had their favorites: Pramnian, Lesbian, Mendaean, Chian, Saprias, and so on. There was even a book in verse on drinking and eating: *The Deipnosophists*. The Greeks, moreover, had a wine-drinking game, *kottabos*.

We do not know whether the ceremonial and mystical use of wine originated from the effects of the alcohol it contained or from the fact that the red wines, at least, were associated with blood and therefore with life itself, or from the mystery of a beverage which produced no behavioral effects one day and marked behavioral effects a few days later (after fermentation). Certain it is, however, that the use of wine in ceremonials was prominent in all early religions and adapted itself naturally to the Christian religion.

The process of making wine was well established by the first century of the Christian Era. The Greeks made wine an article of commerce, and Greek colonies had spread the culture of the vine as far west as Spain and as far east as the shores of the Black Sea. The quality of much of the wines must have been rather poor because of the warm climate and the poor storage containers. Some aged wine of relatively high quality seems to have been available. In spite of the general lack of quality, wine was appreciated as an article of diet and as a part of the culture of peoples of the Mediterranean and the Middle East.

The Romans built upon Greek civilization, adapting from it varieties of grapes and winemaking procedures so that the long period of trial and error in the Middle East and Greece did not have to be repeated in Italy. Greek colonists settled in Italy in the eighth century B.C. They probably found indigenous vines, but doubtless brought some of their own vines and wines. However, the contributions of the Romans to the grape and wine industries are very great.

The first good classifications of grape varieties we owe to the Romans, especially to Pliny, who classified grapes as to color, time of ripening, diseases, soil preferences, and types of wines which might be produced. The Romans had a good idea of the best methods of cultivation of grape varieties. Columella, particularly, favored certain varieties over others. The Romans were rather skilled in pruning the vines and in improving the yield of grapes by fertilization. The pruning knife appears to be their invention; the edict of Numa Pompilius that no wine might be offered to the gods unless it was made from the grapes of pruned vines indicates an appreciation of vine production and wine quality. However, growing grape vines in trees was definitely a retrograde trend which was practiced during the Roman period—the vine cannot be properly pruned, it overcrops, and the fruit seldom ripens properly.

The Romans continued to use the amphora of the Greek period, but in the late Roman period the first wooden cooperage was introduced, possibly in Gaul or northern Italy. This was a very great advance for the wine industry because it permitted wines to be stored out of contact with air for longer periods of time. The art of cooperage was a real achievement, since a barrel is a rather complex engineering invention. It is necessary to have the wooden staves exactly coopered to fit together. They must be bent so that pressure is exerted equally at both ends of the staves. To get the heads to fit into the barrel and be leakproof is a rather difficult engineering problem which some early cooper solved. In their winemaking the Romans were not much better off than the Greeks, for the concept of the bacterial origin of wine spoilage and the methods of control lay nearly 2,000 years in the future. However, they had learned that by putting wine under warm conditions, usually in smoke-filled rooms, the undesirable changes could be slowed down. This heating of wine probably constitutes an early form of pasteurization.

Because the wines had a tendency to spoil, and were frequently acetic, a wide variety of treatments were developed in the Roman period. These included the addition of alkaline materials to reduce the acidity, and of foreign materials to cover up the acidity. The use of salt water to make the colors brighter, and possibly to dilute off-flavors, was also common. The Greek custom of adding spices and herbs to wines was also widespread in Rome. Whether the Greeks or Romans first added resin to wines is not known, but Allen (1932, 1961; see Supplementary Reading list at end of this book) does not believe it was in Greece. The use of gypsum seems to have originated in North Africa and spread to Italy and Spain. It helped to correct deficiencies in the natural acidity.

The blowing of glass became more common in the Roman period, and a few wines were placed in bottles and kept for various periods of time. Wine goblets were common.

Thus the literature of the Roman period in appreciation of wine is much greater and perhaps better than that of the Greek period. Many passages in Horace and Virgil praise the quality of the wines and indicate that something more than an alcoholic beverage had been achieved. Thus a 160-year-old Opimian Falernian wine was praised. Even wine snobs appear, recommending wines to please the smart set in Rome.

The Romans carried vine culture into western and eastern France and as far north as the Rhine in Germany, to the southern part of England, and eastward along the Danube. Wine was exported from Italy to the Roman colonies, but as the latter became better established, particularly in Spain and southern France, they produced the wines they needed for their own use. The wines of the south of France were roundly deprecated by Pliny and other Roman writers, but whether the wines were actually poor or whether this was the sour grapes of regional pride is not known. In fact, in the first century the Emperor Domitian prohibited the growing of grapes in France and even passed a law that the vineyards in the Rhone Valley and other parts of France must be removed. This was apparently to prevent competition from the wines of Gaul with those exported from Italy, though it may also have been due to a need to increase grain production. Not only did the Romans carry vine culture to the far parts of the empire, but they also carried their methods of growing grapes and possibly some grape varieties. And some of their wines must have been great. The famous physician Galen, 130–200 A.D., was a connoisseur who prescribed wine in his medical practice.

With the downfall of the Roman Empire agriculture gradually deteriorated, the vineyard industry with it. There are many indications of this: the lack of appreciation of wine in the Middle Ages, the small amount of wine produced, and the chaos of Europe from 400 A.D. to as late as the thirteenth century. Charlemagne may have planted a vineyard or two, and occasional poets praised wines, probably more for their alcohol than their quality.

One important contribution during the Middle Ages is the probable introduction into Europe of grape varieties brought back from the Middle East by the Crusaders. It is now generally believed that the Petite Sirah was brought to the Rhone by one of the Crusaders, and a number of other varieties were probably introduced into France at this time. The best indications are that most of the varieties now in Europe were present there by the thirteenth century.

The need of the Church for wine for sacramental purposes was an important factor in the preservation of the wine industry through the Middle Ages. The monastic establishments which grew to prominence during the tenth to the fifteenth centuries were relatively stable organizations with an ample supply of labor (Figure 2). Not only were the monasteries free of most of the taxes, but they were also spared much of the marauding which made agriculture hazardous for private individuals. Many of the important wine districts of Europe were either discovered or preserved by monastic organizations, particularly in Burgundy and in Germany, where large monastic orders owned extensive vineyards and developed winemaking to a much higher plane than in the period from 400 to 1200. They not only made wine for sacramental purposes, but used it as a part of their diet and sold some as part of the income of the monastery. Remnants of monastic wineries can still be found in France, Spain, Germany, Austria, Yugoslavia, and other countries.

Not only did the monasteries preserve the growing of grapes and production of wine but they also, for the first time, made a point of the regional classifications of wine. Taking a justifiable pride in the wine industry they were developing, the monasteries naturally praised the local wines of each region. Since the monasteries had a certain stability, they could keep wines over a period of years, especially now that wooden casks were available. Some monasteries kept good records, which made it possible for them to classify the wines and compare them with wines of other districts. Thus by the end of the Middle Ages the monasteries presented to the Western World a well-developed wine industry. In Germany, at least, they became expert coopers and built large and excellent oak casks for wine storage. This is not to imply that only the monastic establishment grew grapes or made wine. Feudal and royal estates owned vineyards and produced wines in many areas.

As the Middle Ages became politically more stable, trade developed and wines were shipped to various parts of the

FIG. 2. Gathering grapes and winemaking in a fifteenth-century monastery vineyard. (Source: Bruckmann Photo.)

Western World. Many documents show that the wine trade was carried on even in the worst periods from the eighth to eleventh centuries, particularly for the use of the Church and the nobility. Trade continued between Bordeaux and England throughout the Middle Ages, and some German wines seem to have been exported as far west as Ireland during this period. In Germany the Hanseatic League of city-states was very active in the importation and exportation of wines, not only between the member states but to foreign countries. But not until the fourteenth and fifteenth centuries did the international wine trade assume large proportions.

The international trade in wines had an important effect on standardization and classifications of wines. When wines are shipped long distances for foreign trade, it is necessary to have some guarantee of their quality. This forced the producers into classifying their wines and selling them at prices appropriate to the quality. Still, wines were probably not as widely distributed among the common people in the Middle Ages as they had been in the Roman period. Nevertheless, as the feudal system gradually dissolved, the improved standard of living of the middle class demanded more and more wines, and the vineyard acreage, particularly in France and Germany, increased rapidly during the fifteenth, sixteenth, and seventeenth centuries. Trade between England and the southern European and Mediterranean countries was especially important. Shakespeare refers to the wines of many countries, but particularly to those of Spain.

By 1850 the wine industry was well established in all parts of Europe south of the Rhine and extending into Austria along the Danube and into the Crimea and Caucasus in Russia. Wines were exported, particularly from France, Spain, Portugal, and Madeira, to England and elsewhere, and from Germany to the countries to the north. Many wines from Germany reached England during this period. The countries which produced no wine, such as Belgium and Holland, developed a flourishing import trade for wine, primarily from France. The trade of port from Portugal to England was particularly important. The fortification of port, dating from the late eighteenth century, led to the aging of these sweet wines, and soon to their popularity with English connoisseurs; the development of vintage claret for the English market followed soon thereafter. Italy was still, in 1850, primarily a collection of city-states, and although winemaking was very common, not much wine was exported from Italy until the end of the nineteenth century, with the exception of vermouth from Turin and of some wine from Tuscany and Sicily. Surprisingly, all the Western countries carried on trade with Cyprus, since there seems to have been more appreciation of sweet wines than of table wines in this period. Constantia, a sweet wine from South Africa, was brought to Europe in the eighteenth and nineteenth centuries and was much appreciated.

There is probably a very good reason for this appreciation of the higher-alcohol sweet wines. They were undoubtedly more stable than the table wines and easier to care for. Furthermore, central heating had not come into use in this period in northern Europe, and the sweet wines gave more calories per volume than the table wines. Nevertheless, Rhine wines and Bordeaux wines as well as Champagne and Burgundy had achieved a recognition for quality by 1850.

In 1850 more wines were being bottled and more wines were being aged than at any previous time. Yet it has been estimated that at least 25 percent of the wine spoiled before fermentation was complete, and much of the wine was certainly of very poor quality. Some, owing to the market with the court and rich merchant classes, must have been very fine.

A series of disastrous vine diseases swept through Europe in the period immediately after 1850: particularly downy mildew, oïdium (powdery mildew), and black rot, which were inadvertently introduced into Europe from America. These diseases made it difficult for the grapes to ripen properly, or indeed to ripen at all. Effective fungicides were soon discovered which ameliorated the effects of these diseases.

About 1870 some American grape species were imported into English and French botanical gardens, and on these vines a root louse, phylloxera, was introduced into Europe. The American species of grapes mostly are resistant to this root louse, but the European grape, *Vitis vinifera*, was not immune and rapidly succumbed. The destruction of vineyards between 1870 and 1900 is unparalleled in agricultural history. Virtually all the vineyards of France were destroyed during this period, most of the vineyards of Spain were ruined before 1910, and the root louse caused widespread damage to vineyards in Austria, southern Germany, Italy, Rumania, southern Russia, and other parts of the world, including California. The French quickly recognized that the only feasible remedy was the importation of vigorous and phylloxera-resistant American rootstocks onto which European grapes could be grafted. Several viticultural expeditions came to this country, and thousands of American cuttings were sent to France. The best of these were selected and widely distributed throughout the world as rootstocks upon which European grapes could be grafted. Unfortunately, in the interim a number of foxy-flavored American varieties which were ill suited to the European climate and the European palate were planted not as rootstocks but as direct producers of grapes, in order that some form of wine industry could carry on. Greece, which was not subject to phylloxera, exported a very large amount of raisins to other European countries to be converted into wine.

The phylloxera-resistant rootstocks now used in California, and indeed most probably the insects themselves, were brought to California from France and not directly from the eastern United States. Phylloxera caused widespread migration of grape growers from France as well as from Italy to North America, South America, and other parts of the world. The economic crisis in the wine industry made the production of quality wines more difficult, and there were few great vintages in France during the period 1875 to 1893. Phylloxera had one beneficial result: when the vineyards were replanted only a few of the best varieties were used, compared to the very mixed plantings in the pre-phylloxera period.

The most important contributions of the mid-nineteenth century to the wine industry we owe to Louis Pasteur. At Lille, where he was teaching, sugar-beet molasses was being fermented for the production of alcohol for distillation. Investigating poor sugar utilization in an alcohol distillery, he found that the conversion of alcohol to acetic acid was the cause of the poor yields of alcohol. Later he turned his attention to the wine industry and demonstrated conclusively that the spoilage of wines was due to aerobic microorganisms of the *Acetobacter* type, i.e., organisms producing acetic acid. He found that if the wines were kept out of contact with the air, *Acetobacter* could not develop. After this great step forward, the acetification of wines has been gradually brought under complete control (except in a few areas and sometimes by careless home winemakers). He also demonstrated a number of anaerobic diseases of wine and prescribed treatments for controlling them.

Louis Pasteur thus represents the application of the scientific revolution to the wine industry. The application of scientific principles to fermentation and the care of wines is still continuing and developing today. The wine industry has made many strides in the application of pure yeast cultures to secure clean fermentations, in the use of mild antiseptics, such as sulfur dioxide, to prevent the growth of undesirable organisms, and in the clarification of wines by means of various fining agents to produce greater stability and clarity.

But another revolution that culminated in the nineteenth century is as important as the scientific revolution: the industrial revolution. New types of machinery were devised for cultivating vineyards, for handling or crushing grapes, for pumping crushed grapes to fermenting tanks, for filtration, and for pumping wines from one tank to the other. The application of technology to the grape and wine industry reduced the cost of production markedly and contributed to a great expansion in the wine industry in the latter part of the nineteenth century.

Thanks to these revolutions and their continuing applications to the wine industry, we are now living in the golden age of wines, for never before has so high a percentage of fine wines been produced. And these are being produced at a lower relative cost than ever before. The production of grapes per acre is also greater. We have developed better varieties, grow them with less injury from insects and fungus diseases, and bring them to the winery in better condition. The scientific revolution has made it possible to process these wines more rapidly, with less cost and greater assurance of success. Much of the guesswork has been taken out of the wine industry.

Within the next twenty years we shall probably be able to control even more of the factors that determine wine quality, and thus further increase the percentage of fine wines produced. The recent excessive prices of some imported and domestic wines is hopefully not a permanent development.

Summary.—The antiquity of the wine industry is recognized by all historians. The Greeks and Romans made wine an item of trade and spread the culture of grapes throughout Europe and the Mediterranean.

During the Middle Ages the monastic orders maintained grape culture, and international trade, an important factor in creating unique types of quality wines, began to develop.

Phylloxera created unprecedented economic problems, and successful grape-growing was only restored by replanting the vineyards on resistant rootstocks. Pasteur personifies the application of scientific principles to the wine industry. The industrial revolution greatly lessened the burdens of growing grapes and making wine.

Because of the scientific and industrial revolutions, we are living today in the golden age of wines as far as quality and availability are concerned.

Wherefore by their fruits shall ye know them. —MATTHEW 7:20

Chapter 2

GRAPES FOR WINE

The wine grape is a unique fruit, and its particular qualities have made "wine" synonymous with "grape wine." It has several characteristics which adapt it to the making of a fermented beverage with less difficulty and fewer problems than is possible with most other fruits or fermentable materials: notably, an unusually high content of fermentable sugar, relatively high nitrogen content, and the natural association of fermenting yeasts with the grape berry. Although limitations of other fruits can be overcome with modern science and technology, and the natural characteristics of the grape have been enhanced by selection, wine would probably not have become a part of the culture of man so early or so importantly without the Old World grape.

The quality of the wine can be affected by the grape variety and its management in the vineyard, by the fermentation technique, and by the processing and aging of the wine. All must be proper for good wine; lack of attention to any one can spoil it. Without grapes that are adapted for the wine intended, the production of good wine is foredoomed to failure. The choice of the grape variety to be grown is crucial to the nature and quality of the wine which can be produced. Once the chosen variety is planted in a vineyard, the grower must usually live with that choice over most of his career. If the choice was unwise, conversion of the vineyard to another variety is costly in time and money.

Grapes belong to the botanical family Vitaceae (order Rhamnales, class Dicotyledoneae, division Spermatophyta-Angiospermae). The Vitaceae (vines) include no food plants of significance other than grapes, but do include several of interest as ornamentals such as Virginia creeper and Boston ivy. There are eleven genera in the family, and that of grapes is *Vitis*.

The major commercial grape of California and most of the rest of the world is the species *Vitis vinifera,* also called the European grape. Native to the area around the Caspian Sea, it was one of the first domesticated plants and has been under cultivation for at least 5,000 years. It was important in the agriculture of ancient Phoenicia, Egypt, Greece, and Rome. Selection over this long time has produced a wide range in size and shape of clusters and berries, color, leaf shape, and growth habit. At least 5,000 named cultivars (the word is a contraction of "cultivated variety") of *V. vinifera* are known, but only a few hundred have achieved any importance. Probably less than 150 different varieties are grown commercially; each may be valued for its flavor, beauty, time of ripening, pest resistance, adaptation to a locale's soil or climate, high yield, or some other special feature.

The European grape was taken along (as seeds, cuttings, or rooted plants) during exploration and colonization. It was brought to Mexico, Argentina, Chile, through Baja California to California, into Australia, and into South Africa. In these areas as well as in Eurasia the European grape was and is the primary grape used for making wine.

The explorers and colonists encountered other grapes growing wild in many parts of the world, especially the north temperate zone. Leif Erikson found so many wild grapes growing in the New World that he called his discovery Vineland. Many old place names reflect the profusion of wild grapes native to America—for example, Martha's Vineyard, Massachusetts. Of American species of *Vitis, V. labrusca* is the most important for fruit production. This species was called the "fox" grape and grew wild in the mid-Atlantic states. The native American species have been domesticated only about

200 years, but at least 2,000 pure varieties and hybrids have been developed. The Concord may be considered the typical *V. labrusca*—more acreage is planted to it (perhaps in the United States 80 percent of non-European grape plantings) and more people are familiar with it in the form of the grape juice and jelly of the North American supermarket or from backyard culture. Other important varieties deriving at least in part from this species include Delaware, Catawba, Dutchess, Isabella, Ives, and Niagara.

Another American native is *Vitis rotundifolia* of the south Atlantic states. These are known as muscadine grapes, of which Scuppernong is one variety. The muscadine grapes are so different that they can be crossed with other grape species only by recently developed special techniques. Botanists classify them in a subgenus *(Muscadinia)* separate from the "true" grapes in the subgenus *Euvitis*. The muscadine has a unique intense fruity aroma. There are many other species of native grapes; some, such as *V. rupestris* (the sand grape) or *V. riparia* (the river grape), are useful as rootstocks or breeding material, but none are themselves important as fruit producers. The fruit from the American species all have distinctive strong "wild" flavors which usually carry over into crosses with *V. vinifera*. These flavors are liked by Americans who are familiar with them and who also like *V. vinifera* flavors, but they are foreign to the European wine types. The drinker of European wines describes the flavor of wine made with *V. labrusca* grapes, such as Concord, as "foxy." Presumably the term comes from the old name of fox grape, although some people claim to note an "animal-den" odor in some old or mistreated wines from *V. labrusca*. The foxy flavor is produced partly by the presence of methyl anthranilate, a flavor substance which is added to synthetic grape "pop" drinks.

Being of rather obvious, simple, strong flavor, wines made with grapes of American varieties are likely to be of limited interest as regular table beverages and monotonous even to those who like these flavors. Although it is often attempted, the matching and justifiable labeling of wines from these varieties with names derived from traditional European wines—

e.g., burgundy, chablis, sauterne, etc.—is nearly impossible and usually disappointing to both those liking Concord flavor and those liking traditional wine types.

The American species do, however, contribute much to viticulture. Growing wild as they did in areas having very cold winters, humid summers, and many natural enemies, they are more resistant to these conditions than the European varieties. The root louse, phylloxera, introduced into Europe from the New World, spread rapidly and became a scourge which nearly wiped out grape growing until it was recognized that scions of the European varieties could be grown as grafts on rootstocks of the resistant American species. Varieties of American species can be grown in areas so humid that European varieties succumb to various pathogens, particularly oidium (powdery mildew), downy mildew, and fruit-spoiling molds. The American varieties resist winter cold better and usually require a shorter growing season. These facts explain the growing of American varieties in preference to European varieties in subtropical (humid) regions as well as in the coldest areas where grapes can be grown. Crossing and back-crossing among American species and *V. vinifera* varieties are being used to develop grapes with fruit like the European and resistance like the American species. These are sometimes referred to as "direct producers," since some of them can be grown on their own roots without grafting in the presence of phylloxera.

Many distinctive wine types require one or more specific grape varieties which contribute much of the distinctiveness of the wine. Many varieties are inherently of poor quality for some wine types, and some varieties can be converted into good or standard qualities of several wine types. In the United States it is common practice to label premium-quality wines which contain mostly a single variety of grapes (51 percent legal minimum) with the name of that grape variety. The use of varietal labels is gaining in popularity in other countries, particularly for wines exported to the United States. This varietal labeling is useful only if the grape variety contributes a generally recognizable distinctive quality to the resulting wine. A wine from a variety of grape without a reputation for some special quality is ordinarily marketed under a class or generic label: red table, chablis, claret, port, etc. In some countries the same result is achieved by using a single variety or a limited number of varieties of grapes for the wines of a given region. Thus, although given geographical labels, the character of the wines reflects the specific variety or varieties grown in the region.

A point that may seem contradictory at first is that wine-makers usually seek to increase or maximize the varietal flavors of *V. vinifera* varieties, but may seek to lower or mini-mize those of varieties derived from *V. labrusca* and other American species. Wine as a table beverage is consumed in fairly generous portions as a complement to food. The *rotundi-folia, labrusca,* and other "wild" flavors are so intense they tend to be overpowering. As a result, their wine may be considered better if blended with more neutral wine, made from less ripe grapes, or otherwise toned down in grape aroma. By contrast, the *vinifera* flavors tend to be more subtle, diverse, and deli-cate. With the exception of the more obvious muscat-flavored group, the best wines tend to be those with the most distinc-tive, most intense (but still mild) flavors among the *V. vinifera* varietals. And certainly the best wines in a series from a single *vinifera* variety are those most intense in characteristic varietal flavor, other things being equal. It is significant that a major goal of breeders of *vinifera* is the production of recognizably distinct new or more intense varietal wines–whereas in cross-ing other species, breeding out the foxy, muscadine, or other "native" flavor is often a major goal.

It is notoriously difficult to describe flavors in a generally meaningful way, but it is possible to divide grapes into a few classes which can be readily recognized with a little experience in tasting their wines. The flavor of the wine, even when freshly made and certainly after aging or further processing, may be different from that of the fruit as picked. However, if the wine from one variety is distinctive and usually recogniz-able by experienced tasters, compared to the same type of wine from other varieties, the difference is attributable to the nature of the grape. Not every lot of wine produced from grapes of varieties ordinarily having distinctive flavors will be flavored intensely and characteristically enough to be recognized even by the expert taster. The subtlety and variability in flavor qualities between wine from different varieties of grapes, and even from the same variety as produced by different wineries, in different lots, and in different years, contribute much to the enjoyment of wine by those who observe and become acquainted with these differences.

A classification of varietal flavors into four groups will help the novice become acquainted with the broad range of possible flavors: non-*vinifera*-flavored varieties, muscat-flavored varieties, other distinctively flavored varieties, and nondistinctively flavored varieties. The non-*vinifera*-flavored variety group is dominated by grapes such as Concord which have a flavor described as "foxy," "wild-grape," or perhaps preferably, *labrusca*. Muscadines and grapes of other species are included here, although their flavors are not the same as the Concord-*labrusca* types. The muscat-flavored group are *vinifera* varieties and a few *vinifera* crosses with other species that have a distinctive perfumy, floral aroma which is often quite intense and is easily recognized, once experienced, both in the grape and in the wine. *Vinifera* varietals which are not muscat-flavored and yet are recognizable are a heterogeneous group which includes a wide range of flavors and most of the varieties famous for quality wine production. The nondistinctive varieties include those that produce wines with a flavor which is generally best described as "vinous." Good standard wines are produced from members of this group, and owing to high yields or other factors, some of the most widely planted and largest-total-tonnage varieties fall here, but the flavors are very similar. As an illustration, most of the *vinifera* grapes seen in the fresh-fruit market, such as Thompson Seedless, make wines which would place them in this class. Such varieties are often used in wine types whose characteristic flavors depend on processing rather than grape variety.

An attempt has been made to list most of the major and some of the minor varieties (in terms of use in wines which are commercially available) according to these groups in the accompanying tabulation. There is no substitute, of course, for personal experience in recognizing flavors, and listings are subject to differences of opinion based upon personal experience and interpretation. We are *not* saying that within these four classes there are no differences between varieties—far from it! Not all *labrusca* varieties make wines with the same flavor, nor do muscats, or the other two classes. Even if the basic flavor is similar, differing levels of intensity, different nuances, and differing features other than flavor, such as red versus white color, produce a wide range of very noticeably different grapes and wines in each general class.

GROUPINGS ACCORDING TO RECOGNIZABLE
FLAVORS OF THE FRUIT (AS WINE)

A. *Non*-vinifera *varieties with distinctive flavors* (derived from American species and hybrids thereof, they carry more or less strong native-grape flavors into young table, sparkling, or dessert-type wines made from them)
  1. Vitis labrusca-*type flavors, "foxy" aromas*
     a. *Red and pink wine types* (owing to low natural pigment, some are frequently used to make white wines): Concord (the classic "foxy" variety); Agawam; Black Pearl; Campbell's Early; Catawba; Clinton; Delaware (spicy, aromatic); Diana; Iona; Isabella ("foxy" plus raspberry); Ives (Ives Seedling); Niabell; Early Niabell; Pierce; Steuben; Vergennes (Vergeness)
     b. *White wine types:* Niagara; Diamond (Moore's Diamond); Dutchess (Duchess); Elvira; Golden Muscat ("foxy," with little muscat aroma); Missouri Riesling; Noah
  2. Vitis rotundifolia-*type flavor, muscadine grape aroma* (an intense, characteristic, fruity aroma, *not* muscat or "foxy")
     a. *Red wine types:* Burgaw; Eden; Hunt; James; Mish; Thomas
     b. *White wine types:* Scuppernong (loosely used for all muscadine grapes and wines); Topsail; Willard

FIG. 3. Pinot noir grapes, illustrating the tight cluster of thin-skinned berries common among *Vitis vinifera* varieties for wine. (Source: The Wine Institute.)

3. *Other North American species and hybrid varieties thereof* (these species contribute various flavors described as raw, grassy, herbaceous, post-oak, mustang, harsh, bitter, horehound, etc., but generally not foxy and *not* muscadine; as more species are crossed—seven or more are known in the parentage of single hybrid varieties— the wines become less obvious in specific "wild grape" flavors, and particularly as they are back-crossed with *Vitis vinifera,* the aromas of the wines become more subtle and less easily distinguished from pure *vinifera* varieties; in some the distinction can become meaningless from a flavor viewpoint)

   a. *Red and pink varieties:* Alicante Bouschet, Baco noir (Baco No. 1—herbaceous, astringent); Beta (grassy); Cascade (Seibel 13053—prunish, bituminous odor); Chambourcin (Joannes Seyve 26205—fruity-tarry); Chancellor (Seibel 7053); Chelois (Seibel 10878— fruity, spicy); Colobel (Seibel 8357—bitter "hybrid" taste); Cynthiana; De Chaunac (Seibel 9549); Foch (Maréchal Foch, Kuhlmann 188-2); Herbemont; Jacquez (Lenoir); Landal (Landot 244); Léon Millot (Kuhlmann 194-2); Rosette (Seibel 1000—bitter); Royalty (horehound); Rubired (horehound); Salvador (harsh); Seyve-Villard 5247

   b. *White wine varieties:* Aurore (Seibel 5279); Seyval blanc (Seyve Villard 5276—fruity, pommade); Verdelet (Seibel 9110—fruity, spicy); Vidal blanc (Vidal 256—"hybrid" taste, coarse); Vignoles (Ravat 51—fruity, crisp)

B. Vitis vinifera *varieties*

   1. *Muscat-flavored varieties* (fruity-floral aroma of the muscats—likened to daphne flower—makes them very attractive as fresh fruit, and carries very recognizably into the wines, usually dessert wines)

      a. *Red or pink wine types:* Aleatico; Muscat Hamburg

      b. *White wine types:* Muscat blanc (Muscat Canelli, Muscat Frontignan); Gold; July Muscat; Malvasia bianca; Muscat of Alexandria; Muscat Otonel; Orange Muscat

FIG. 4. Sauvignon blanc grapes. (Source: The Wine Institute.)

2. *Other distinctively flavored varieties, besides muscat or native-grape-flavored* (this group is the most important for the high-quality wines of the world, but it is very heterogeneous as to nature and degree of distinctiveness of the grape's aroma and wine's flavor; suggested descriptive adjectives are intended to be complimentary, and flavors are much more delicate than the terms imply —these descriptions may aid in developing your own tasting vocabulary, but are *not* to be taken too literally)

   a. *Red wine types:* Barbera (very fruity, tart); Cabernet franc (green olive, weedy); Cabernet Sauvignon (green olive, bell pepper); Carnelian (fruity, tart); Gamay Beaujolais (fruity, tart, spicy); Grenache (fruity, estery, may become harsh); Grignolino (more than one variety sold under this name, also frequently blended—spicy-fruity, sometimes tannic, tends to pinkish-orange color); Malbec (fruity young, olive or krautish old, soft); Merlot (green olive); Meunier (Pinot Meunier—fruity, spicy); Napa Gamay (fruity, tart, spicy); Nebbiolo (fruity, licorice); Petite Sirah (possibly Durif, Shiraz, more than one variety carries this name—fruity, tannic); Pinot noir (Figure 3) (pepperminty); Pinot St.-George (Red Pinot—not highly distinctive); Ruby Cabernet (green olive, weedy, tannic); Souzão (rich, fruity); Tinta Madeira (prunish, cheddar, rich), Tinta Cão (rich, fruity); Zinfandel (raspberry)

   b. *White wine types* (fruity-floral aromas are sometimes difficult to distinguish from muscat, but other flavor factors distinguish them): White Riesling (Johannisberg Riesling—fruity-floral, tart); Chardonnay (Pinot Chardonnay—applish, ripe-grape, intensity increases with degree of ripeness of grapes); Chenin blanc (Pineau blanc de la Loire, White Pinot—fruity, appetizing, not highly distinctive); Emerald Riesling (fruity, sometimes spicy, slight muscat, tart if not blended); Fernão Pires (very fruity-floral); Flora (fruity, spicy); Folle blanche (fruity, tart); Gewürztraminer (spicy, resembles muscat); Grey Riesling (spicy-fruity, not highly distinctive except when grapes are very ripe); Helena (fruity); Melon (similar to Pinot blanc); Müller-Thurgau (slight muscat); Pinot blanc (weedy, rich); Sauvignon blanc (Figure 4) (Fumé blanc, fruity, faintly herbaceous); Sauvignon vert (fruity, spicy, slight muscat); Sémillon (figs, faintly cigar-like); Sylvaner (Franken Riesling—fruity, tart, not highly distinctive)

3. *Nondistinctive varieties* (very important on acreage and gallonage basis; quality of wines ranges from very ordinary to good or even excellent, but generally no recognizably distinctive flavors derive from the grape itself)

   a. *Red varieties* (low-colored varieties can be used in white dessert wines and sherries): Aramon, Carignane, Charbono, Emperor, Flame Tokay, Mataro, Mission, Pagadebito, Picpoule noir, Red Malaga, Refosco, Terret, Valdepeñas

   b. *White varieties:* Aligoté, Burger, Chasselas doré (Gutedel, Fendant, Sweetwater), Clairette blanche, Feher Szagos, French Colombard, Green Hungarian, Grillo, Palomino (Golden Chasselas), Saint-Émilion (Ugni blanc, Trebbiano), Thompson Seedless (Sultanina), Veltliner

Summary. —The characteristic composition, flavor, and other qualities of the grape variety are extremely important variables in the making of wine. No one can be personally acquainted with all the world's grape varieties and the wines that could be made from them. New varieties are continually being bred and selected. Each variety must be tested for several wine types, over several seasons, and in different areas before its distinctiveness and value can be estimated. Decades may elapse before the place of a variety in a given viticultural economy is secure, and even then it can be upset by many factors. The wine producer and the wine consumer can profit from this diversity by learning to exploit it according to their own needs and tastes. A grouping of varieties with respect to their recognizably different flavors has been presented. Together with later discussions on the effects of climatic differences, vinification practices, and adaptation of certain varieties for certain wine types, this table and some tasting experience should help the novice to advance rapidly in understanding and appreciation of wine.

No great thing is created suddenly, any more than a bunch of grapes or a fig.
Let it first blossom, then bear fruit, then ripen. —EPICTETUS

Chapter 3

GROWING WINE GRAPES

Viticulture—the growing of grapes—is a very large agricultural industry. According to the statistics available to us, the total world commercial tonnage of grapes approaches 75 percent of that of all other fruits combined. On a world basis, the grape probably enters the human diet in a larger amount per capita and in more different forms of commercial importance (raisins, many kinds of wine, fresh fruit, canned fruit, juice, jellies, etc.) than any other fruit.

California is by far the most important state viticulturally in the United States. It produces about 90 percent of all grapes, 100 percent of the raisins, about 95 percent of the table grapes, and about 72 percent of the wine consumed in this country. This production had a farm value estimated at $480 million in 1975, involving 330 wineries (of a national total of 579) and 647,000 acres of vineyard (about 83 percent in bearing). The total annual production of grapes in the United States is over 4 million tons, and about 60 percent of this is crushed by wineries. Although this production is of great importance from the national viewpoint, in terms of the world's total commercial output California produces nearly 4 percent of the wine, 40 percent of the raisins, and 8 percent of the fresh table grapes. Since the acreage is about 3.5 percent of the world's total,

California's viticulture is seen to be relatively efficient. Several other states, notably New York, Ohio, Pennsylvania, Michigan, and Washington, have appreciable wine-grape production, and some grapes are grown in most states, adding a total of about 400,000 tons per year to the commercial grape crop of the United States.

The total commercial wine production of the world, as of 1975, is estimated to be about 8.4 billion gallons per year. Of this total, European countries produce about 6.6 billion gallons. The remaining 1.8 billion gallons are produced in Africa (405 million gallons), Argentina (584 million gallons), and several other countries including the United States (804 million gallons). Generally speaking, the countries with the largest production of wine also have high consumption and as a result do not export a major proportion of their wines. The foreign wines seen in the United States do not usually reflect the typical wine of the country of origin. In many cases only a small proportion of the wine, that with the most renown and highest price, may be selected for export. However, wines which can be sold at low prices on the American market are also often exported. Therefore, we cannot speak knowingly of the "wines of country X" without understanding many details of weather, viticultural practices, and winemaking procedures and their relation to the typical wines as well as to the wines exported from country X. Writers have tended to emphasize wines worthy of export, not the standard district wines. This encourages snobbism and shallow knowledge of both domestic and foreign products.

The sources and types of wines consumed in the United States in 1975 are shown in the accompanying table. The figures for the rest of the United States were obtained by subtracting the California wine entering distribution channels from the total consumption of wine produced in the United States. The transfer of California grapes, juice, concentrate, and wine spirits directly to wineries in other states for blending or further processing is believed to have inflated the apparent proportion of wine contributed by the rest of the country.

PERCENTAGE OF UNITED STATES WINE CONSUMPTION (1975)

Source	Table wine	Dessert wine	Sparkling wine	Vermouth	Other flavored	Total
California	71.0	67.6	73.9	37.3	96.0	73.5
Other states	10.0	28.5	16.6	17.9	4.0	13.1
Foreign	19.0	3.9	9.5	44.8		13.4
Percentage of total U.S. consumption	58.2	18.2	5.5	2.6	15.5	100.0

Viticulture is a complex science. Each viticultural area has its own problems. Considering the great number of varieties of grapes and the several types of wine, it is fortunate for the student of wines that it is not possible to grow every variety of grapes and produce every type of wine efficiently in every area, and that certain guiding principles govern the choice. A general knowledge of the growing of grapes and the production of wine is necessary for those who would understand wine.

In the spring as soon as the average daily temperature reaches about 50° F. (10° C.), the dormant vine begins to grow and put out the shoots which will bear this year's crop. The flower-clusters emerge with the new shoots, and about 45 days later the inconspicuous flowers bloom. After the small, hard, green, acid berries set they grow rapidly for a time, then undergo no great visible change until the beginning of ripening. By then cell division in the berries has ceased, but a second period of growth owing to cell enlargement begins. Just prior to the start of ripening, the concentration of tartaric and malic acids in the cell fluids of the berry is at its maximum, totaling about 3 percent; the sugar content is very low, less than 4 percent. From this stage until the fruit is ripe, the concentration of sugar in the fruit will rise to over 20 percent. This means that the plant is using its tremendous photosynthetic capacity to produce sucrose, which is translocated in low concentration (0.5 percent or so) from the leaf to the fruit and concentrated there.

The grape is very unusual among fruits in that the disaccharide sucrose is hydrolyzed as it is translocated into the berry, where it is stored in high concentrations of approximately equal proportions of the constituent monosaccharides, glucose and fructose. Most other fruits store carbohydrates as either starch or sucrose and do not produce so high a concentration of soluble, fermentable sugar. During the final cell enlargement stage the volume of the berry increases about fourfold to fivefold; if the *amount* of acid in a berry remained constant during this period, the *concentration* would decrease in proportion to the dilution produced by the accumulation of juice in the enlarged state. But part of the acid is respired, so the concentration of acid decreases even more than can be accounted for by dilution. The proportion of the acid which is respired is affected by the temperature: in hot weather most of the malic and perhaps part of the tartaric acid may be lost by respiration in the fruit; in cooler weather more is retained. As an example, if 100 green berries at 1 gram each contain a total of 3 grams of acid (3 percent), they may weigh 5 grams when ripe and contain 2.5 grams of acid, giving a concentration of 0.5 percent acid in the ripe berry. Thus, in this example, dilution by enlargement can account for dropping the acidity to 0.6 percent, and respiration explains the additional 0.1 percent drop. Other changes occur, of course, during the later stages of ripening: flavor compounds are produced, chlorophyll is lost, and in red varieties the red anthocyanin pigments form. Anthocyanins are the natural phenolic glycoside colors of red and blue fruits, flowers, and leaves.

As an example of this grand sequence in the northern central valley region of California, say the Lodi district, the grapes should "push"—begin to sprout from the dormant buds— about April 1. Blooming should occur about May 15, ripening begins about July 15, and the berries should be fully mature about September 15. These estimates are approximate, of course, for a midseason ripening in an average year. Individual grape varieties vary in their required growing season from as short as 90 days for a very early-ripening variety to about 195 days for a late variety. The vine itself should continue green and active, but with limited growth after fruit maturity. As the weather turns cool in the fall, the vine becomes dormant and drops its leaves, often with a brilliant display of fall colors which makes vineyard areas tourist attractions at that time of year. After the vines are dormant, the vineyardist prunes them and the process is ready to begin again in the spring.

The manner of pruning can affect the yield and quality of the next crop. The fruit for next year's crop develops from buds upon the canes which grew this year. Thus the number of fruitful buds left when the vines are pruned helps control the size of the following crop. If too many are left, the vine probably cannot mature all the fruit; the result is that the fruit matures slowly and its quality may be impaired. If too few fruitful buds are left, the quality is generally good, but the yield is impaired. Economics and human nature conspire to produce more errors on the "too many" side. Much skill and considerable luck are required to prune every year to obtain the maximum yield consistent with optimum quality, since grape variety, vine health, the weather, berries set per cluster, and the wine to be made all contribute in determining the optimum crop in any one season for a certain vineyard. The heaviest-producing varieties of grapes, particularly if over-cropped, may produce 16 tons of fruit per acre; but California production averaged 9.2 tons per acre for raisin varieties, 6.1 tons per acre for table-grape varieties, and 5.6 tons per acre for wine varieties in 1975. Production in Europe is usually only 2 to 5 tons per acre, depending upon variety.

The varieties of grape which can be recommended for planting in a given vineyard are limited by the local climate and the marketing situation. If the growing season (between frost-free conditions) averages 120 days, it is obvious that varieties requiring 180 days to mature should not be planted. For less obvious reasons, among them the fact that early varieties tend to be shy producers and to produce lower-quality wine under hot conditions, it is not usually a good idea to plant early-maturing wine-grape varieties in an area with a long, hot growing season. In latitudes toward the poles, grape growing is limited by a short growing season and severe winter cold. Several days of 0° F. (−18° C.) is likely to kill even dormant European vines. Nearer the equator, grapes suffer from the lack of a winter dormant period and perhaps from high humidity which induces fungus diseases. Hence, the planting of grapes for commercial-scale wine production is limited to an ill-defined belt in the Northern Hemisphere including California and the Mediterranean area, and in the Southern Hemisphere including South Africa, Australia, Chile, and Argentina (Figure 5). However, grapes are not grown in all places where they could be, and local geography, pest prevalence, and weather may limit profitable grape growing to a much greater degree than is implied by the extent of this "double belt" around the earth.

By special viticultural techniques and greater risks, of course, grape growing can be extended outside its normal geographic range. In tropical countries green pruning can throw the vines into an artificial and temporary "dormancy," and two (but generally about half as large) crops may be produced each year. In colder climates special protection such as burying the vines in winter, or even greenhouse culture, may make grape growing possible and perhaps economically attractive under special circumstances. In such conditions the most modern scientific viticulture and specially adapted cultivars are essential to long-term success.

Grape vines are adaptable to most well-drained soils, even relatively infertile ones (Figure 6). They have very extensive root systems and can withstand more drought than many other crops. If irrigation is possible, grapes are not limited by lack of rainfall. In fact, since the grape vines dislike cold, waterlogged soil and are susceptible to pathogens such as mildew in wet or too humid conditions, the absence of summer rains is often a favorable characteristic for a wine-growing area. If summer rains do occur (as in many European areas), their timing, the amount of rain, and the time before the excess water drains away and drying conditions return are critical.

Since moisture is moisture to the vine root, the opinion that irrigation is detrimental to wine quality, compared to rainfall, is erroneous; but the purity of irrigation water and the timing of its application can be very important. Rains during blooming may cause a poor set of berries, resulting in a light crop.

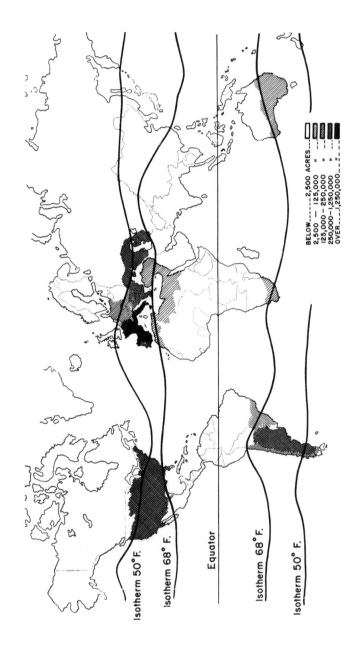

Fig. 5. Distribution of wine grape plantings in the world.

Rains late in the ripening period, particularly if followed by several humid days, may delay ripening and produce lowered quality or perhaps complete loss by encouraging berry cracking, bunch rot, and so on. Fog and high humidity without rain may have similar effects, encouraging mildew on the leaves and causing berry damage. Localities with frequent hailstorms are undesirable for grapes. When the shoots are small and brittle, hail can damage a vineyard severely. Later, hail decreases the yield and quality of the year's vintage and may weaken the vine.

The effects of wind can be severe on grapes; areas of strong or poorly timed windstorms are unsuitable for grapes. Tender shoots may break off and the crop will be reduced by high winds. Leaves may be ripped from the vine, decreasing its ability to produce sugar and mature the fruit. If strong winds occur later in the season, the fruit may be damaged by whipping and may be exposed to decay and sun damage.

Sunburn and heat damage have various effects depending upon the timing. At temperatures of about 105° F. (40° C.) or more the grape berries are likely to be damaged, particularly those exposed to the direct sun. If this occurs early in the season, the damaged berries will be shrunken and hard. The yield will be decreased, but the remaining berries will develop normally and the quality of the wine will not be impaired. Later in the season the damaged berries will sunburn and become raisined and caramelized in flavor. This may not cause much reduction in yield, but off-flavors will lower the quality of the wine. Relatively uniform and gradual changes in temperatures are important, especially in the spring and fall. Below-freezing temperatures after the shoots have begun to develop, or before the vine has turned dormant, will seriously damage or kill the vine and affect the amount of the crop in the spring or its quality, if it is still on the vine, in the fall. Prolonged unseasonable warm spells during the dormant period may cause premature sprouting followed by frost damage.

All these factors influence the success of grape growing and the quality of the wine in a given area. However, not only the climate of a viticultural area is important, but also the "microclimate" of each vineyard. By establishing vineyards on gentle slopes with maximum exposure to the sun, or in valleys protected from wind, the vineyardist can minimize possible climatic problems. By centuries of observation of success and failure in the older viticultural countries, and more recently by scientific study, especially in the newer viticultural areas, the locally successful viticulture and grape-wine complex is developed. The types of wine produced, the varieties of grapes which should be grown, the proper management of vineyards and wineries, are characteristic of a given area. There is always room for the innovator, and the "best" management practice today may be superseded by better information tomorrow; but the producer who flouts the fundamental viticultural, enological, or economic "laws" in his operations is doomed to failure. We have been emphasizing the environmental variables largely out of the control of the viticulturist once the vineyard is planted. Many details of propagation, nurture, and pest defense contribute heavily to the wine quality and economic success of a given producer, of course.

One of the most successful methods of clarifying the relationships among different areas, both for grape growing and winemaking, has been the "heat-summation" method of classifying vineyard regions. The grape does not grow or mature its fruit when the temperature is below about 50° F. (10° C.). The growing season for grapes is the total number of days during the summer (based upon a ten-year average) when the average daily temperature is above 50° F. The rate of metabolism and growth of plants is generally faster under warmer conditions. The heat-summation scale used for grapes is obtained by totaling the number of degrees above 50° F. for the days of the growing season. Thus if the average daily temperature is 70° F. (21.1° C.) today, this contributes $70 - 50 = 20$ "heat-summation" units, air-temperature growth units, or "degree-days" to the grape-growing season ($21.1 - 10 = 11.1$ "degree-days" on the Celsius scale; to convert degree-days on the Fahrenheit scale to Celsius, divide by 1.8). Ten days at 51° F. would be equivalent in these units to one day at 60° F. average temperature. (The average daily temperature is ordinarily estimated

FIG. 6. A Sémillon head-pruned vine showing the location of the clusters. The rocky soil might be poor for other crops, but it is typical of many areas famous for grapes. (Source: The Wine Institute.)

by averaging the minimum and maximum temperatures for each 24-hour period.)

Based upon these units, the coldest regions where grapes are grown commercially have annual heat summations of about 1,700 degree-days (using the Fahrenheit scale), and the hottest regions reach about 5,200 degree-days. The grape-growing areas have been conveniently classified into five "regions" of heat summation (Figure 7). The coldest, Region I, has 2,500 or fewer degree-days and would be represented by areas near the towns of Napa, Salinas, Santa Cruz, and Santa Rosa in California, much of Switzerland, and the districts of the Rhine, Moselle, and Champagne in Europe. Region II, still fairly cool, has a heat summation of 2,501 to 3,000 degree-days and would characterize the middle of the Napa Valley, the Sonoma Valley, the Santa Clara Valley, and the central Salinas Valley of California, and the region near the city of Bordeaux, France. Region III, 3,001 to 3,500 degree-days, is typical of the northern Napa Valley, the central Salinas Valley, and Livermore in California, and Tuscany in Italy. Region IV, 3,501 to 4,000 degree-days, characterizes areas near the California towns of Ukiah, Davis, Lodi, and Cucamonga, and much of Sicily, Greece, and central Spain. Region V is the hottest, 4,001 degree-days or more, and characterizes most of the northern Sacramento and central and southern San Joaquin valleys of California, as well as the vineyard areas of North Africa, southern Spain, and parts of Australia.

The general characteristics of these regions, and more specifically the average heat summation in a specific vineyard, tell us much about the type of grapes and wines that should be produced in the vineyard and why this is so. In a Region I vineyard the growing season is short, temperature is low, and only early-ripening varieties will mature. Obtaining sufficient sugar in the grapes may be a problem, and the acidity of the juice tends to be high. As a result, table wines are the preferable type to produce, since they are dry or nearly so, tart, and of relatively low alcohol content. In a vineyard in Region V the grapes can mature later and will tend to have high sugar content but low acidity, with the result that good dessert wines can be produced.

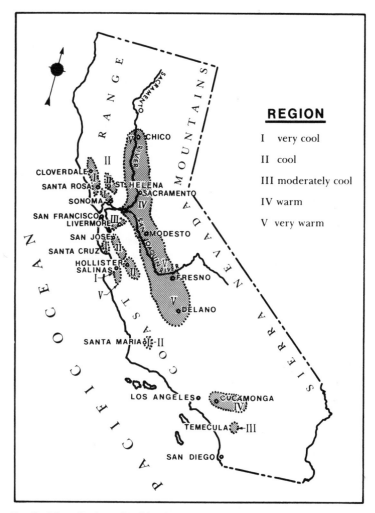

FIG. 7. Wine districts of California.

By growing high-acid varieties and with improving modern technology, table wines of acceptable and improving quality are now produced in the warmer regions, IV and V.

A grape variety grown in Region III will have more total acid when ripe than the same grape variety grown in Region V, because a higher proportion of the acid is respired under warmer conditions. The fruit will reach a higher sugar content on the same date, or reach a given sugar content earlier, in V (warmer) than in III (cooler). A variety of grape with red-pigmented fruit will ordinarily have more red pigment in the cooler region than in the warmer at the same degree of ripeness. The fruit from the cooler region will ordinarily taste fruitier and more tart; the fruit of the same variety from the warmer region will be sweeter but more flat.

The interrelationships described here help make it clear that as grape-growing regions, the cooler coastal valleys of California have much in common with such cool regions as Germany and Burgundy and Bordeaux in France. The hotter parts of the San Joaquin Valley have much in common, viticulturally, with southern France, Spain, and Algeria. The range of conditions in California is unusually wide and makes possible the production of good quality wines of all the basic types.

The heat-summation figures given are based upon a ten-year average and do not reveal another important feature. For consistent success and a stable wine-growing industry, wide deviations from the average climate are undesirable. The climate of inland areas is more variable than that of areas modified and made more uniform by nearness to the oceans or other sizable bodies of water. The growing of wine grapes beside the Finger Lakes in New York, and the influence of the Mediterranean Sea upon the countries surrounding it, are examples of this. Many of the vineyards in the important viticultural areas of the world which are noted for their grapes and wines depend partly on the more equable climate which results from the influence of an adjacent body of water. California is particularly fortunate in the relative uniformity of its climate. This is one reason why the climatic-region (I–V) concept has been developed and made particularly useful in this state.

The statement is often heard that every year is a vintage year in California. In the sense that the grapes are able to ripen to an adequate sugar level in California and are not unduly threatened by late rains, this is generally true. In many regions of the world, in as many as three or four years out of five sugar must be added to the grapes and lowering of the acidity must be encouraged in order to produce a properly balanced wine. The vintage years traditionally extolled for these areas are the years in which the grapes were able to ripen optimally. Although California, the source of most of America's wine, is relatively fortunate in this respect, vagaries of storm and season still cause variation in the product from year to year and from vineyard to vineyard. The fact that wine, in contrast to most food products, does vary and is still often handled in small batch lots, and similar products from several years' production may be available simultaneously, enables the student of wine to seek out and enjoy these variations. High-quality milk is envisioned as having a single identical flavor regardless of source. Standardization of wine to the same degree is, fortunately, unlikely. Wine surely would lose most of its interest for the sophisticated adult if it did not display so many variations, both obvious and subtle, in its qualities and attributes from the vineyard to the dining table and fireside.

Summary.—Commercial viticulture is limited to certain areas of the world with 1,700 (using the Fahrenheit scale; 940 using the Celsius scale) or more heat-summation units during the summer season, without excessive rain or humidity in summer, and having a continuous winter dormant period with no excessive or prolonged cold temperatures nor un-seasonable warm spells. Vineyard sites and cultural practices are selected in order to produce the best grapes of the chosen variety for the type of wine to be made. The environment of the vine has important effects upon its metabolism and influences the composition of the fruit and, in turn, the quality of the wine. Consistently successful commercial growing of high-quality wine grapes depends upon a correct matching to wine type of cultivar, viticultural operations, climate, and, at times, not a little good fortune.

Chapter 4

MICROORGANISMS AND WINE

Two plants are necessary to make wine: the fruit from the grapevine and yeasts for fermentation. The grape, a seed-bearing member of the plant kingdom, or spermatophyte, has been discussed. The other essential plant for wine, the yeast, is a member of the thallophytes. This division includes the algae, lichens, and fungi or mycetes. In this broad group will be found the yeasts, bacteria, and molds, all of interest to students of wine. The genus called *Saccharomyces* (sugar fungus) includes the yeasts of most significance in all forms of commercial production of alcohol from sugar. The species *Saccharomyces cerevisiae* (the name referring to cereal and the goddess Ceres) is the yeast commonly used in panary (bakery) and vinous fermentations. Selections of S. *cerevisiae* and another species, S. *uvarum,* are generally used for distillery and brewery fermentations also.

S. *cerevisiae,* which is most important in wine fermentations sometimes has a slightly elongated oval shape compared to the more nearly spherical form of other yeasts. (In older books this wine yeast may be listed as S. *ellipsoideus* or as S. *cerevisiae* var. *ellipsoideus.*) Strains of this yeast are well adapted to fermenting grapes to wine and are often found on the skin of the ripe wine grape in sufficient numbers to make possible the fermentation of the crushed grape without further inoculation. The visible white coating of the grape berry, the bloom,

52

is a waxy material produced by the fruit and *not* yeast cells, although a considerable yeast population may stick to it.

Yeasts are widely distributed in nature, and most other fruits as well as the grape carry some associated yeasts. The numbers and species of the natural microflora on the surface of a healthy fruit are influenced by many factors. While the ripe grapes in wine-producing areas often carry sufficient cells of the wine yeast *S. cerevisiae* on their skins to ferment the grape to wine when crushed, it is more usual today to add an inoculum of a strain of this "tame" or "domesticated" yeast selected for its desirable attributes. Several problems are avoided by this procedure. The relatively high cell numbers and the known growth characteristics of the strain added produce more prompt and predictable fermentations. If microorganisms are present in the crushed grapes which would otherwise begin to multiply, they are "swamped" by the large number of wine-yeast cells added, and the resultant rapid vinous fermentation prevents appreciable modification of the wine by these other organisms.

Among the microorganisms that may be present on grapes for wine are the "wild" yeasts, which often belong to other genera such as *Hansenula, Kloeckera, Pichia,* and *Torulopsis.* Some of these are also referred to as the apiculate yeasts, because the cells have pointed ends (apices) somewhat like the shape of a lemon. Cells of these yeasts as a group are usually more numerous on grapes than are wine-yeast cells. During the early stages of fermentation, particularly if no inoculum has been added, these wild yeasts multiply. The relative growth of the wine yeasts in comparison with the wild strains is favored by the addition of sulfur dioxide. Most of the wild yeasts are more susceptible to its inhibitory effects than are the wine yeasts. In addition, the wild yeasts are usually inhibited by about 4 to 6 percent or more alcohol; as soon as this level is exceeded, the wine yeasts become predominant and most of the wild yeasts cease appreciable growth or fermentation.

There has been much speculation with little firm conclusion as to the importance of the type or strain of yeast to the flavor and quality of the wine. A particular strain of *S. cerevisiae* is usually chosen for such attributes as rapid fermentation, high alcohol yield per gram of sugar consumed, high alcohol tolerance before cessation of fermentation, ease of removal of the yeast cells from the finished wine, and ability to ferment at low temperatures, rather than for specific flavor effects. Differences in respect to flavor contribution among fermentations of the same juice with single pure strains within this variety appear to be relatively minor. This may not be true when other species and genera become involved in the fermentation. Although the wild yeasts produce alcohol, they can also produce a higher proportion of other products which contribute to flavor. *Hansenula,* for example, is noted for a relatively high production of odorous esters. Even though the growth of most of them stops at 4 to 6 percent alcohol, the wild yeasts are believed occasionally to contribute special flavors from their activity in the early stages of fermentation. Moreover, some species of *Torulopsis* will ferment to 10 percent alcohol.

Other species within the genus *Saccharomyces* are important in special wine types: *S. bayanus, S. capensis,* or *S. fermentati* contribute a special flavor to *flor* sherry. On the other hand, *S. bayanus* is used to produce table wines and champagnes without obvious compositional and sensory differences from similar wines fermented with *S. cerevisiae.* Wines made in different areas from the same grape variety with apparently similar fruit composition and processing often do taste noticeably different. It may be that differences in the microflora naturally present in the two areas are important in producing the subtle flavor differences in the wines. The natural flora on grapes in vineyard regions where wine has been made for many years usually differ from that found on grapes in an isolated new planting, and often few wine yeasts are found on grapes from new plantings. As a new vineyard produces fruit, some falls on the ground, and insects and other vectors bring in yeasts which multiply in the fallen fruit and perhaps on the surface of healthy fruit. Yeasts can survive from season to season in the soil; as the cycle is repeated over the years, a complex flora of microorganisms is built up which may be fairly stable in one vineyard area but differ from that in other areas. Not only the vineyard flora but the winery flora may be important. In parts of Europe it is believed that special qualities and distinctiveness are introduced into wines by the complex microflora present on the grapes, and inoculation with pure cultures of wine yeasts is only now entering commercial practice. While these differences may be small, we believe they can be significant, but they are difficult to control and often tend to be undesirable rather than desirable.

Many studies have indeed shown that a great variety of yeasts, including *Saccharomyces* species other than the typical wine yeasts, do occur on grapes and can participate in fermentation of the grapes to produce fine wines. It is also true, however, that wines of the highest quality are produced (and more consistently so) in countries where the most modern and scientific technology is used, usually including routine inoculations with pure cultures of selected strains of wine yeasts.

Yeasts, like most living organisms, require as nutrients a metabolizable source of carbon and of nitrogen, minerals, and certain trace substances or vitamins. The usual carbon source is a fermentable carbohydrate. Grape juice contains approximately equal proportions of the 6-carbon sugars (hexoses) glucose and fructose, both of which are readily fermented and support growth of the majority of yeasts. Maltose, a sugar formed from starch breakdown—but not starch itself—can be fermented by the yeasts used in commercial fermentations. Sucrose—table sugar—can be fermented by yeasts, since they produce invertase, the enzyme which converts sucrose to invert sugar—an equal mixture of glucose and fructose. Sucrose is sometimes added to grapes and often is added to berry fermentations, but it does not occur in important amounts in ripe grapes.

Starch conversion to sugar, and then fermentation of the resultant glucose and maltose, is not involved in wine preparation, since grapes do not contain starch; but it is, of course, an important step in beer and spirit production from cereals and starchy materials. Other sugars such as galactose, mannose, and melibiose may or may not be fermented readily at first or even after the yeasts become accustomed to them, but this is primarily of interest as a means of distinguishing strains and species of yeasts from each other, since these sugars are not found widely in fruits. Certain other carbohydrates, particularly pentose sugars such as arabinose, ribose, and xylose, do occur in fruit juices in small amounts and are not fermentable by wine yeasts. As a result, a residue of nonfermentable sugars of the order of a gram per liter remains in the wine even when it is fermented completely "dry"—that is, all of the fermentable sugar has been consumed.

As a nitrogen source for producing its own proteins, the yeast cell can make use of the amino acids (protein building blocks) in the grape juice. Wine yeasts and yeasts in general, however, do not ordinarily require the presence of amino acids or other complex nitrogen sources. Yeasts can grow, ferment, and multiply simply by using ammonia or ammonium salts. They also can use the nitrogen of many simple organic compounds such as carbamide, but they cannot use nitrates as many higher plants can. Ordinarily grapes contain sufficient amino acids and other forms of available nitrogen to satisfactorily support yeast metabolism during wine fermentation. Grapes are almost unique among fruits in this regard. For satisfactory fermentation of honey, apple juice, and so on, some extra nitrogen source frequently must be added; raisins may be used for this purpose.

The minerals required by yeasts are known to include most of those required by living organisms. The natural substrates such as grape juice ordinarily contain more than enough of each to meet the needs of fermenting yeasts. In fact, the amount of most of the mineral elements required by yeasts is so small that it is difficult to produce a medium sufficiently low to demonstrate the requirement. Occasionally phosphorus in the form of phosphate ions, and less often smaller amounts of other elements such as potassium or magnesium, may be needed for fermenting diluted or partially purified mixtures such as sugar syrup.

The vitamin requirements of yeasts are of interest as diagnostic agents to determine identity or nonidentity of two cultures of yeast cells. Many yeasts have an absolute requirement for biotin; the biotin must be present in the medium or the yeast will not grow. Requirements may also be partial: growth will occur without the substance but will be slower than if it is added. The requirements may also be adaptive: after becoming accustomed to the absence of a substance yeasts will grow well without it, but will not do so at first. Although such requirements are less common and less frequently absolute than the requirement for biotin, a yeast strain may require one or more of the other water-soluble or B family of growth substances such as thiamine, pantothenic acid, pyridoxine, nicotinic acid, para-aminobenzoic acid, or inositol. Riboflavin is readily produced by most yeasts and is produced commercially in high yields from cultures of a yeast, though not a fermenting species. All these vitamins and growth factors are commonly found in grape juice in sufficient amounts to permit rapid fermentation by wine yeasts.

Crushed grapes or grape juice ready to be fermented (commonly called *must* in the wine industry) are, then, ordinarily adequate nutritionally for yeasts to develop in them and convert them into wine. Under special circumstances such as refermenting wine, restarting a stopped fermentation, or fermenting fruits and materials other than grapes, yeast "foods" may be necessary. Various proprietary mixtures have been sold, primarily to home winemakers, to ensure rapid completion of fermentation if the amount of an essential nutrient (other than sugar) is inadequate. These yeast foods usually include ammonium phosphate and perhaps other minerals. As a source of the other trace substances, an extract or lysis product from yeast cells (called yeast extract) which is rich in vitamins, growth factors, and amino acids may be used.

The production of alcohol during the usual anaerobic (protected from air, i.e., oxygen) fermentation of must to wine parallels yeast growth. By growth, when speaking of microorganisms, is meant cell multiplication. Yeasts multiply somewhat differently than do most bacteria and other one-celled microorganisms. Bacterial cells commonly multiply by splitting into two equal new cells; this is called binary fission. Since the new cells are both equally young, and at each new "generation" all the cells are again "young," there is no such thing as an old *cell* present, but only an older culture. Yeasts, on the other hand, reproduce by forming a daughter bud on the mother cell (Figure 8). This bud grows until it eventually (with most yeasts) splits away and begins to bud itself. The mother cell retains a bud scar; only a few dozen buds can be produced before a given mother cell is "old" and dies. The break-up *(autolysis)* of the old cells can contribute nutrients to the remaining active cells. This may be one reason yeast fermentations compared to bacterial fermentations generally go more smoothly and without difficulty to completion under suboptimal conditions.

The growth curve of yeast cells during fermentation follows the typical S-shaped form. There is a lag period during which the total number of yeast cells (whether added or naturally present) remains constant and the number of living cells may even decrease as some die from the shock of the new environment. As budding begins and new cells form, there is a rapid transition to the second phase—the period of logarithmic growth. During this period the number of cells increases more and more rapidly as each cell becomes two, the two become four, the four turn into eight, and so on. This period continues until some factor begins to become limiting (too little sugar, too much alcohol, etc.), at which time the multiplication slows and eventually stops, marking the third and final phase of the process. If some of the cells are removed to a new container of fresh must, the process begins again. If they are allowed to stay in the fermented wine, they gradually die, but a few survive for a long time. Any sugar added at a later time is therefore very likely to be fermented, unless special treatments are used to remove or kill the remaining viable yeasts.

The growth and fermentation process for a single organism, the wine yeast, can be complicated by the presence of other organisms. Grape juice from ripe grapes is rather acidic, having a pH between about 3 and 4 (pH units from 7 downward indicate a more and more acidic solution). Many microorganisms (particularly animal pathogens) will not multiply in or even survive such acidic conditions. During the fermen-

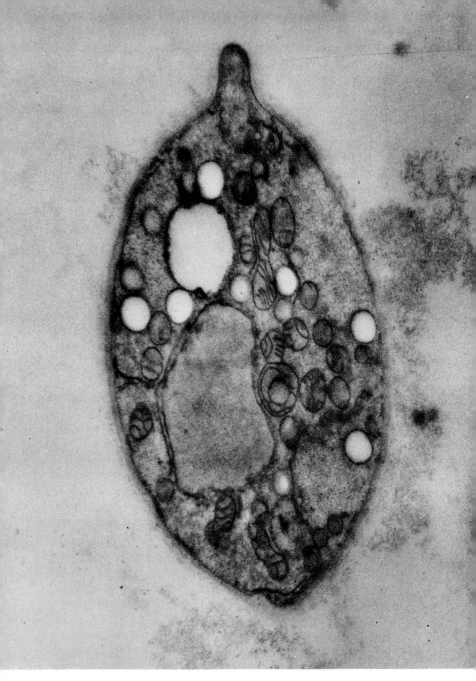

FIG. 8. A yeast cell just beginning to form a bud, as shown by electron microscopy at about 20,000-fold magnification. (Source: Dr. S. F. Conti, Dartmouth Medical School.)

tation, the anaerobic conditions and probably the high carbon-dioxide content prevent the growth of a further large group of organisms, molds for example. As fermentation proceeds, the increasing content of alcohol limits even more the organisms which might survive. As a result of all these and other similar factors, relatively few microorganisms can be present and survive, much less multiply, in wine. This is perhaps less important today with modern sanitation and scientific technology, but in the days of polluted water and general ignorance of good sanitation this fact no doubt explained the healthfulness of wine compared to many other foods. No human pathogens or dangerous food toxin producers occur in wine nor, indeed, would they be likely to survive if deliberately added. Certainly this is a source of comfort to both producers and consumers.

The fact that most of the wild yeasts do not develop beyond about 4 to 6 percent alcohol means that variations in the time it takes different lots of wine to reach about 4 percent alcohol would permit variations in the contributions of wild yeasts to the final quality and flavor of wine. This is true also of the activity of other organisms present in wine during fermentation. A cleaner-flavored, better product results more consistently when the major fermentation (i.e., that of the wine yeasts) is prompt in starting and properly carried to completion. Again the value of inoculation with a selected yeast is apparent.

Among the limited number of kinds of microorganisms other than yeasts which may grow in wine are the bacteria which produce acetic acid. Several species of *Acetobacter*, such as *Acetobacter aceti* and *A. mesoxydans*, are used to produce vinegar by conversion of ethanol to acetic acid. They are aerobic (requiring oxygen) and are inhibited by sulfur dioxide, so that they are not usually a problem during fermentation. However, they occur in most wineries, and a few of their cells may be found in or can get into most wines by contact with previously used casks. Owing to their general presence, nearly any wine produced by natural fermentation (without added alcohol) will become acetic *if exposed to the air*. As the bacteria multiply, more and more of the alcohol is oxidized to acetic acid and part of the acetic acid is combined with more of the ethanol to produce ethyl acetate. Ethyl acetate may also be produced directly. Although a small amount of acetic acid and ethyl acetate occur in wine as natural constituents from the grape and from the yeast fermentation, any appreciable amount indicates activity of acetic-souring bacteria. Most countries have legal limits upon the maximum amount of acetic acid which can be present in products sold as wine.

When the growth of *Acetobacter* is encouraged, wine vinegar will result. Encouragement usually takes the form of inoculating the wine with *Acetobacter* cells and allowing free air contact with the wine so that these aerobic organisms can grow. On undisturbed wine, these bacteria grow as a characteristic thin whitish film or scum on the surface, but with aeration and vigorous stirring they will grow throughout the solution.

Conversely, the winemaker can prevent his wine from becoming vinegar by keeping his equipment and containers clean to minimize the possibility of appreciable numbers of acetic-acid-producing bacteria being added to his lots of wine. Since some *Acetobacter* cells can be found in most wines, he prevents their multiplication also by keeping the wine containers full to the top to prevent air contact (and thus the growth of these air-requiring bacteria) and by judicious use of sulfur dioxide or other inhibitory additives.

The other major group of bacteria important in wine are the lactic acid bacteria. Organisms of this general class are active in the souring of milk, cheese making, sauerkraut production, and other useful fermentations. Some of them may be spoilage organisms in wine or they may have beneficial action, depending upon their effect and manner of occurrence. Several genera of these organisms may occur in wine, notably *Lactobacillus, Pediococcus,* and *Leuconostoc.* These genera include many species, each with very definite and often complex arrays of nutritional requirements and metabolic products. These bacteria are widely distributed in nature and thus can and usually do occur in grape musts and in wineries. They are essentially anaerobes, tolerant to the acidity of wines, and some are able to multiply even in solutions with ethanol concentrations too high for yeasts. Hence they can occur in wine and multiply during the yeast fermentation, although they are usually susceptible to sulfur dioxide. They can metabolize sugars to produce lactic acid and other products; however, they are relatively slow-growing organisms (compared to yeasts during active fermentation) and seldom are a problem at this stage. After the alcoholic fermentation is finished they may still develop in wine by consuming nutrients not consumed (or not consumable) by the yeasts.

The most important result of the multiplication of lactic-acid bacteria in wine is the so-called malo-lactic fermentation. Malic acid, $HOOC—CH_2CHOH—COOH$ (the name referring to its isolation from *Malus*, apples), is converted by these organisms to lactic acid, $CH_3—CHOH—COOH$, the acid of sour milk, and carbon dioxide is given off. As a result of this action the acidity of the wine is decreased and the pH raised because the two carboxylic-acid functions of malic acid are reduced to the single carboxylic-acid function of lactic acid. The proportion of the wine's total acidity resulting from malic acid is thus reduced to half its former amount. Ordinarily, when the malo-lactic fermentation occurs, malic acid is completely converted to lactic acid. The proportion of the total acidity of a wine which is contributed by malic acid is variable by season and by grape variety, but is particularly high when the total acidity is high, sometimes amounting to as much as half. The total acidity may be too high for the most palatable wine, and therefore lowering of the acidity by a malo-lactic fermentation is desirable. This is frequently true in countries with relatively cool weather during the grape-growing and harvesting season. In warm regions (such as parts of California) the malo-lactic fermentation might not be desirable, since it might lower the already low acidity too much and produce "flat"-tasting wine.

Considering the malo-lactic conversion alone is, however, an oversimplification, for the growth of lactic-acid bacteria produces other effects than converting malic to lactic acid. A study of premium-priced California wines showed that a higher proportion of them (nearly all the red table wines) had undergone the malo-lactic conversion than was true of popular-priced wines. The subtle complexities introduced into the wine's flavor may be advantageous even if acidity-lowering per se is not particularly desirable. Generally, a completed malo-lactic fermentation is considered desirable in aged, premium-quality red table wines, but is avoided in most fruity white table wines. The species or strain of lactic-acid bacterium which is present is evidently important. The special flavor effects are sometimes noticeably favorable, but in other cases the growth of lactic-acid bacteria produces undesirable off-flavors such as "mousiness" or excessive "krautiness."

The timing of the malo-lactic fermentation is important. If the malo-lactic fermentation occurs after the wine is bottled, the increase in cells may produce noticeable and undesirable turbidity. The same is true, of course, of any other cellular growth, yeasts included. The wine is then said to have been biologically unstable with respect to clarity. Other effects may also result from the activity of lactic-acid bacteria. If the malo-lactic fermentation occurs in the bottle, or if the carbon dioxide produced is not allowed to escape, the wine will be "gassy." With the exception of a few kinds of wine which make a virtue of this effect, gassiness in table wines is considered a negative quality factor. Another type of defect may result from a few members of the malo-lactic group of organisms—"ropy" wine. The causal organism produces a gelatinous thickening agent much like the dextran used as a transfusion blood-substitute. These are very rare in modern wines.

Molds do not grow in wine and are not a problem in a winery except for occasional localized "mildew" problems on the outside of casks, on or in corks, or in improperly maintained empty containers. This situation is not serious as it is easily controlled by proper and frequent housecleaning. Molds can be a problem on grapes, however, particularly after prolonged early-fall rains and inside shipping containers of fresh table grapes.

One of the most commonly troublesome molds on table and wine grapes is an ash-gray mold, *Botrytis cinerea*. This and certain other molds may attack unripened grapes on the vines under high humidity conditions, and berries with cracked skins may be attacked by secondary infections of molds, yeasts, and bacteria. The results are lower yield and reduced suitability of the grapes for wine. But *B. cinerea* can have special effects which have aided in the development of some of the most luscious and expensive wines from grapes upon which this mold has grown. If the humidity is high for a period, spores of *B. cinerea* can germinate, and the mold will grow on and through the skin of the healthy grape. If this is followed by a period of low humidity, much of the moisture of the berry is lost through the penetrated skin. The berry becomes shriveled like a raisin, but without the caramelized taste of the raisin. The juice obtained from these grapes has a higher sugar content owing to the water loss. Not only is a special delicate flavor introduced by the growth of the mold, but also the grape's natural flavor seems to be more concentrated. As a final dividend, the mold preferentially metabolizes a portion of the acid of the grape so that the resulting juice has about the same acidity as the original juice. Thus a small amount of a very rich, sweet wine can be made from the remaining concentrated juice from grapes infected by this "noble mold." The happy combination and sequence of events leading to this result rarely occur in nature except in certain small regions of the grape-growing world. More will be said about this later, in connection with the Sauternes of France, the *Trockenbeerenauslese* wines of Germany, and the Tokay of Hungary. In California the proper conditions rarely occur in the vineyards, although in some areas and seasons wines with a botrytis flavor are being produced. Study of the right conditions for inoculation, the control of humidity, and development of the correct equipment and technique has led to the production in California of luscious wines from picked grapes inoculated with spores of *B. cinerea,* although owing to higher cost they are not now regularly produced.

Summary—The major microorganisms of importance to students of wine have been briefly described. The yeasts are the agents for the alcoholic fermentation necessary to convert grape juice to wine. Limited activity of "wild" yeasts may sometimes be important for development of particular flavors, but excessive growth of wild yeasts can be harmful. Since the growth of mixed cultures is unpredictable, the use of inocula of selected true wine yeasts is the only procedure which can be recommended. Organisms other than yeasts are sources of negative or sometimes positive effects on grape or wine quality. Some are used in producing other fermented food products. None constitutes a health hazard. With proper winemaking techniques and the necessary precautions, the microbiological problems of wine production can be controlled and wine quality maintained. Winemakers capitalize upon the special effects of some of these organisms to produce improved and more elegant wines.

Chapter 5

ALCOHOLIC FERMENTATION

In this chapter we shall consider how the yeast acts during the conversion of grape juice to wine and how some of the major constituents of wine arise during fermentation. The word "yeast" is believed to have reached English from the Anglo-Saxon *gist* via Greek *zestos* (boiled) and Sanskrit *yasyati* (it seethes). To ferment is to seethe, or "boil" without a great deal of heat. The term "fermentation" today is used loosely to include all processes in which chemical changes are brought about in organic substances by the action of microorganisms (or less commonly by other cells or free enzymes). Important commercial examples include the production of antibiotics by submerged aerobic mold and actinomycete fermentations. With some exceptions, such as vinegar production, the "natural" food fermentations observed by housewives and farmers of long ago were usually capable of changing foods in sealed or deep containers—that is, were anaerobic. This includes sauerkraut, pickle, and olive fermentations by lactic-acid bacteria, as well as the alcoholic fermentation by yeasts. This "boiling" without heat was a great mystery to the ancients and was one of the first subjects studied by the emerging life sciences. The knowledge resulting from the study of wine fermentations and the so-called diseases of wine was a major contributor to the development and early progress of the modern sciences of microbiology and biochemistry.

66

Only a little over a hundred years ago it was discovered that alcoholic fermentation could occur naturally only in the presence of small living "ferments," the yeasts. Pasteur, from his studies in the 1860s, defined fermentation as life without air (anaerobic life), in contrast to the respiration of animals and higher plants which require air (are aerobic). In 1897 Edward Buchner reported that yeasts could be broken up and the cell-free juice would still produce alcohol from sugar. Thus the idea arose that there were "organized" ferments (cells of microorganisms) which could be broken down to "unorganized" ferments. These we know now as the enzymes, proteinaceous molecules which catalyze each of the metabolic reactions of the cell. Originally it was assumed that one enzyme of the yeast produced alcohol from sugar, but further study revealed that separate enzymes carry on steps in the process. The process of sugar catabolism to ethyl alcohol by yeasts and to lactic acid by the muscles of animals was eventually found to be essentially the same process except for the very last steps. This pathway of carbohydrate utilization by living organisms is usually called the Embden-Meyerhof pathway, after two of the many scientists who have contributed to our present understanding of this biochemical process.

The process of fermentation of one molecule of a simple sugar to alcohol was shown to result in two molecules of ethyl alcohol (more simply called ethanol) and two molecules of carbon dioxide. This was formulated by Gay-Lussac in 1810 into the equation which bears his name. This equation on the overall process can be written in a slightly modernized version as:

$$1 \text{ glucose } (C_6H_{12}O_6) \rightarrow 2 \text{ ethanol } (CH_3CH_2OH) +$$
$$2CO_2 + \text{ about 56 kilocalories of energy}$$

Thus 180 grams of glucose (the molecular weight in grams computed from the atomic weights of carbon 12, hydrogen 1, and oxygen 16) should produce a total of 92 grams of ethanol and 88 grams of carbon dioxide when completely fermented. This represents the maximum theoretical ethanol yield, which is 51.1 percent of the weight of the sugar (hexose) fermented.

Although actual yields in winemaking approach this level, they are slightly lower owing to the diversion of some of the sugar's atoms to other products, incorporation of sugar derivatives into the yeast cells, losses by volatilization, and so on.

The Embden-Meyerhof pathway of conversion of sugars to ethanol does not require oxygen, and in fact the mixture of air into the fermenting solution decreases the yield of ethanol. Under truly aerobic conditions no alcohol is produced even though yeast growth is excellent, and if ethanol is already present the yeast cells, in the presence of air, can eventually metabolize it completely to carbon dioxide and water. The normal condition for alcoholic fermentation, then, is the absence of air or oxygen. This is relatively simple to accomplish, since any oxygen dissolved in the solution to be fermented is rapidly consumed by the yeast cells during initial (aerobic) multiplication. Access of further oxygen during fermentation in the typical deep liquid layer is not usually a serious problem, particularly since carbon dioxide is produced in large volume, and as it escapes it sweeps away the air.

The 56 kilocalories of energy indicated in the Gay-Lussac equation above as a product of fermentation of one gram molecular weight of glucose represents the total energy change during the reaction. If glucose is "burned" either actually or by complete metabolic combustion to carbon dioxide and water, the total heat energy released is 673 kilocalories. The yeast cell ferments sugar *not* to get alcohol and carbon dioxide; it has no use for them and thus they accumulate or escape. It does need energy, and this is the "profit" the yeast gains from fermenting the sugar. The energy is needed to do the chemical work of synthesizing the substances of more yeast cells; without it no reproduction of the yeast can occur. It is obvious that if 673 kilocalories are produced when yeast converts 180 grams of glucose to carbon dioxide and water by complete oxidation, and only 56 kilocalories are produced by alcoholic fermentation, more than twelve times the amount of energy is potentially available for producing new yeast cells aerobically than anaerobically. To put it another way, yeasts must metabolize more than twelve times as much sugar to produce the same amount of cellular growth when growing anaerobically as they would if oxygen were available to them. This is fortunate for us, because it means that during alcoholic fermentation the yeasts must "process" a great deal of sugar to alcohol with relatively little cell multiplication and therefore relatively little consumption of the sugar and other nutrients to build cells. If our object is to produce a large number of yeast cells, whether for use in inoculation of musts for wine fermentation or as pressed yeast cakes for the baker, the pumping of oxygen (air) through the solution containing the yeast will produce up to twelvefold more cells per unit of sugar consumed and lower or eliminate the production of ethanol. The fact that the addition of oxygen to fermenting yeasts inhibits the conversion of glucose to ethanol, and gives more cells per unit of glucose consumed, was observed by Pasteur and is termed the Pasteur effect.

The total amount of energy released during conversion of glucose to ethanol by yeasts (about 56 kilocalories/mole) is not available to the yeast for metabolic work. About 40 percent of this amount, or 22 kilocalories, is captured in a usable form by the yeast. The rest is lost to the yeast and appears as heat. Thus the temperature of the fermenting solution is increased significantly. The usable energy is captured and transferred to other uses by the yeast cell in the form of a complex chemical, adenosine triphosphate, usually abbreviated ATP. A phosphate ion from the fermenting solution is combined by enzymes of the yeast with adenosine diphosphate, ADP, to give ATP. This illustrates one important reason why yeasts require the presence of phosphate for growth. The formation of ATP requires energy, and the energy is obtained by the yeast from specific steps in the conversion of sugar to ethanol. Once "built into" ATP, this energy can be temporarily stored, transferred, and used by the yeast for a multitude of metabolic reactions requiring energy. In fact, ATP is the primary energy-exchanging substance for all activities of living organisms including the muscular work you are doing right now as you breathe.

Converting sugar to alcohol requires at least a dozen enzymes, each of which catalyzes one step in the process sequence of the Embden-Meyerhof pathway. The enzymes acting first are those necessary to get the particular sugar being fermented phosphorylated and isomerized into the form of fructose-1,6-diphosphate. This hexose phosphate is necessary for starting the remainder of the breakdown reactions, and two molecules of ATP are consumed in its formation from the fermentable simple sugars. The next reaction splits the 6-carbon unit, fructose-1,6-diphosphate, into two 3-carbon triose phosphates. These are dihydroxyacetone phosphate and glyceraldehyde-3-phosphate, which can be converted one into the other by the action of an isomerase (enzyme). A series of reaction steps, each with its own enzyme, then occurs, and eventually two molecules of pyruvic acid result. During these reactions hydrogen is transferred to a coenzyme carrier and two new molecules of ATP are formed for each 3-carbon unit, or a total of four, giving a net gain of two ATP per sugar molecule fermented. Each new gram molecule of ATP represents about 11 kilocalories of useful energy gained by the yeast, and therefore accounts for the 22 kilocalories of energy yeasts gain in converting one mole of glucose to two moles of ethanol.

The pyruvic acid (CH_3—CO—COOH) is converted to acetaldehyde (CH_3CHO) by loss of one molecule of carbon dioxide (or two per original hexose sugar). This escaping carbon dioxide is one of the major products of fermentation. The acetaldehyde is ordinarily reduced by the addition to it of the hydrogen transferred to the coenzyme carrier at the earlier step mentioned. This final reaction:

$$CH_3CHO + H_2 \rightarrow CH_3CH_2OH,$$

is catalyzed by the enzyme alcohol dehydrogenase. It is a reversible reaction, and acetaldehyde can be produced from ethanol. All the reactions in this sequence are reversible if the proper conditions, enzymes, and energy are supplied, except that of the decarboxylation (carbon dioxide loss) of pyruvic acid. The reversal of the sequence would produce sugars from smaller molecules, and has several features in common with the way in which the grapevine makes its sugar.

This reaction system may seem a bit complicated, but it has been substantiated by chemists and is one of the fundamentals of modern biochemistry. It clearly explains the origin of the major products of alcoholic fermentation. It also explains the presence of at least small amounts of many of the intermediate compounds in the sequence, such as acetaldehyde and pyruvic acid. Acetaldehyde reacts with sulfur dioxide, or rather the bisulfite ion in solution, to form an addition product which cannot be reduced to ethanol by the coenzyme hydrogen carrier system. The hydrogen is diverted under this condition to reduce the triose dihydroxyacetone to glycerol. Some glycerol (also called glycerine, $CH_2OH—CHOH—CH_2OH$) is produced to the extent of about 0.2 to 1.5 percent in every wine fermentation, but considerably more may be produced under certain conditions, including the presence of high amounts of bisulfite. Glycerol production for explosives (nitroglycerine) by fermentation was an important development in the First World War. Glycerol is a slightly sweet substance and *may* contribute to the viscosity and apparent "body" of some wines.

Glycerol is a constituent of fats, and as such some of it is incorporated into the yeast cell. Pyruvic acid is partly converted to alanine, one of the amino acids of yeast proteins. Reactions such as these divert some of the atoms from the original sugar molecule into yeast-cell constituents and decrease the yield of ethanol. Other reactions, such as the enzymatic reduction of a small amount of pyruvic acid to lactic acid or the conversion of some acetaldehyde to acetic acid, not only divert some of the carbon source to products other than alcohol, but also explain the presence of small amounts of these compounds which may contribute to a wine's flavor.

Yeasts are able to grow aerobically and can convert ethanol to acetaldehyde and then, via a series of reactions known as the Krebs cycle, after its discoverer, to carbon dioxide and water. Various degrees of temporary, partial, or incomplete aerobic metabolism can occur or be produced in wine fermentation. In the production of *flor* sherry, for example, the level of acetaldehyde and certain other flavor-producing substances is much increased by aerobic growth of yeast in or on the surface of previously fermented wine. In any typical wine fermentation, some oxygen gains access to the wine even though relatively anaerobic conditions must exist to produce wine. Again, as a result, more or less of the carbon source is diverted from ethanol production to other products. Among these products are citric acid, succinic acid, fumaric acid, malic acid, and α-ketoglutaric acid. Not all compounds that are found in wine got there from the action of yeasts, however, for the Krebs cycle occurs in grapes, too, and produces the greater part of the total acids found in wine.

These many possible and actual diversions of the carbon of sugar during wine fermentation explain the fact that whereas 51.1 percent of the weight of glucose theoretically should appear as ethanol, only about 48 percent actually does so. Since the yeast does produce 90 to 95 percent of the theoretical amount of ethanol, it might be assumed that the small amounts of other products are unimportant. This is far from the truth, because many of the constituents minor in amount in wine are major in importance to flavor and aroma. Many of the important esters and other odorous constituents are present in very small amounts and in complex mixtures which are difficult to analyze; yet they determine the quality and distinctiveness of wines and most other food products. In wines many of these important trace compounds arise from the grapes themselves, but many are produced or are modified as the yeasts play their role in the process of wine making.

Higher alcohols, sometimes called fusel oils, occur in fermented beverages. By higher alcohols is meant those like ethanol, but with more than two carbon atoms. Particularly the 5-carbon or amyl alcohols, 4-carbon butanols, and 3-carbon propyl alcohols or propanols may occur in wine in various isomers and proportions. These compounds arise in large part during alcoholic fermentation, and their relative concentration in wines and spirits is a factor in the flavor and quality of the product, although they ordinarily total rather less than 0.1 percent of the wine. It was believed, based upon the work of Ehrlich, that these compounds arose by the action of yeast enzymes upon the amino acids in wine musts. An example is the conversion of leucine into isoamyl alcohol:

$$(CH_3)_2—CH—CH_2—CH(NH_2)—COOH + H_2O$$
$$\rightarrow (CH_3)_2—CH—CH_2—CH_2OH + NH_3 + CO_2$$

This is an oversimplification because, among other things, more higher alcohols are produced under some conditions than can be accounted for by complete conversion of all the respective amino acids present in the medium. Rather, it is now known, the carbon skeletons which the yeast produces to make its amino acids can also be diverted to produce these alcohols. This is another example of the complex and intimate interplay among the numerous chemical reactions which characterize the metabolism of living cells, and alcoholic fermentation in particular.

As we have seen, the grape berry contains sugars, acids, pigments, tannins, and odorous compounds; and some of these ingredients, particularly sugars and amino-acid derivatives, are used and transformed by yeasts during fermentation. Fermentation, particularly the alcohol produced, affects the solvent powers of the fluid and influences the composition of the wine. The pigments, many of the odorous compounds, and part of the tannin compounds are localized within the cells of the skin of the grape berry. Another large portion of the total tannin of the berry is found in the seeds. Some of these compounds are not released at all and some do not go completely into the solution merely as a result of the crushing of the grapes. Time for diffusion from the cells and the extractive effect of alcohol are both provided during fermentation, if the solid parts of the berry remain in the must during this period. The turbulence in the fermentation vessel and perhaps the enzymic actions of the yeast also affect the transfer of less soluble grape-cell components to the solution. Thus, although the grape produces the tannin, anthocyanin pigment, and aroma compounds, and the yeast may not produce any synthesis or chemical change of these compounds, their content in the wine can be strongly influenced by events during the fermentation process.

Summary.—The juice from the freshly crushed grape berry contains sugars, acids, and other cell-sap-soluble components of the easily disrupted cells. Juice-insoluble substances and the contents of cells not easily broken, which may be important to the composition and quality of the wine, are dissolved in the wine by the alcohol and by other effects produced by fermentation. The metabolic activities of the fermenting wine yeast produce a theoretical conversion of 51 percent of the weight of sugar fermented to ethanol and the rest to carbon dioxide. Actual yields are slightly lower because the yeast produces a series of compounds other than alcohol. Some of the sugar is used to synthesize new yeast cells. The energy necessary for this synthesis and waste heat energy are produced by the yeast during the sequence of fermentation reactions terminating in ethanol, a byproduct of the activity of anaerobic yeast. The ethanol, acetaldehyde, higher alcohols (fusel oils), and other products of alcoholic fermentation are important attributes of wine. The variable proportions of them contribute to type, flavor, and quality differences among wines. Some yeast cells die and "leak" or break up (autolyze) to contribute their soluble constituents to the solution. Therefore, the composition of the wine may be affected by the grape, by the direct and indirect reactions of alcoholic fermentation on grape must, by yeast-cell breakdown products, by activity of other microorganisms, and by reactions during processing.

The biochemistry of fermentation not only beautifully illuminates and clarifies the ancient art of making wine, but also explains and makes possible a calculated control of many of the "mysteries" which baffled the artisan winemaker. Aesthetics, however, is still a part of (and should not be displaced from) wine production and wine appreciation, but mystique should not remain if knowledge can be substituted.

It is true that taste can be educated. It is also true that taste can be perverted. . . . If any man gives you a wine you can't bear, don't say it is beastly. . . . But don't say you like it. You are endangering your soul and the use of wine as well. . . . Seek out some other wine good to your taste. . . .
—HILAIRE BELLOC

Chapter 6

CLASSIFICATION OF WINES

Wines can be classified on the basis of geographical origin, color, the amount of carbon dioxide, sugar, or alcohol they contain, or many other chemical characteristics.

Actual commercial sales of wines are generally made according to country and district of origin. Climatic conditions, grape varieties used, winemaking procedures, and customs of processing and aging usually do make the wines of different viticultural regions different from each other. However, the geographical origin of wines requires a special classification for each country and for the many microclimates of each country. For nondefective ordinary wines, which differ little from one region or country to another, the distinction is unnecessary on the basis of either quality or composition.

The classification we shall use is based primarily upon easily recognizable characteristics, such as whether herbs or flavoring materials have been added, the amount of carbon-dioxide pressure, the percentage of sugar, and the presence or absence of distinguishable varietal aromas. This classification is intended primarily for students and consumers who are interested in distinguishing one wine from another by means of their own senses. It is basically an amplification of the scheme already outlined in the Introduction.

The question whether a varietal aroma is "distinguishable" is not so easily established. Different varieties contribute more or less distinctive flavors to wines. The distinctiveness varies with the maturity of the grapes (which, in turn, depends on climatic conditions) and on the winemaking and aging procedures. Moreover, individuals vary in their ability to recognize and remember varietal aromas: the novice may barely be able to distinguish muscats from nonmuscats, while the expert can distinguish a fairly large number of varietal aromas. But the beginner, though unable to identify the varietal aroma, will often be able to distinguish the odor of a wine from that of other varieties.

Even within a single varietal aroma there may be a good deal of variation. For example, the origin of most of the wines of Burgundy is Pinot noir. Nevertheless, many experts on the wines of Burgundy are able to distinguish the wines made in one part of the region from those made in another part, and even those of one vintage from another. The same is true of the wines of Bordeaux, although there the varietal composition is likely to be more complex. This also leads to differences among wines of different chateaux. Long experience with the wines of a region is necessary to be able to distinguish such subtle nuances of character; an expert on the wines of one region may be unable to identify the wines of another region with which he is unfamiliar. California's large area and climatically diverse vineyard regions can produce relatively wide differences among wines of the same type, even if 100 percent from a single grape variety.

In the following classification we have listed as "distinguishable" only those varieties and types of wines which are normally distinctive. A number of varieties listed as having indistinguishable varietal odors may, under certain conditions, be distinguishable. A good example is Nebbiolo, which is listed as being without a distinguishable varietal aroma, whereas the wines of Barolo sometimes have a distinguishable varietal aroma. Since Barolo wines are made from Nebbiolo, this would appear to be a contradiction—but when grown in the Barolo district, the Nebbiolo seems to have more varietal aroma than it does when it is grown in California and even in other regions of Italy. The examples given in this list are mainly of American wines, but include a representative number of European wine types. Note that the classification is generally dichotomous; so if the wine does not fall into one group, it must be found in the other. Inevitably there are some wines that overlap categories, as technological improvements or law changes permit new products.Where does one classify a 12-percent-alcohol flavored sweet wine with a hint of carbonation—such as now may be found at the corner grocery? More to the point, how should such a wine be used? Not in the "usual" connoisseur's fashion, that's certain!

WINES WITH ADDED HERBS
OR FLAVORING CONSTITUENTS

Wines with anthocyanin (red) pigments.—The exact flavoring materials which are added to red wines to produce bitter-tasting wines are not always known. One of the most popular proprietary wines of this type, Byrrh, contains some cinchona and has a distinctly bitter quinine taste. While most *retsina* is white, occasionally you find a red one containing the typical pine resin or turpentine odor. A few of the flavored California wines (with copyrighted proprietary names) have been at least pink in color. The Dubonnet and Byrrh types of wines are consumed in France as aperitifs with or without ice and with or without soda; in the United States Dubonnet is also used as an aperitif, as well as for making cocktails with gin. Several Italian types of wines might also be placed in this category, but none that we have sampled is likely to be popular with Americans. A number of red sangria-like (citrus-flavored) wines are now bottled in Spain and California, usually with less than 14 percent alcohol.

Wines without anthocyanin pigments.—The most characteristic of these are the herb-flavored wines of the dry or French type of vermouth and the sweet or Italian type of vermouth. The dry vermouths have a slight amber color when produced and sold in France or Italy. Those exported to or made in this country are mostly very light in color—this is obviously so that more vermouth can be blended with gin for martini cocktails (vermouth being less costly than gin). These vermouths are not actually dry, as most of them contain from 2 to 4 percent of sugar. The sweet type of vermouth is very sweet, usually with 14 to 16 percent sugar and 16 to 20 percent alcohol. Sweet vermouth has an amber color, sometimes with a reddish hue. Both types have distinct and complex odors from the herbs and spices from which they are made. Some dry vermouths on the American market have a low herb character. Even if strong in total herb character, the herb mixture should be adjusted so that the odor of no single herb or spice predominates.

Besides the true herb-flavored wines, we have nowadays a wide variety of wines to which other kinds of flavoring constituents have been added. These, known as "special natural-flavored" wines in this country, carry proprietary labels, such as Thunderbird and Silver Satin. Many of them are very light in color and appear to have been intended as substitutes for the gin or vodka type of highballs. A few have been produced with an amber color and have even been bottled in whiskey-type bottles. These may have been intended as substitutes for the whiskey highball. They formerly had 18 to 20 percent alcohol, but at present several have less than 14 percent alcohol. They usually contain 8 to 14 percent sugar. They have been moderately popular in this country, and there certainly is a market for them. It is probable that new and different types of flavoring materials may continue to be used in producing these types of wines. Several imported types appear to be imitations of the original American prototypes. The increase in consumption of such wines has been a partial cause for the lessened demand for standard dessert wines such as port and muscatel.

Very few medicinal types of wines are produced nowadays. Occasionally one finds a home-made gentian or rhubarb wine, and a small but widespread home industry is engaged in the making of flavored wines for home use. During and just after World War II, there was a fad for a flavored wine which was said to have medicinal property, but this eventually ran afoul of the internal-revenue laws and disappeared from the market. Some of the favored and widely advertised prescriptions of the past, especially tonics and those for "female complaints," may have owed their attraction and alleged beneficial properties to the alcohol they contained. Medicine was genteel; alcohol was not.

WINES WITHOUT ADDED HERBS
OR FLAVORING MATERIALS

Most of the wines produced in the world contain no added flavoring material. Their flavor comes from the variety of grape from which they were produced, from the fermentation process, or from treatments during aging or from the aging itself.

Wines with excess carbon dioxide—Excess (in the sense of supersaturation and increased pressure) carbon dioxide in wines may arise from (1) the fermentation of sugar which has been added to the finished wine, and which leads to the production of two to six atmospheres of pressure; (2) the fermentation of constituents normally present in the wine, such as residual sugar or malic acid; or (3) the addition of carbon dioxide directly to the wine. In the latter two cases, the amount of pressure produced is usually much less. Wines containing excess carbon dioxide from the fermentation of added sugar may be further classified as those containing anthocyanin pigments and those which do not contain anthocyanin pigments.

Sparkling wines containing anthocyanin pigments are commonly sold as either pink or red sparkling wines such as sparkling burgundy, cold duck, or champagne rouge. A small amount of sparkling Burgundy is imported from France. Because of their tannin content in juxtaposition with the carbon dioxide, these wines usually have a slightly bitter taste. Therefore they are normally sweetened and hence are abhorred, justifiably or not, by many wine connoisseurs.

Sparkling wines that do not contain anthocyanin pigments may be subdivided into those which have a muscat flavor and those which do not. The most important types of muscat-flavored sparkling wines are produced near Asti in northern Italy and known as *muscato spumante.* A small amount of sparkling muscat is also made in California and elsewhere.

The sparkling wines that do not contain a muscat flavor include those labeled simply as California or New York champagne, *Sekt* (Germany), *spumante* (Italy), *espumoso* (Spain, Portugal), *shampanskii* (Soviet Union), and Champagne or *mousseux* (France). In this country, if the wine has been fermented in bulk in large tanks it is labeled California or New York or American champagne, bulk or Charmat process. These nonred types of sparkling wines may be further labeled *brut, sec* (dry or extra dry), *demi-sec,* or *doux.* These usually refer to wines containing less than 1.5 percent of sugar for the *brut* types, and from 2.5 to 4.5 percent of sugar for the *sec,* 5 for *demi-sec,* and 10 for *doux.* However, some *brut* types, unfortunately, contain more than 1.5 percent sugar.

The sparkling wines that derive their gassiness from constituents normally present in still wines are of two types. Both contain very little pressure, usually about one to two atmospheres. More common are the wines which are gassy from the fermentation of residual sugar. These include occasional wines from Germany, France, and Italy, and the *muscato amabile* of California. The last is a particularly interesting type in that it is made from very sweet muscat musts which are allowed to ferment at a very low temperature. It is then bottled with a certain amount of gassiness. In France a number of the Vouvray types are gassy from the fermentation of the residual sugar.

Technically more interesting are the wines which are gassy from the malo-lactic fermentation, if this is characteristic and not an occasional defect. The most important types of these are the red and the white *vinho verde* types from the Minho district of northern Portugal (see Chapter 15). A number of wines in the Piedmont district of Italy are also gassy from the fermentation of malic acid.

Addition of carbon dioxide is an old practice, and formerly a number of these carbonated wines were found on the market. Those containing anthocyanin pigments were sold as

California carbonated burgundy and those not containing anthocyanin pigments were sold as California carbonated wines of the moselle or even of the sauterne type. A number of Swiss wines are bottled with enough added carbon dioxide to give them a slight gassiness. In California some wines contain about an atmosphere of pressure, sufficient to give a slightly prickly sensation to the tongue. These may not be called carbonated wines either on the bottle or in their advertising, since that would cause their tax to be increased, but the title of one of them, Ripple, seems to suggest subtly that carbon dioxide may be present. Under the new (1975) regulations, which again increased the permissible level of carbon dioxide in "still" wines, more of this type of wine will probably be produced in the future.

Wines without obvious excess carbon dioxide. —These wines, the major portion produced in the world, can be classified as still (i.e., not gassy) wines. There are three very broad groups on the basis of alcohol content: below 14 percent alcohol, those between about 14 and 17 percent alcohol, and those containing over 17 but below about 21 percent alcohol. The first are commonly known as table wines, and the others as aperitif or dessert wines. Judgment of the relative alcohol level by taste requires some experience and a few percentage differences within categories, but it is relatively easy to distinguish between the usual 12-percent table wine and the 17 to 20 percent group by the intensity of the alcohol odor and the sensation of warmth in the mouth.

Alcohol 8 to 14 percent: California regulations call for wines to be between 10.5 and 14 percent alcohol if they are red, and between 10 and 14 percent if they are white. Federal regulations require a minimum of 9 percent by volume of alcohol. The usual European minimum is 8 or 9 percent. For districts with an *appellation d'origine* in France (see Chapter 13), the minimum percentage of alcohol is specified by regulations. For example, a wine labeled simply Bordeaux rouge can have a lower minimum of alcohol than one labeled Médoc. The regulations in other countries are likewise very diverse.

Two broad subgroups of these wines may be differentiated:

those with anthocyanin pigments and those without such pigments. The wines containing anthocyanin pigments can be subdivided, in turn, into those which are pink and those which have a full red color.

The pink wines are usually dry and are labeled as rosé types, sometimes varietal such as California Gamay rosé or California Grenache rosé, or in a few cases Grignolino. Some come from a specific district in France, such as Anjou, Provence, or Tavel, or in Italy, such as Calabria, Puglia, or Tuscany. Some proprietary blended rosé wines, both American and imported from Portugal, Spain, and elsewhere, have appeared on the market. Some of these are lightly carbonated. There has been a tendency to make the rosés with about 1 to 2 percent sugar. A number of the more popular brands are decidedly on the sweet side. Some eastern United States proprietary-named rosés are very sweet. Unfortunately, sugar levels do not now appear on the labels.

The table wines with a red color are generally and traditionally dry, although a few have a small amount of sugar. The dry red wines can be classified as to whether they have or do not have a distinguishable varietal aroma.

Among these with a distinguishable varietal aroma, the Barbera usually has a high acidity although, because of the use of the malo-lactic fermentation or late harvesting, this may not always be true. Those with a moderate acidity include Barolo, produced from the Nebbiolo grape; Beaujolais, a product of the Gamay variety; the various Bordeaux wines such as Médoc, Saint-Émilion, and château wines from the various districts, all of which contain some Cabernet aroma; the wines of Burgundy, produced from Pinot noir; the California, Chilean, Australian, Argentinean, Russian, etc., Cabernets; Châteauneuf-du-Pape, produced from Grenache and several other varieties; Chianti, a product of Sangioveto and Colorino; Freisa, named after the variety; Gamay (at least some Gamays in California have a varietal aroma); Hermitage, which owes its distinguishable character to Petite Sirah; California, Chilean, and other Pinot noirs; Rioja, a mixture of Grenache and Tempranilla; Zinfandel; and many others.

Wines without a distinguishable varietal aroma include California burgundy, California claret, California dry red table wine, California red chianti; Carignane; Charbono; Durif; Malvoisie; Mourastel; Pinot St.-George (Red Pinot by error); and many of the *vins ordinaires* and local wines of France, Portugal, Spain, Italy, and other countries. Under the best conditions, some of the varietal types may have a distinctive flavor. Although many attempts have been made to introduce characteristic distinctions between these nonvarietal types—for example, greater color and alcohol in California burgundy compared to California claret—none has been successful. The California burgundy of one producer may resemble the California claret of another, and vice versa. In France the *vin ordinaire* is often sold (with increasing price) on the basis of alcohol content—usually 9 to 11 percent.

Stable sweet red wines of only 8 to 14 percent alcohol are easily produced with the modern methods of stabilization and pasteurization, and a number of them are found on the market. They include wines of the California vino da tavola (mellow red) type which contain about 1.5 percent sugar, but they also include a number of kosher-type wines which would be classified as sweet red table wines, but which have a distinct Concord aroma.

White wines (without anthocyanin pigments) can be classified into those which have a distinguishable varietal aroma and those which do not. Among those which have a distinguishable varietal aroma, some are sweet and others contain no noticeable sugar. The sweet wines include various German types; Hungarian Tokay; the California light muscat, Malvasia bianca, and other light sweet muscats; the Loire wines in years when *Botrytis* develops well; French Sauternes; Sweet Catawba; some California Sauvignon blancs and Sémillons; and some California and South African Chenin blancs. There are also eastern United States wines with proprietary, varietal and semi-generic labels which are sweet and have an anthranilate (Concord) type of odor.

The dry wines with distinguishable varietal aromas include Catawba; Chablis; Chardonnay (sometimes labeled Pinot

Chardonnay); Chenin blanc (sometimes slightly sweet, and occasionally labeled White Pinot by error); Delaware (also pink); Folle blanche (not always with a varietal aroma); Gewürztraminer; Graves; Grey Riesling (sometimes); some Loire wines, particularly from Vouvray; Moselle; California Pinot blanc; Rhine; California White Riesling (called Johannisberg Riesling by error); California Dry Sauvignon blanc (also called Fumé blanc); California Sauvignon vert; California Dry Sémillon; Sylvaner; and Traminer.

Many California, French, Italian, and other white table wines do not have a distinguishable varietal character. Thus California chablis, dry sauterne, rhine, white chianti, and similar types are usually blends of several wines—often wines of ordinary varieties of grapes. Even wines labeled Riesling, Green Hungarian, Veltliner, Rotgipfler, Chasselas doré (or Gutedel) can seldom be distinguished, at least in most years or from most producers. Many Italian, Austrian, Swiss, Spanish, and Greek white table wines are of this type. As with the reds, many attempts to persuade California producers to make some distinction in flavor and chemical composition between the generic types have been without success—e.g., to distinguish California chablis from California rhine. One company's products may be quite different from another's with the same generic name; or in some instances, there is little difference between two generic wines from the same company.

Alcohol 14 to 17 percent: This is a sort of no-man's-land for wines. There is a good reason for this. Fermentation of sugar often ceases at about 14 percent alcohol, but bacterial activity continues through 17 or 18 percent. Consequently, wines which contain residual sugar are usually fortified up to something over 17 percent of alcohol so that they will rarely be subject to bacterial spoilage.

The Catholic Church has preferred that alcohol be added to wines only toward the end of the tumultuous fermentation and, in addition, that the alcohol should not normally exceed about 18 percent. Therefore, a number of wines with an alcohol content in this range are produced for ecclesiastical use. A few dry Spanish wines of the *fino* and *manzanilla* types with an alcohol content of about 15 to 16 percent are regularly sold in Spain and occasionally exported.

Among the wines in this alcohol range which contain anthocyanin pigments are miscellaneous red sweet wines which are shipped to certain states because of legal restrictions. Sometimes these are called American port; others have proprietary names. A number of these are kosher or for ecclesiastical use and employ either proprietary names or names that would indicate that they are not dessert wines. Recently some late-harvested California varietal reds of over 14 percent alcohol have appeared on the market. These appear to us to be too high in alcohol to be considered as table wines. Certainly they will be very slow to mature by bottle aging.

The wines in this range that do not contain anthocyanin pigments include a variety of ecclesiastical types which may be labeled California angelica or California muscatel or have various kinds of proprietary labels. The Spanish *fino* and *manzanilla* wines are usually labeled under these names, but would, of course, also carry the name of the producer. A number of the *montilla* and some Málaga wines in Spain have an alcohol content in this intermediate range. The Soviet Union produces a number of very sweet wines which have an alcohol content of not more than 16 percent. These wines, sometimes labeled muscatel or Pinot gris, contain up to 20 or 23 percent sugar. For most purposes, this alcohol range can be ignored and its wines considered with the most closely related table or appetizer or dessert wines.

Alcohol 17 to 21 percent: This is the main group of appetizer and dessert wines, with the most common minimum alcohol level now 18 percent, except for sherries at 17 percent. It too can be divided into two subgroups: those which contain anthocyanin pigments and those which do not. Those which contain anthocyanin pigments can be divided into those with a muscat aroma and those without a muscat aroma. In this country very little muscat-flavored wine, red or pink, is now produced. Aleatico wine is seldom on the market at the present time, but a number of sweet table wines made from it in Tuscany and Sardinia in Italy do have a pink color and muscat aroma. Only a few California companies are producing a red or black muscatel.

We have a number of types of red dessert wines which do not have a muscat aroma. A wine with very tawny-red or pink color and baked odor is California tokay. It obviously has some of the characteristics of a sherry, very few characteristics of port, and some of the sugary characteristics of angelica. It is not normally aged very long in California, and enjoys only a limited market, usually among consumers desiring a low-priced dessert wine.

The more important group of red fortified wines without a muscat aroma are those which carry the name port. Those which have a slight brownish red or amber tint are usually sold as tawny port, whether from Portugal, California, Australia, or South Africa. The red color is more pronounced than in California tokay. The tawny color should be clearly due to aging and not to baking, since wines made by baking usually have a caramel or burnt odor. The remainder of the ports available in this country are called simply port or ruby port. Vintage ports include the wines that are bottled after only two years in wood, or in some cases wines which may be bottled somewhat later, but before they become brown in color. The classical type of vintage port was that produced in Portugal, but bottled and most appreciated in Great Britain. Vintage-type wines with wood- and bottle-aging are made also in California, Australia, and South Africa.

For the wines not containing anthocyanin pigments, we can also distinguish those which have a muscat aroma from those which do not. A great many white dessert wines with a muscat aroma are produced in various parts of the world: for example, the muscatel of Frontignan and of Lunel from the south of France, and the Muscato Canelli from near Asti in the Piedmont district of Italy. Some Italian muscatels are slightly less than 17 percent alcohol, rather than above. There are also the very sweet muscat wines from the Island of Samos in Asia Minor, the Setúbal wine from near Lisbon in Portugal, and the varieties of muscatel from Russia, South Africa, Australia, and California. While many of these have developed an amber color through aging, some are amber because they were made from excessively ripe grapes or were heated. These latter have a raisin or caramel flavor which is undesirable.

A number of white dessert wines have a special odor because of treatment or aging; others have no special odor caused by treatment or aging. The first group includes a diverse collection of wines having a raisin odor (Málaga); a baked odor (California dry, medium, or sweet sherry, and Madeira of Sercial, Boal, and Malmsey types); wines with a reduced-must or burnt odor (Marsala type); and wines with a *rancio* odor from long aging of sweet wines (such as the Banyuls from the south of France and the wines from the Priorato region near Tarragona in northern Spain).

In another group of wines, the special odor arises from the film-yeast process. These film-yeast wines can be divided into dry and slightly sweet types. Among the dry types are California, Australian, South African, and Russian *flor* sherry; many of the *montilla* wines from near Cordoba in Spain; the wines from Château Chalon in France; and some of the Spanish *manzanillas* which have been prepared for export. Among the slightly sweet *flor* types are the *amontillados* and Australian, Russian, Californian or South African medium or sweet *flor* sherries. Some of the sweet types of Spanish sherries *(olorosos* and some *montillas)* contain little film-yeast wine and belong in the next category.

The last grouping includes wines which do not have a special odor because of treatment or aging. The most important of these is the amber-colored wine called California angelica. The *olorosos* which do not have any *flor*-type odor could also be placed in this category. Some of the cream sherries from Spain might belong here, too. The classification becomes difficult because extensive blending occurs. Wines which are somewhat lighter in color, owing to the use of very light-colored juice and possibly, for some wines, the use of charcoal, are sold as California white port. White port from Portugal is more nearly in the category of the California angelica.

Summary.—Wines can be classified on the basis of whether or not they contain added flavoring materials, such as herbs or spices. The nonflavored wines can be separated into sparkling and nonsparkling wines, depending on whether or not they contain a visible excess of carbon dioxide at room temperature. Most of the wines of the world are of the nonsparkling type. These can best be distinguished on the basis of percentage of alcohol: 8 to 14, 14 to 17, and 17 to 21 percent. The intermediate group is of importance primarily for wines produced for certain localities or for sacramental purposes. In all groups, wines can be classified on the basis of color, varietal aroma, and sugar content, and additionally in the 17 to 21 percent group, by production or processing techniques. Some understanding of all categories, and the exceptions difficult to classify, is necessary to grasp the diversity and fascination of wine as a whole. Features expected in one wine type may be defects in another—sparkling *versus* gassy table wines, or sherries *versus* oxidized table wines, for examples.

Wine is made to be drunk as women are to be loved: profit by the freshness of youth or the splendor of maturity; do not await decrepitude.
—THEOPHILE MALVEZIN

Chapter 7

OPERATIONS IN WINEMAKING

Most of the descriptions of winemaking processes given here are based upon commercial practice. This may appear unfortunate to persons interested in home winemaking; for this reason, a few words on making wine at home are in order. The United States has very detailed and stringent laws regulating the production of alcoholic beverages; the Bureau of Alcohol, Tobacco, and Firearms (often referred to as the B.A.T.F.) of the federal Treasury Department must be consulted regarding the latest pertinent federal laws before one engages in such production. The federal laws permit, upon obtaining specific permission, the tax-free production of up to 200 gallons of still wine per year by the head of a family, for the exclusive use of the family. This ruling reflects the special place that wine holds as a dietary beverage; such permission is not granted for distilled beverages or beer. In fact, even possessing an unregistered still is illegal; home registrations are rarely approved, and then only for uses other than producing alcoholic beverages (distilled water, etc.).

Assuming that you are the head of a household and have obtained governmental permission to make wine at home, can you can be successful? The answer depends upon your idea of success. Many who dabble in home vegetable gardening soon learn that it is difficult to show a profit. Even if land and labor are assumed to be free, satisfactory gardens are rare without expenditure for fertilizer, sprays, and tools. If accounting is honest, you may find that better and cheaper carrots can be obtained from the grocery store than from your garden. The "money-savers" and the "let's-try-it-oncers" are usually better advised not to start gardening (or winemaking).

If you care to learn how and follow the rules, it is possible to produce carrots of prize-winning quality—or, for that matter, orchids—at home. Winemaking is similar. If you want the pride and thrill of being able to say "I made it myself," or if you have an abiding interest in making a special product not otherwise obtainable (such as wine from your own rare variety of grapes), you can learn to make good wine in small lots (about 5 gallons recommended minimum) in your own basement or garage. However, success depends on attention to all the enological facts which govern the production of good wines commercially. Therefore, a description of commercial practices and the reasons behind them will suffice for the home winemaker if he does not cut too many corners. He may be willing to accept a small amount of sediment in his wine, and can do without filtration and tartrate removal; but if he does not keep his storage containers full and sealed, the wine will become vinegar even more quickly than it does in large commercial operations.Some pamphlets with specific descriptions of home winemaking procedures are listed in the list of Supplementary Reading: Amerine and Marsh (1962), Eakin and Ace (1970), and Robinson (1963). Too many other books for the would-be home winemaker take the form of recipes which are deceptively simple, but rarely culminate in a worthwhile product.

COMMERCIAL WINE ANALYSIS

To make the best wine possible with the raw materials available, and do so every time, the process must be *controlled* from grape to glass. Control implies learning the necessary facts and acting upon them to modify the process in the desired direction. The facts relate to the microbiological status, chemical composition, and sensory quality of the grapes and the wine at all the important stages. To obtain these facts, every winery must use laboratory examination and several analytical procedures. A few of the larger wineries have elaborate quality control and developmental research laboratories staffed with enologists, bacteriologists, chemists, statisticians, engineers, and other specialists. All wineries have at least modest facilities for obtaining the essential minimum of data.

It may be sufficient for the winery to determine sugar, total acid, volatile acid, alcohol, and extract in the musts and wines. Analyses for sulfur dioxide, tannin, pigment, aldehydes, esters, iron, copper, calcium, postassium, and malic acid are frequently very helpful. Sensory examination (careful, unbiased comparison and judgment of appearance and flavor) is necessary, and microscopic and microbiological control are frequently needed. Consulting organizations, both private and (especially in Europe) governmental, may be utilized by smaller wineries, particularly for the more complex or less commonly required laboratory procedures.

Total acid content is usually determined by neutralizing a sample of the wine with a solution of alkali. Calculation of the total acid (as tartaric acid) from the amount of alkali required is then possible. The total acid value is a measure of the tartness of the wine or must, and is useful in determining the time to pick the grapes, in preparing blends, and in estimating a wine's stability. Volatile acidity is determined similarly, upon a distillate from a wine sample, and indicates the soundness or defectiveness of the wine from its acetic acid (vinegar) content.

Alcohol (ethanol or ethyl alcohol), sugar, and extract can be determined in several ways, depending upon the accuracy and specific data needed. Modifications of a single simple method can be used to estimate all three to a degree of accuracy sufficient for most winery purposes. Extract refers to the nonvolatile, soluble solids present in a wine. It is determined on the residual solution after distilling the alcohol from a wine sample. The distillate is trapped and condensed and used to determine the alcohol content of the samples. Sugar is not usually determined directly but is estimated as dissolved solids, since the major portion of the soluble solids in must and sweet wine is sugar, and correction can be made if desired for the nonsugar solids, i.e., the extract in a sample of the same must fermented dry. The total dissolved solids in an aqueous solution (such as must) or the alcohol in a distillate can be determined by measuring the density of the solution. Density, the weight per unit of volume, is affected by temperature— the volume of a given weight of solution increases as the temperature rises. Therefore, the density determined at the solution's temperature is corrected to a standard temperature and compared to the appropriate table of known density values for sugar or ethanol solutions in water at the standard temperature. To avoid using density tables, it is possible to determine the density by means of hydrometers calibrated directly in units of sugar or alcohol concentration.

Hydrometry is based upon Archimedes' discovery that a floating object will sink in a liquid just to the point that the weight of the volume of liquid displaced by the submerged portion equals the weight of the object itself. The hydrometer (sometimes called a "stem" or "spindle" in the winery vernacular) is a sealed hollow glass tube with a bulbous end weighted at the bottom so that it floats vertically (Figure 9). The top portion is made narrow so that a considerable length represents a relatively small increase in displaced volume. This drawn-out portion is calibrated and marked to indicate the density, or a density-related value, of the liquid at the point on this scale intersected by the surface of the liquid when the hydrometer is floating freely. In order that the whole range of values possible in the winery can be read to the desired degree of accuracy (usually ± 0.05 percent), a set of hydrometers, each covering only a part of the range, is needed.

When ethanol is added to water, the density decreases and the hydrometer sinks deeper and deeper.Hydrometers for use in determining alcohol in wine distillates are usually calibrated to read ethanol volume per hundred units of solution volume (percentage by volume) at 60°F. (15.6° C.) It is usual to distill the alcohol from a certain volume of wine and dilute the distillate back to that same volume in order that the alcohol content of the wine may be read directly from the distillate

Fig. 9. Hydrometers illustrating measurement of dissolved solids
in the juice (left) and ethanol in distillates (right), with a
thermometer for use in correcting the values to a standard
temperature.

(corrected if necessary to 60° F.). The residual aqueous
solution in the distillation flask can be diluted to the original
wine volume also, and the dissolved solids (extract) determined with a different set of hydrometers.

Dissolving solids like sugar and organic acids in water raises
the density and causes hydrometers to float higher and higher.
Hydrometers used for the measurement of dissolved solids in
wineries are usually calibrated to read zero in pure water at
(68° F.) 20° C., and weight units of sucrose (table sugar) per 100
weight units (percentage by weight) for higher density solutions at that temperature. The tables of density values upon
which these calibrations are based were first calculated by Balling, and later recalculated and improved by Brix. Since the dissolved solid being measured in the winery is not primarily
sucrose, it is common to refer to a reading corresponding to
the density of 20.0 grams of sucrose per 100 grams of solution

at 20° C. as 20.0° Brix (pronounced "bricks") or simply Brix 20.0. Degrees Balling may also be used in wineries, but Brix is the preferred term and is used in the other branches of the food industry. The numerical values are now the same in any case.

Brix values for the extract of a completely fermented dry wine generally are below 2 for thin white wines and over 3 for the richer red wines. The extract of sweet wines is higher in proportion to the sugar content. For most winery operations, the temperature-corrected Brix values are ordinarily used directly for determining the time to pick grapes, for estimating the alcohol yield to be expected from grapes received at the winery, and for following the course of a fermentation. For these purposes it is important to recognize the approximations involved. Since sugar solutions are denser and alcohol solutions less dense than water, the Brix readings will drop faster during fermentation than does the actual consumption of sugar. At a hydrometer reading of 0° Brix, unfermented sugar is usually present; when the sugar of a sweet grape must is completely fermented, the alcohol level produces a minus Brix hydrometer reading directly in the wine. Serious errors in Brix values may result if care is not taken to prevent the effects of high levels of suspended insoluble solids, foam in the solution, and unclean hydrometers.

Values for dissolved solids equivalent to the Brix hydrometer readings may be obtained on grape juice by using a refractometer, which measures sugar and other dissolved substances by their effect on the refractive index of the aqueous solution. Pocket-sized models calibrated in Brix equivalents covering the range of about 0 to 40 percent sugar are very convenient for use in the vineyard to observe the ripening of the grapes and select the time for harvesting. Only a few drops of juice are needed for a reading, and readings can be taken from several vines in a few minutes. A hydrometer requires a cupful or more of juice, and is more fragile and inconvenient for field use.

A convenient formula for estimating the alcohol content to expect in a dry wine is: degrees Brix of the crushed grapes (original unfermented must) times 0.55 equals alcohol in percentage by volume after fermentation. This estimate corrects for the conversion of some sugar to other products, takes into account the extract, and expresses the alcohol in the usual wine units. Therefore, grapes testing 20° Brix can be expected to give wine of about 11 percent alcohol by volume, or numerically slightly more alcohol than half the "sugar" (dissolved solids) in the proper units.

PREPARING THE GRAPES

The making of wine actually starts with the harvesting of the grapes. Not only must they be picked at the proper stage of development for the particular wine to be made, but they must arrive at the winery in good condition. They should arrive at the winery as cool as possible, with clusters intact and berries without damaged skins or freed juice. The time between picking and the start of actual processing in the winery should be short. If mechanically harvesting, it is generally better to destem, crush, and add sulfur dioxide in the field. The must can then be transported to the winery in a closed tank protected from air. If the picked grapes are handled roughly and held for even a short time, organisms begin to develop. Some of these organisms are likely to be undesirable under these uncontrolled, aerobic conditions. The subsequent wine fermentation may not be as "clean," and the yield of alcohol and the quality of the wine may be lowered. Loss of free juice may reduce the yield of wine. The modern American practice is to wash the grape containers after each trip from the vineyard to the winery. If the grapes are broken or juice dries on the containers, the cleaning process is more difficult. A final important reason for care and dispatch in handling grapes is that enzymes of the fruit, particularly those that cause browning (as on a peeled apple), begin to act when the berry is broken. This may contribute an undesirable brown color and possibly other defects to the wine.

Stemming and crushing.—The processing of grapes into wine begins as soon as the grapes arrive at the winery. Although there are several stages in the process, there is no stopping-place until the wine has passed at least the fermentation and initial clarification steps. The first operation at the winery is ordinarily the removal of the stems, and the next is the crushing of the grape berries. Usually both operations are accomplished together in a crusher-stemmer. Various models are used, but the Garolla type is common. It consists of a horizontal cylinder or tube a foot or more in diameter and several feet long, covered with slots or holes large enough to pass the berries but not the stems from the cluster (Figure 10). Along the center of this tube is an axle carrying a series of paddles which rotate at fairly high speed, 500 r.p.m. or more. The tube itself also rotates, at a moderate speed—about 25 r.p.m. The grape clusters are conveyed into one end of the tube, and as they travel along it the paddles whip the berries through the holes and the stems remain inside to be carried out the other end. The berries are whipped or knocked through the holes in the rotating cylinder with some force, and are thereby crushed either by the paddles in going through the holes or by hitting the walls of another stationary cylinder surrounding the first, which catches and drains the crushed grape mass, called must, into a basin or sump from which it is pumped to the next operation.

The ease of removing the stems and crushing the berries depends upon the variety of grapes. Large clusters with long, tough stems cause problems from the stems' winding around parts of the machinery. Withered or raisined berries may hang onto the stems or resist crushing. Berries of thick-skinned or pulpy varieties may crush poorly. Table-grape varieties have been selected for stronger skins and large clusters with strong stem attachment, to withstand shipment as fresh fruit; as a result, they are often relatively difficult to destem and crush for winery use. The objective of crushing is to break open every one of the berries to free the juice for removal or for contact and fermentation by the yeast; the intact berry may pass through a fermentation unchanged and not yield its juice when pressed, thus reducing the yield of wine. Grinding or overly forceful breaking of the berries is usually undesirable: an excess of suspended solids may be introduced, and the wine will be difficult to clarify later; also,

FIG. 10. Internal view of a crusher-stemmer. (Source: The Wine
    Institute.)

seeds may be broken up, and then contribute too much tannin,
astringency, and bitterness, as well as seed oils, to the wine.

The dry stems amount to only about 40 to 150 pounds per
ton of grapes, depending upon the variety, and average about
80 pounds. They contain very little fermentable carbohydrate,
and no appreciable loss is sustained by their removal unless

an unusual amount of juice or tightly-held raisins are carried off with them. Removal of the stems from grapes for wines is common practice in California and most other modern wine-growing areas of the world. The stems contain a fairly high concentration of tannin, and this tannin and other substances from the stems add astringency, bitterness, and resinous or peppery flavors to the wine if they are not removed. Stems are also relatively high in ash (mineral) and acid, which may contribute undesirably. Musts without stems are reduced in volume, and pump and handle more easily. Rarely (in California), stems may be left in the must to contribute some tannin to wines otherwise too low in this group of substances for proper flavor and keeping qualities. Sometimes stems are left in or are added back to aid in pressing juice from troublesome lots of freshly crushed grapes that are pulpy and tend to squirt through the press openings instead of yielding their juice.

Sulfur dioxide addition. —Wine yeasts tolerate moderate concentrations of sulfur dioxide, while most undesirable organisms in musts and wine are inhibited by it. Sulfur dioxide is the pungent gas which is given off as sulfur is burned in air. Formerly, sulfur-containing candles and cloth wicks were burned in casks to produce the sterilizing gas. Now, however, metal cylinders of the liquefied SO_2 gas are more commonly used, because they give a more precise and controllable treatment. The sulfur dioxide may be metered directly into the solution (must or wine), or it may be dissolved as a concentrated solution (6 percent or more) in water (sulfurous acid is the hydrated form of sulfur dioxide) for addition. The bisulfite ion and sulfurous acid may be generated in musts, and in wine also, by the addition of sodium or potassium metabisulfite ($Na_2S_2O_5$ or $K_2S_2O_5$), sodium sulfite (Na_2SO_3), or sodium bisulfite ($NaHSO_3$). These white crystalline solids are no longer used commercially as often as sulfur-dioxide gas or solution, but are perhaps more convenient to obtain and to store for use in small operations, such as in home wine-making. In acid solutions (e.g., musts), they yield about half of their weight as sulfur dioxide.

Sulfur dioxide has three major functions in winemaking: to control undesirable microorganisms, to inhibit the browning enzymes, and to serve as an antioxidant. The action of the browning enzymes of grapes is directly inhibited by sulfurous acid, which denatures these enzymes. Sulfur dioxide also helps prevent browning and other oxidative reactions by keeping the system under reducing conditions and reacting with the oxygen present. By this action it becomes an antioxidant and resists or even temporarily reverses the effects of air. Other effects of sulfur dioxide include combination with acetaldehyde, thus causing the formation of more glycerol by fermentation. The amounts used in normal winemaking are too small to change the glycerol content appreciably, but the technique has been used to alleviate glycerol shortages during wartime. Sulfur dioxide may aid in clarification, especially of juice before fermentation. It helps kill the cells of the grape skin and thereby aids the release of the red pigment for red wines, but it also reacts with the red pigments to bleach some of the color, at least temporarily.

No other substance is known which has the combination of desirable attributes of sulfur dioxide, but several different substances are coming into use or are being tested to reduce the total amount of sulfur dioxide needed. Substitutes are desired because its burnt-sulfur, pungent odor becomes noticeable, and a negative quality factor, at rather low levels. There are also objections from public-health authorities to excessive daily intake of sulfur dioxide from all sources. Its use should therefore be held to the absolute minimum; and with close attention to good winery practices, it is not necessary to use objectionable levels of sulfur dioxide. The legal maximum in finished wine in the United States and most other countries has been 350 p.p.m.; there is some pressure for this to be lowered toward about 200 p.p.m. Some sulfur dioxide is naturally present as a result of yeast's reduction of sulfate during fermentation.

Owing to the need to inhibit the browning enzymes and "wild" microorganisms as soon as the grapes are crushed, the sulfur dioxide is often metered in at the crusher-stemmer as the must is pumped to the next operation. Thus the action of the sulfur dioxide begins immediately, and the necessary uniform mixing of the sulfur dioxide with the must is accomplished more easily. Since the bound forms of sulfur dioxide, such as the aldehyde bisulfite addition compound formed during fermentation, are not active as are the free forms, it is usually necessary to make further small additions of sulfur dioxide at later stages of winemaking.

PRESSING

After the grapes are destemmed and crushed and sulfur dioxide is added, the must is ready for further processing. If white grapes are being vinified (converted to wine), the usual next step is separation of the fluid must or juice from the solids (skins, seeds, and part of the pulp), called pomace, specifically sweet pomace in this case. If red wines are being produced, the separation of fluid (wine) from solid (fermented or dry pomace) occurs during fermentation, but the same type of equipment is used. The must may be held in a large tank for a time, and pectin-splitting enzymes may be added to allow some breakdown of the tissues to occur. The free juice may then be drained off through a slotted false bottom in the tank. This juice, or wine similarly obtained, is termed *free-run* as opposed to *press-run*. With care, particularly with juicy wine-grape varieties, it is often possible to obtain 60 to 70 percent of the fluid as free-run. Even if this particular method is not followed, it is usual to collect a free-run fraction which drains off from the press under no pressure or very light pressure, and then to collect one or more subsequent portions as the pressing becomes more complete. The wine resulting from the later, more drastic pressings may be used in blending, sold as a lower-quality grade, or used for distilling, since it may contain a high level of tannins or other potentially undesirable extractives and may resist clarification.

Vitis labrusca varieties are called "slip-skin" grapes and are difficult to press; other pulpy varieties also are troublesome. Muscat varieties, some table-grape varieties, and a few others, such as Palomino, are noted for the difficulty with which the juice is recovered from the pulp. Not only is good juice recovery difficult from such grapes, but the pulp and skins tend to squirt explosively from the openings in the press as pressure is applied. To resist this effect, pressure is applied very slowly and the press may be lined with cloth or stems.

On the other hand, after fermentation the remaining grape pulp is usually disintegrated to the point that pressing the pomace is less troublesome. Thus, pressing of pomace from red-wine fermentations is rarely a problem. The total direct yield of juice (or wine) from grapes is from 140 to 190 gallons per ton and averages about 175 gallons commercially. White wines (pressed as juice) usually yield 15 to 20 gallons less per ton of grapes than red wines (pressed after fermentation). The dry weight of the pomace amounts to 40 to 160 pounds per ton of grapes, averaging 100 pounds.

Several types and many models of presses are in use in wineries. The major types of presses are rack and cloth presses, basket presses and modifications thereof, and continuous presses. In the rack and cloth procedure, a slotted shallow box, usually wooden, is lined with a coarse-weave cloth. The crushed grape must, perhaps mixed with cellulose fibers or other press aid, is distributed a few inches thick on the cloth, the cloth is folded over the top, and the whole "cheese," or several stacked on each other, is squeezed in a screw or hydraulic-pressure frame until the juice desired has run out and been collected in a catch basin at the bottom. This procedure is laborious and slow, but it can handle Concord and other slippery varieties of grapes that are very difficult to press. With the increasing costs of labor and new types of presses, this procedure has nearly disappeared.

Basket presses—the familiar slotted wooden basket with screw or hydraulically operated central piston and press-plate, used for cider and other juices as well as wines—are used particularly in small table-wine wineries (Figure 11). They are rather slow and laborious, and are rapidly being replaced by modern semiautomatic presses. By pressing less forcefully on a thinner layer of grape pomace, the newer models produce a better combination of good recovery with high-quality musts. One press of this kind (the Willmes-type bag or bladder press) receives the must into a slotted horizontal cylinder (slots too small to pass seeds and skins) with closed ends. The cylinder is rotated to distribute the must around the periphery, and a rubber bag along the axis of the cylinder is inflated with air pressure, forcing the solid portion (pomace) against the sides. The juice (or wine) is caught in a pan at the bottom. The pressure may be released, the cylinder rotated, and pressure reapplied to improved the yield. The dry pomace is then expelled, and the cycle is repeated.

Continuous presses on the market today are usually of the screw-press type, although continuous-belt presses are available. The screw press operates by accepting must or partly pressed pomace at one end, and compresses it by passing it along a screw rotating in a slotted cylinder. The screw threads and cylinder are pitched at an angle such that progressively higher pressure is applied and the fluid is expressed from the solid mass through the slots. The pomace expelled from the end of the screw may be actually hot from the pressure and friction produced. Although extremely high recovery can be obtained, the quality of the product is apt to be low (high in astringency and bitterness, difficult to clarify, perhaps heated or browned). However, the newer types of continuous presses separate the clearer juice into several fractions and perhaps produce more clear juice, with only the last fraction reserved for wine for distilling.

FERMENTATION

The fermentation of the juice for white wines, or the whole crushed grape mass for red wines, is the next operation. The fermentation is accomplished in any suitable container large enough so that it is only half to three-quarters full when the must has been added. This precaution is frequently necessary owing to the considerable volume of carbon dioxide produced during rapid fermentation, and the resultant expansion in volume and surface foam. The sulfured must is pumped into this tank and the inoculum of wine yeast added

Fig. 11. Hydraulic press and press cake after pressing. (Source: Presse- und Informationsamt der Bundesregierung, Bonn.)

(usually about 1 percent by volume of a rapidly fermenting culture, or equivalent amounts of commercial pressed granules or cakes of a selected wine yeast). The whole mass is then mixed well.

Fermentation starts slowly, but after twelve to twenty-four hours should be quite active. The lower the initial temperature, the slower the start of active fermentation. As heat is released from fermentation, the temperature in the container and hence the rate of fermentation increase. If the fermentations are conducted in small lots in a cool place, the heat loss from the container may be sufficient to prevent excessive temperature rise in the fermentor. In large commercial lots, however, the temperature rise must be controlled.

As a rule of thumb, the heat produced by fermentation, if it is not removed, will raise the temperature of the fermenting mass about 2.3° F. (1.3° C.) for each drop of 1° Brix. If the must contains 20 pounds of dissolved solids (primarily sugar) per 100 pounds (20° Brix), and is allowed to ferment to 0° Brix—that is, not quite dry—the temperature could rise about 46° F. (26° C.). This rise, starting from normal summer temperatures, is sufficient to be highly discouraging if not lethal to yeasts. Therefore, it is possible in large fermentors with low rates of heat dissipation for the yeasts to "pasteurize" themselves with their own heat production and halt the fermentation. This or any fermentation which spontaneously stops with fermentable sugar remaining is said to be "stuck." It is often difficult and always a nuisance to restart a stuck fermentation; cooling, aeration, and often addition of more yeast and extra yeast "food," such as yeast extract and ammonium phosphate, are required. It may be preferable to gradually blend the stuck wine into another actively fermenting must. The final product, though, is usually of poorer quality than it might have been if the initial fermentation had been completed with- "sticking." It is much better to avoid the problem than to try to correct it after it has arisen. This is particularly important in winemaking, because during the relatively short vintage season (two or three months) all the wine for the year is made. During this very busy period, efficient haste without waste is crucial, and the investment in extra fermentation tanks to hold "mistakes" while you correct them is not likely to return a profit.

In large wineries, especially in warm climates such as that of California, high-capacity cooling systems are required. A common type of temperature-controlling system consists of a large central mechanical refrigeration unit connected to one side of a heat exchanger (an apparatus giving a large conductive surface for exchange of heat between two fluids without any contact or mixing of the fluids) with facilities to pump the fermenting must to be cooled through the other side and back to the fermentor. An alternative, especially for smaller operations, might be one or more portable refrigeration units with cooling coils to be lowered into the fermentors. If the fermentors are small and the climatic conditions moderate, cooling of the fermenting room, or a cooling coil operated with cold running water, may be adequate.

Cooling not only removes the extra heat produced by fermentation, but also, by lowering the fermentation rate, decreases the rate of heat production. Other means, such as maintaining a high pressure (4 atmospheres or so) in the fermentors, can be used to slow the fermentation and allow the heat to escape. The pressure-controlled fermentation method was popular in some countries, notably Germany, but has not been found particularly advantageous in California. Besides, the equipment is costly.

The fermentation is allowed to proceed to the desired point. This may be until it terminates naturally with all the sugar fermented, or the fermentation of the remaining sugar may be arrested by such means as the addition of wine spirits. These details and the related problems of when to remove the grape skins from red-wine fermentations are discussed later with the specific wine types.

AGING AND CLARIFICTION

After the pomace has been separated from the wine and the fermentation has been completed or stopped, the next step is the first racking. The wine is allowed to stand until a major portion of the yeast cells and other fine suspended materials has collected at the bottom of the container as sediment or lees. It is then racked: the relatively clear wine is carefully pumped or siphoned off without disturbing the lees (deposited precipitate). It is important to remove the first or yeast lees and complete the first racking as soon as possible for if the yeast cells are allowed to remain in a thick layer at the bottom they will begin to autolyze and possibly introduce off-flavors into the wine. Early racking also tends to prevent further growth of yeasts and other microorganisms by removing much of the potential nutrients with the lees. Conversely, leaving the wine for a time on the yeast lees may encourage liberation of some nutrients for the malo-lactic organisms, and encourage that fermentation if it is desired.

During the transition period between the tumultuous fermentation and the first racking, there is likely to be a slow release of carbon dioxide as the last portion of fermentable sugar is converted and the dissolved carbon dioxide escapes from the wine. The wine cannot be sealed tight without causing pressure increase—and yet the carbon-dioxide evolution is too slow to prevent air from entering the wine cask. This dilemma is solved by the use of a fermentation bung: an arrangement of valves or water-sealed tubes which allows escape of gas but keeps air from mixing freely with the headspace gas (Figure 12). The problem is especially critical with small containers. Generally, after the first racking, much of the carbon dioxide has escaped and the wine cask or tank can be bunged tight. Contact between the wine and the air must be kept to a minimum to prevent excessive oxidation, browning, and the growth of the aerobic vinegar bacteria. This can be accomplished by keeping the container as full as possible and closed except during essential operations.

Wooden containers such as white-oak barrels (usually 50 to 60 gallons) and casks (100 to 1,000 gallons) and oak and redwood tanks (several thousand gallons) are believed to serve a special role in aging wine by allowing a very slow access of oxygen to the wine—which, if sufficiently slow and limited,

FIG. 12. A simple fermentation bung which allows the escape of carbon dioxide. The water seal prevents access of air to the wine in the barrel.

produces some of the desirable changes of aging. The oak of the barrel or tank stave also contributes some flavor and extractives, and the wine becomes more complex and mellow. A small but steady diffusion of water and ethanol vapor out of the cask also occurs. Depending upon the relative humidity, the wine usually becomes more concentrated in alcohol (dry conditions), but might become weaker in alcohol (moist conditions) because of different relative rates of loss of ethanol and water through the wood. As water and alcohol escape, the nonvolatile constituents become slightly more concentrated, and the decrease in volume appears as ullage: more headspace. This allows more air to enter the cask. To prevent harmful effects of this air, the ullage is made up every week or so by adding more of the same wine from another container. This is called topping in many California wineries. Ullage occurs even in impervious containers as the young wine cools to cellar temperature, or there may be overflow if a full container is allowed to rise in temperature.

Because of the necessity of keeping all containers full and yet allowing for a continual slow loss, the winery must have a variety of sizes of cooperage (winery containers collectively). As the "fill" wine for the ullage of a large cask is used up, the cask is "broken down"; that is, the wine is transferred to fill one or more smaller containers, more "fill" is set aside (perhaps in a small barrel or glass jars), and the process starts all over. This has always been a problem for wineries which age wine in wooden containers. It is difficult to have stainless steel, glass-lined, or coated concrete tanks just the right size for each lot of wine (Figure 13). This problem is solved today in some wineries by using nitrogen or carbon dioxide atmospheres in the headspace of partly full tanks to flush out and keep out the air. Owing to the penetration of oxygen by diffusion, this is successful only with tanks having impervious walls.

One quality criterion for wine is clarity. The American consumer is conditioned to suspect any product with sediment, and discriminates against it. Brilliantly clear wine is not achieved at the first racking, by any means. Several additional rackings, along with filtrations, and *fining* (the use of certain

FIG. 13. Oak ovals, stainless steel tanks, and redwood tanks in a
California table-wine winery. (Source: The Wine Institute.)

agents to produce a brilliant clarity), and stabilization treatments are required to produce wine that is and will stay clear
until purchased by the consumer: stable wine. The clarification of wine is partly accomplished by aging the wine, but it
is also partly opposed by aging. With time, the proteins, other
colloidal substances, and microbial cells tend to precipitate
out, and the wine becomes clarified. Also with time, however,
metal ions may be picked up from containers and equipment,
oxidation may be producing turbidity, and some microbes may
multiply. Even though a wine has been made brilliantly clear,
small amounts of sediment often continue to form.

There is much justification for the statement often found upon the labels of bottles of red wine that it is *natural* for fine wines to form a deposit when aged in the bottle. This does not mean that murky wine is better, nor does it justify slipshod clarification practices by the winery, but the consumer is ill informed who objects to all types of slight imperfections in brilliance and stability of clarity. He will never know the "bottle bouquet" and extra quality produced by proper bottle age, of red wines especially, nor will he learn to buy and keep wines in his own wine closet or cellar for extra aging and quality improvement.

Various types of turbidity can be present in wine: microbial cells, amorphous precipitates of materials such as proteins and some forms of pigments and tannins, and crystalline precipitates, particularly of potassium acid tartrate. Microbiological stability is achieved by removing, killing, or preventing development of the microbes by use of sulfur dioxide and other permitted agents such as sorbic acid, by pasteurization, and by such fine filtration that the cells are removed and the product emerges effectively sterile. The combination of treatments chosen depends upon the type of product and degree of stability desired. It is possible to produce microbiologically stable dry table wines and fortified dessert wines with only a modest amount of sulfur dioxide and ordinary fining and filtration or centrifugation procedures. With low-alcohol wines having residual sugar, such as naturally sweet table wines and some of the other more recently popularized types ("mellow" reds and slightly sweet rosés), additional treatment is often required.

Fining agents produce a flocculent precipitate which removes (by coprecipitation and adsorption) dispersed hazes and colloids which would not readily settle out by themselves. Three major types of fining agent are proteins, adsorbents, and metal-removing substances. Egg white, skim milk, and even beef blood were formerly used as proteinaceous fining agents. More purified and predictable proteins are generally used today, gelatin and casein being the most common. A solution or fine suspension of the protein is made up in some of the wine and then is well mixed into the rest of the wine at the rate of about 1 ounce per 100 gallons (7 g/100 l). Tests on small portions should be made to determine the optimum dosage for a particular wine. The protein forms a coagulum which settles over a period of several days to a few weeks and leaves the supernatant wine clarified. A major factor in the coagulation and precipitation of proteins from wine is reaction with tannins. If insufficient tannin is present or too much protein is added, clarification may not be satisfactory. Ordinarily, red wines contain sufficient tannin to clarify well, and removal of some of the astringency of the tannin may be a desirable effect of the fining. With white wines, addition of an equivalent amount of tannin before fining with proteins may be necessary. The removal of some color with the fining precipitate may reduce the intensity of red-wine color and may lighten the color of white wines.

The most commonly used adsorbent fining agent is the clay-like mineral bentonite. This is added as a finely powdered and well-hydrated slurry at the rate of about 4 pounds to 1,000 gallons (480 g/kl) of wine, again based on preliminary tests. Bentonite adsorbs finely dispersed substances and clarifies as it settles to the bottom. It is particularly effective in removing protein which might cause turbidity in wine. Its use may thus supplement the use of protein fining agents and even correct the results of overfining with too much protein.

A metal-removing fining agent, not permitted in the United States but in use in Germany and other countries, is potassium ferrocyanide. The process is known as blue fining, because a blue precipitate is formed. This procedure requires careful control, but is very effective in clarifying wine and is particularly valuable in removing small amounts of copper, iron, and other metal ions that cause troublesome precipitates and catalyze oxidation. In the United States a trade-named substance is permitted which accomplishes similar effects.

Various other agents have special uses or are being studied for use in wine clarification. Among these are activated charcoal for selective removal of color or odor, pectin-splitting and other enzymes for clarification (particularly of fruit wines), and fining agents derived from plastics such as polyamide powder and polyvinylpyrrolidone. Since winemaking is a "permissive" industry, the use of all these agents is closely controlled by governmental regulations, and a new agent must be approved before it can be used commercially. In some cases samples taken before and after treatment are submitted to a federal Bureau of Alcohol, Tobacco, and Firearms (B.A.T.F.) laboratory for each lot of wine treated before it can be released for marketing.

Tartrate stabilization.—Potassium bitartrate, the potassium half-salt of tartaric acid, is familiar to the housewife as cream of tartar. Grape juice contains considerable amounts of this compound. As the juice is fermented the wine becomes supersaturated, since alcohol lowers the solubility of potassium bitartrate. As a result, this salt crystallizes slowly from the wine and forms argols, or crusts, in the wine tanks. If all excess is not removed by proper stabilization procedures, it may continue to form deposits in the bottled wine. Although no real harm is done by this crystallization, and the crystals are often sparklingly pretty, the consumer dislikes what seems to him to be "sand" or even "glass splinters" in the wine. Two common procedures are in use to see that the wine is stable with respect to tartrate deposition: cold stabilization and ion-exchange treatment. Cold stabilization involves hastening and completing the precipitation of all the potassium bitartrate which would in time come out of solution at normal storage temperature, by chilling the wine nearly to its freezing point (lower than water's freezing point, 32° F. (0° C.), because of the presence of alcohol). The wine is held at this temperature until the precipitable tartrate (and incidentally some other insoluble substances) has crystallized out; it is then filtered while cold to remove the precipitate and to prevent it from redissolving as the wine warms. This is a controlled form of the effect of winter temperatures upon wine in storage cellars.

The other stabilization practice, ion-exchange treatment, is more modern. Minerals or resins such as those used in water softening are converted to the sodium form. This means that the insoluble substances are loaded with sodium ions; when a fluid such as wine or hard water is passed through a bed of these particles, other positively charged metal ions may be taken up and the sodium ions released. Thus the potassium of wine is taken up and at least part of the potassium bitartrate is converted to sodium bitartrate. The sodium salt is more soluble in wine than the potassium salt, and therefore the precipitation of tartrate from the wine can be prevented. The ion-exchanging materials can be regenerated and reused, and the process can be precisely controlled.

If the regenerant is an acid, hydrogen ions and not sodium ions are exchanged for the wine's potassium, and the resultant tartaric acid not only stabilizes the wine but also lowers the pH and increases the acidity. This is generally the preferred procedure today. Variations in the process can be used to produce other modifications in the wine's composition, and troublesome ions such as those of calcium, magnesium, iron, and copper may be removed by ion-exchange treatment. As with any beverage process, ion-exchange treatment must be properly done and closely supervised to prevent undesirable taste and quality effects. Excessive sodium contents are especially to be avoided, to preserve the naturally low sodium content of wine.

Metal ions in wine. —The undesirable effects of certain metal ions have been mentioned. The inorganic fraction of grape juice, the ash that would be left upon complete evaporation and combustion, is a complex mixture which contains at least trace amounts of most of the common elements found in the soil, including potassium, iron, copper, calcium, magnesium, sodium, aluminum, manganese, phosphorus, sulfur, and boron. With the exception of potassium, the natural constituents may, but do not usually, amount to enough to cause trouble. Wine is slightly acidic, however, and *if allowed to do so* will readily pick up iron and copper from metal equipment, and calcium from concrete tanks. Iron at more than about ten parts per million and copper at one part per million or less are likely to promote oxidative and other reactions and produce changes in color, flavor, and clarity in wine. For this reason brass and mild steel equipment has been largely replaced by stainless steel, glass, and other materials in the wine industry.

Calcium ions produce turbidity in wines because their salts, with tartaric and other organic acids, are relatively insoluble. Calcium ions may be picked up not only from concrete tanks, but also from diatomaceous earth filter-aids used in filtering wines. This is usually avoided by washing these materials with citric acid solutions before use, or perhaps by discarding a little of the first wine through a filter. Pick-up of calcium from concrete storage tanks is avoided by acid cleaning and by use of coatings, usually waxes or plastics. Concrete storage tanks are rapidly disappearing in favor of stainless steel containers.

OTHER FINISHING OPERATIONS

Care is needed at each step in the fermentation, aging, clarification, and stabilization procedures for wine production. Fortunately, wine is *not* subject to all the problems and hazards of many other foods, but its quality can be damaged at any point along its relatively prolonged production path. A tank with brass fittings may contaminate the wine with a trace of copper. A pump may be operated improperly and the wine become aerated and eventually oxidized. If such errors are not prevented, the wine will often be ruined.

The final acts in the drama of wine production—preparation for market—are no less important. If the wine is to be blended, this should be done well in advance so that a "marrying" period can reveal any further need for treatment (fining, etc.). Wines ready for marketing are usually given a final "polishing" filtration on the way to the bottling machine. The potentially harmful effects of oxidation by air in the headspace of the bottle and dissolved in the wine are minimized or prevented by various procedures. The wine may be stripped of dissolved oxygen by passing bubbles of nitrogen through it. Bottles may be purged with nitrogen or carbon dioxide and filled so as to displace the gas without introducing air, and may be sealed under vacuum.

The bottles used by commercial wineries in this country are almost invariably new, owing to legal requirements and for reasons of sanitation, economy, uniformity, and convenience. In Europe bottles sometimes are reused, and crushed bottles are recycled in this country. The appropriate size and shape of bottle for the type and brand of wine are used (see Chapter 19). Since many types of wine are damaged by sunlight, the bottles are usually of colored glass, commonly dark green or brown. A small amount of sulfur dioxide is often added just before bottling. Other antioxidants such as ascorbic acid (vitamin C) might be substituted, or other microbial inhibitors may be used. The wine may be pasteurized or filtered so as to be effectively sterile as it is bottled. The bottles are often capped with screw caps, except for wines which are to be aged in the bottle. For these, natural corks have been preferred. If wines are to be bottle-aged at the winery they may be binned— stacked in the cellar—without labels. Otherwise they are usually labeled and cased immediately and, after a short period of observation to check for unexpected problems, shipped to the market. It is becoming more common to bottle-age at the premium winery in the shipping case rather than binning, owing to the decreased handling involved and the fact that wines are seldom bottle-aged more than a year or two at the winery.

Many more details of winemaking could be discussed. Some will be covered in later chapters; others require explanations which would be tedious in a book of this sort. If possible, you should visit some wineries; most of them welcome visitors. They often give conducted tours and offer samples for tasting. Not only is this a good way to increase your understanding of the process of winemaking, but also it offers an excellent opportunity to find and purchase wines which suit your taste.

Summary.—The home winemaker may not be particularly dismayed if some of his production is poor or is even a total loss. The commercial winemaker cannot afford such results. He must control each step of the vinification process so that possible deficiencies are avoided or minimized and each wine's quality is maximized. Chemical analyses, microbiological examinations, and systematic tasting are helpful and necessary for rational control and consistent success in modern winemaking.

The wine grapes must be picked at the proper time and handled quickly and carefully. They are crushed, destemmed, treated with sulfur dioxide, and fermented. According to the requirements of the wine type, the wine is drained and pressed from the pomace. Approximately 175 gallons of wine may be obtained from a ton of grapes. Dry wines should ferment to an alcohol content about 0.55 times the original Brix of the must. Temperature control during fermentation, avoidance of metal pick-up—particularly copper and iron—and the proper minimum of access of oxygen are positive quality factors with most wines. Appropriate aging to produce the desired level of maturity and complexity of flavor, and treatments to achieve stable clarity, are followed by bottling.

The consumer can influence the quality of wine by learning what experts consider to be important quality factors, adding his own preferences, and then selecting types and styles of wine which please him and do not violate accepted quality standards. By this selectivity, he gets better wine now and encourages the conscientious producer for the future. The consumer can participate more directly in improving the quality of wine by experimenting with bottle-aging of commercial wines, particularly dry table wines. He might add to his enjoyment and certainly his range of experience by making some of his own wine at home, and may produce high-quality wines if he follows good commercial practices.

We went to see the hermit
In the mountain.
He is plain and joyful,
He lives on a handful of rice,
The water in the spring contents him,
And yet he has kept his wine cup.

—Li Po

Chapter 8

MAKING TABLE WINES

The term "winegrowing" is often used. Grapes are more perishable and difficult to transport than wines. The grower of wine grapes has historically made them into table wine which he later sold. His agricultural produce left his farm in the form of bulk table wine. The product of many small winegrowers was often collected by brokers, and blended and processed by vintners (wine merchants, especially wholesale) before reaching the retail market in the cities. This cottage-industry type of winemaking still exists in several parts of the world. Under this system the average quality of the blended wine is likely to be low, because of some very poor lots resulting from ignorance or errors made by some of the growers. The price received by the grower tends to the least common denominator, and this will dissatisfy the grower who produces good wine.

This unsatisfactory situation has led to the development of modern winemaking in several directions. The former broker-vintner may operate a modern central winery and buy grapes from growers, thereby avoiding the poor-quality wine produced by the careless maker of wine on the farm. Several grape

117

growers may join forces to build and staff a coöperative winery to produce and market quality wine, either directly to the consumer or through a bottler with an established wholesale and retail trade.

The large centralized winery makes possible the production of good wines in large volume and, particularly with wines which require expensive equipment, such as brandy stills, this results in more efficient and economical production. If, however, only dry table wines are to be produced, these call for relatively little expensive equipment and can be produced economically in small wineries. Thus a place remains in the table-wine industry for the small producer. Of course, these small wineries need a certain minimum production if they are to be money-making operations. The most successful have concentrated upon producing premium-quality table wines, usually vintage-labeled varietal wines, and a sizable part of their production is often based upon their own vineyards. Since high-quality vintage varietal type wines are almost of necessity produced in lots no larger than a few thousand gallons, the small winery has competed effectively in this area with larger organizations.

An interesting and worldwide phenomenon in the wine industry is the wine producer who has been successful in another line of work and then taken up winery operation as a serious vocation or avocation. The story of one such winery illustrates the possibilities. The late Mr. J. D. Zellerbach, former United States Ambassador to Italy, knew and liked fine table wines. After retirement from his duties with the Crown-Zellerbach Paper Company and the United States Department of State, he planted a vineyard and erected a model winery in the Sonoma Valley of California. His objective was to produce Chardonnay and Pinot noir table wines as fine as or greater than any in the world. With the guidance of a scientifically-trained enological biochemist and using the most modern techniques, his winery, at his untimely death, was selling wines which proved his goal to be realistic. There are a number of other examples of such operations in this country and abroad.

Part of the charm and fascination of wine and winegrowing

lies in the fact that it is possible to find, tucked away in some valley, a small winery producing very fine wines which may be in demand all over the world. It is also part of the fun that the products of many fine wineries are not known outside a certain district, because production is limited and most of it is snapped up by local connoisseurs as soon as it is released. This lends zest to the search for unfamiliar labels and special lots of wine. If one educates and trusts his own palate rather than the pronouncements of wine snobs, one can drink better wine, sometimes at lower prices, by such searching.

We do not intend to leave the impression that only small wineries are capable of producing high-quality table wines. It is almost impossible to obtain a bad bottle of wine with the label of a large modern producer, and if one is found it undoubtedly was the result of an accident after it left the winery. The same statement cannot be made about all small producers. In producing wine in large volume to a standard of uniformity as well as quality, however, the large company may be forced to blend its smaller lots of superlative wine with the rest, whereas the small producer may sell his wine selectively, lot by lot. The resultant great diversity of wine by producer, by lot, by season, and of course by type, is a dividend to the consumer, and sets wine apart from most other foods in this age of mass production.

WHITE TABLE WINES

It is possible to make white wines from red grapes except for the few varieties which have red flesh (Teinturier types), since the red pigment does not readily or quickly escape from the cells of the skin unless the grape is overripe, damaged by mold, or beginning to ferment. This practice is not widely followed for table wines because it has no particular advantage, and extra work is necessary to ensure that no red color appears in the wine. A few varieties commonly made into white table wine (e.g., Grey Riesling, Veltliner, Gewürztraminer, and several eastern varieties like Delaware) have a faint red or pink blush on the ripe berries, but this causes little problem. The grapes which are made into white table wine and are likely to be named on the label of wines produced in California include Chardonnay (Pinot Chardonnay); Chenin blanc (White Pinot by error); Emerald Riesling; Folle blanche; French Colombard; Gewürztraminer; Grey Reisling; Malvasia bianca; light muscat (specific variety not usually named); Pinot blanc; Sauvignon blanc (Fumé blanc); Sémillon; Sylvaner (Franken Riesling); and White Riesling (usually, and less desirably, Johannisberg Riesling in California). The wines of a few of these (Folle blanche, French Colombard, Grey Riesling) may not be distinctive enough to enable one to name the variety in blind tasting, but they often are good, well-balanced, fruity wines.

The eastern U.S. varieties Delaware and Catawba may be found as white table wines with distinctive *labrusca* flavors (see Chapter 2 for further examples). Other white grapes used in producing table wines which are not usually or logically labeled as varietal wines include Aligoté; Burger; Clairette blanche; Green Hungarian; Palomino (Golden Chasselas); Saint-Émilion; Sauvignon vert; and Thompson Seedless. In addition to a relatively neutral flavor, these grapes may have properties which make them less suitable or more troublesome for winemaking. For example, Palomino tends to have low acidity and to make a flat-tasting wine. Owing to the presence of existing plantings and good viticultural properties —particularly high yields—such varieties are used. However, in recent years in California and elsewhere, the use of these less desirable neutral-flavored wines has decreased as large acreages of better varieties have been planted.

The climatic region where the vineyard lies also influences the wine quality considerably. The best Chardonnay, White Riesling, and Gewürztraminer wines are produced from the coolest regions (I and II). Most of the other varieties also give better white table wines, as a rule, in the less hot regions (II, III). Acceptable white table wines can be made in the warmest regions, and they may be excellent when extra attention has been paid to picking at the proper time and refrigerated processing. In the warmest regions (IV and V), the best white table wines are likely to be produced in the cooler vintages and from varieties like Chenin blanc, Emerald Riesling, and French Colombard, which retain acid well or ripen after the hottest part of the summer.

High-quality white table wines in general, and the dry ones particularly, are not easily made. When well made, they have a delicate fruity yet vinous odor (with the appropriate varietal notes) and a light straw to bright medium-golden color, with no muddiness or brown and no off-flavors. Overripeness must be avoided by picking the grapes at 20–23° Brix. By our estimate of Brix × 0.55, the wines should then be 11 to 12.6 percent alcohol by volume. This level is enough for preservation and good quality; a higher level in dry white table wines usually indicates overripe grapes. The acidity should be determined and the harvesting adjusted as much as possible to keep acidity up in a warm climate, or down in a cold one, to about 0.8 percent calculated as tartaric acid.

Once the decision to harvest has been made, the grapes must be handled with care at every step. White wines are particularly susceptible to damage by oxidation and browning, and any off-flavors permitted to develop will be noticeable over their normally delicate aroma and crisp flavor. Precautions must be taken to avoid browning. Sulfur dioxide should be added to the must as soon as possible at the rate of 75 to 150 parts per million, depending upon the tendency of the variety to brown and the condition of the grapes. The separation of the juice from the pomace, and the inoculation of the juice with yeasts, ordinarily should be accomplished as soon as possible, but this general rule may require modification. A short period of holding (4 to 12 hours) of the sulfited whole must may be desired for adequate clear juice yield or increased robustness of flavor. Settling and partial clarification of the must before fermentation is usually desirable to give the best quality and to aid in complete and rapid clarification later; centrifugation is now often used for this purpose. The pressed sweet pomace may be diluted and fermented for distillation, but it is not used directly in white table-wine production, and the pressed juice is blended into lower-priced wines or also used for distilling.

Improved quality results if white table-wine fermentations are carried on at a relatively low temperature. Fermentation at 80° F. (26.7° C.) or more is undesirable, causing loss of grape aroma and perhaps the development of "hot fermentation" off-flavors. The recommended temperature for fermentation of white musts is 50–60° F. (10–15.6° C.). In California and other warm climates, especially if very large containers are used, this low temperature requires cooling of the must before inoculation, and more or less continuous cooling during fermentation. Fermentation is slow at this temperature, and takes four to six weeks to reach completion. The longer time, slower carbon dioxide evolution, and greater susceptibility of the wine to damage by the oxygen of the air make it preferable that the fermentors for white table wine be closed and fitted with a suitable air-restricting fermentation vent.

After fermentation, the wine is racked, fined, and cold-stabilized or ion-exchanged, as previously described, except that with these wines extra precautions are necessary to keep air contact low and minimize pick-up of metals. The use of casein or casein-plus-tannin fining is often helpful in keeping the color light by removing part of any brown pigment which may have formed. Some producers, both in Europe and in California, no longer use wooden cooperage or only in very large sizes for dry white wines. Others believe that storage of certain whites (e.g., Chardonnay) for a few months in previously conditioned new or used wooden casks produces a desirable minimal degree of oxidation and improved flavor. Barrel aging should not be so prolonged as to contribute a too obvious woodiness or oxidation flavor.

Since the flavors of most of the wines in this class emphasize light grapy aromas, they are usually finished and sold relatively young—within one to two years after vintage. All white table wines receive some "rest" in the bottle to recover from the effects of bottling. The lots and types of wine with less delicate, more full and rich flavors may be stored in the bottle an additional one to four years, or occasionally even more. This can produce a desirable bottle bouquet and subtle flavors which result in a more interesting and complex wine.

The consumer can do this for himself by buying several bottles of the same wine and keeping them. Each bottle should be stored on the side so the cork is moist. Storage should be at a uniform, cool temperature, preferably 50–55° F. (10°–12.8° C.). A bottle should be served occasionally to observe progress and avoid overlong storage and eventual decline in quality. It is an exceptional white dry wine that will improve appreciably after three to five years of such storage (or a total age of four to seven years), and many should not stay that long. The lighter, more neutral wines are probably best when purchased, and are unlikely to benefit from such treatment. They have probably been treated with sulfur dioxide and perhaps other antioxidants just before bottling, and as these diminish to a low level with time, undesirable changes may occur. In selecting wines for bottle aging, some attention should be paid to the objective of the producer. A very fresh, fruity, slightly sweet wine sold at a modest price in a bottle with a short-lived closure was obviously not intended for long storage by the retailer or the customer.

Owing to the useful effects of sulfur dioxide in bleaching brown pigments and resisting oxidation, the tendency is to use too much of it. A not uncommon defect in white table wines is excessive free sulfur dioxide. The odor is not only easily noticeable in these light wines, but tends to anaesthetize the nose and prevent enjoyment of the desirable aromas. If the color was light before addition of excessive sulfur dioxide, it is likely to be colorless and water-like afterward.

White table wines that retain some sweetness may be made by various procedures such as arresting fermentation by chilling and centrifugation or clarification and filtration to remove the yeasts, or by adding sugar (illegal in California), unfermented juice, or concentrated grape juice. Such wines do not have sufficient alcohol to prevent further fermentation and are by nature subject to biological instability. They can be rendered stable for marketing by adding a high level of sulfur dioxide, 250 parts per million or less, and then aging them until the free sulfur dioxide decreases and becomes less objectionable by gradual oxidation and fixation in the form of reaction products. Pasteurization, newer inhibitors such as sorbic acid, and, preferably, sterile filtration may also be used to prevent yeast growth in these wines after bottling. Natural sweet wines result from botrytised or otherwise dehydrated grapes whose musts are so high in sugar that the yeasts are unable to ferment it all before the alcohol level becomes inhibitory. These are more readily stabilized, but the same considerations apply. The longest-lived white table wines fall in this class; some improve for two to three years in wood and five or more years in bottle, and they may last indefinitely under good storage conditions.

PINK OR ROSÉ TABLE WINES

Rosé table wines are much like white wines in their preparation and properties. They should have a bright pink to light red color without excessive orange or purple shading.They should be light, fruity, and quick-maturing. They contain more tannin and are therefore less subject to oxidation, browning, and clarification problems, but only slightly so, than white wines. Rosé wines are usually made from grapes which have insufficient color to make a normal red wine. They can be made from red grapes by limiting the time the skins are in contact with the fermenting must. Rosé wines can also be made by blending red and white grapes or red and white wines. The best of these procedures is the use of red grapes and a short fermentation on the skins. If the grapes are very low in red pigment content or if a blend of a high proportion of white grapes is used, the wine is likely to be tannic and unbalanced, since longer contact with the skins is required. If the grapes are low in color from being grown in a hot region, they are likely to make easily oxidized (orange from slight browning), low-tannin, flat wines. The usual practice is to use varieties of grapes which produce the desired bright color and fruity flavor and are moderate in the amount of red pigment. The varieties Cinsaut, Grenache, Gamay, etc., are used in France. Grignolino is employed in Italy, and occasionally by a few growers in California. Grenache and Napa Gamay are also favored for rosés in California, but Carnelian, Zinfandel, and other varieties are being used. Some varieties contribute distinctive varietal qualities to the wine, especially when grown under the proper conditions, and often are named on the label. Obviously, these wines should truly have a varietal character. Other varietally distinctive red grapes can be used, such as Cabernet Sauvignon or Pinot noir, but this is not common, for they are likely to be in demand for red wine production. Muscat-flavored pink (Aleatico) and light red varieties (Muscat Hamburg) are commonly made into dessert wines rather than into pink light muscat-type wines. Rosés are also made from standard nondistinctive red wine-grape varieties such as Carignane.

Grapes for rosé wines should have a composition similar to those for white wine, with moderate sugar (20–23° Brix) and reasonable tartness (at least 0.7 percent titratable acid). Freedom from bruised or damaged grapes, rapid sulfiting (75 to 150 parts per million of sulfur dioxide), inoculation with wine yeast, and a brief fermentation on the skins (12 to 36 hours) are desirable. As the preferred degree of color extraction is reached, the wine is separated from the skins by draining or pressing. Since some sugar and red pigment remain in the pomace, it may be added to fresh must and used to make ordinary red wine. It is probably more appropriate, if the winery also distills wine spirits, to convert this sweet pomace and that from white-wine production to alcohol by dilution with water and fermentation to dryness. The resultant dilute wine and the other residues, such as lees, can be distilled to recover the alcohol.

Rosé wines are ordinarily not aged in oak containers; if they are so aged, they are stored in wood for only a few months. They are not ordinarily aged very long in bottles, either, and are stabilized, finished, and marketed as fresh fruity young wines, often the same year they are produced and rarely more than two years later. For the American market, a rosé with some residual sugar (1 to 4 percent) has proved popular, and the stabilization practices mentioned for sweet white table wine are necessary. It is unfortunate that the dry and sweet rosé types are not easily distinguished by the labels.

RED TABLE WINES

Grape varieties commonly used for dry red table wines that are distinctive enough to warrant a varietal label, and are usually so labeled, include Barbera; Cabernet Sauvignon (often labeled just Cabernet); Ruby Cabernet; Concord; Gamay; Merlot; Pinot noir; and Zinfandel. Many other varieties of grapes can make distinctive red wines when all conditions are favorable. A few of the less common which may be found on California varietally labeled red table wines include Grignolino; Petite Sirah; Pinot St.-George (Red Pinot); and Charbono. Some widely planted distinctive varieties, notably Zinfandel and Grenache, go also into nonvarietally labeled red table wines along with less prestigious varieties such as Alicante Bouschet, Carignane, and Refosco. Further examples, including more *labrusca* varieties and hybrids grown outside California, are given in Chapter 2.

In general, the best red table wines are from grapes grown in climatic Regions II and III. Pinot noir, the earliest-ripening red *vinifera* grape of importance, is best in Regions I and II. Some other varieties, if they ripen sufficiently, also tend to be better in the coolest regions. Grenache, for example, will usually have insufficient color for red wine and less varietal flavor in Regions III, IV, and V. Acceptable, often good, and sometimes excellent red table wines can be made in Region IV and even Region V from grape varieties adapted to hotter weather by characteristics including good color production, better acid retention, later (cooler) ripening, and adequate tannin production. Such varieties include Barbera, Petite Sirah, and—as a result of breeding specifically for such characteristics—Ruby Cabernet and the new releases Carnelian and Carmine.

Red grapes for table wines are ordinarily picked when they are slightly higher in sugar (21–23° Brix) than grapes for white or rosé wines. They should retain a moderate acidity— at least 0.6 percent titratable acidity. The requirements for good red-wine processing are perhaps a little less stringent, since the product is more robust in constitution and flavor than white wine, but many of the same considerations apply.

The grapes must reach the winery in good condition. About 75 to 150 parts per million of sulfur dioxide are added as the grapes are crushed, or immediately afterward. The must, consisting of the entire crushed grape mass—perhaps even including the stems in very warm regions, to raise the tannin level—is then inoculated, and the fermentation begins. The fermentation temperature, cap management, and the aging procedure distinguish red-wine production from that of white and rosé wines.

The fermentation temperature should be kept from rising above 85° F. (29.4° C.), but should be above 70° F. (21.1° C.) during the tumultuous fermentation. The evolution of the carbon dioxide causes the skins to rise to the surface of the wine and form a dense cap there. This cap is partly exposed to the air, since red-wine fermentors are usually open-topped, and is frequently partly covered with foam (Figure 14). Owing to the rapid fermentation occurring within it, and its insulating nature, the cap is as much as 15° F. (8.3° C.) warmer than the body of the fluid. These factors favor development in the cap of organisms other than yeasts, particularly heat-tolerant and aerobic bacteria which may produce off-flavors and high volatile acidity (acetic acid). Also, extraction of the requisite amount of red color from the skins is not obtained unless there is contact between the fluid and the cap.

These ill effects are avoided by keeping the cap wet and periodically mixing it with the body of the fluid. This can be accomplished by *punching down* the cap with a suitable plunger by hand, at least twice and preferably several times, during a 24-hour period. Punching down the cap is too laborious for a large winery, and a similar result can be achieved by *pumping over:* the fermenting fluid is drawn off below the cap and is pumped and distributed or sprayed over the cap; this also is repeated several times a day. Several types of special fermentors with screens or other arrangements are designed to hold the grapeskin mass below the surface or to use the pressure from the fermentation carbon dioxide to force wine over the cap. None of these is in wide use because of expense of construction, difficult cleaning of equipment between lots, and

Fig. 14. Sampling fermenting red-wine must for hydrometric testing; note the cap. (Source: The Wine Institute.)

sanitation problems. Closed fermentors with features installed for semi-automatic or continuous pumping over or other special methods of effecting red-color extraction are becoming increasingly popular.

When the desired level of red pigment and tannin has been extracted, the skins and seeds are removed by draining and pressing. The apparent Brix at this time is usually 6–10°. The fermentation and the cap manipulation cause the breakdown of the pulp; the recovery of the wine is easier and the yield better than is the juice recovery for white wine. Today's consumer is interested in lighter, early-maturing wines, and unfortunately seldom does he or the retailer do any aging in their own wine cellars. To meet this changing demand, the winemaker the world over has been cutting down the time the wine is in contact with the pomace in order to extract less tannin. Before World War II, a fermentation period of fifteen days on the skins was not uncommon for premium wines which were to be aged. At the present time, a period of three to five days on the skins is probably typical for most California producers, and only slightly longer elsewhere. For popular-priced wines, heat treatments to release the red color before fermentation, rather than extraction by alcohol during fermentation, may be used, and therefore the contact time cut to hours rather than days. However, the heat treatments developed so far tend to produce some browning, undesirable flavor changes, and clarification difficulties. Botrytis-infected musts cannot be used to make red table wines, because the red color is oxidized by the enzymes. Heat treatment can salvage botrytised red must by destroying the enzymes responsible.

After the wine has been separated from the pomace, the fermentation is allowed to go to completion at moderate temperatures (60–70° F., 15.6–21.1° C.) and with the usual precautions of closed fermentors, a fermentation bung, and so on. For the "mellow" reds, a small amount (1 to 5 percent) of residual sugar may be retained in those to be marketed and consumed young. As the yeast and other lees settle out, the wine is racked periodically. If the malo-lactic fermentation is desired, it may be encouraged by leaving the wine in contact with the yeast longer than usual and continuing storage at a relatively warm temperature. The relatively high tannin level of red wines promotes good fining with proteinaceous agents such as gelatin; if the tannin is excessively high and the wine too astringent, the level can be reduced by such fining. The wine may be cold-stabilized or ion-exchanged to control tartrate precipitation. During these treatments, the wine is ordinarily stored in large tanks; the surface-to-volume ratio is such that, even if they are wooden, not much effect from the wood as compared to other tank materials can be noted in the wine. If the wine is to command a premium price it is usually placed, after the initial clarification and stabilization treatments, in smaller white-oak containers (50 to 500 gallons).

A few European wineries use new barrels for aging red wine, often after fermenting in them first. In most American wineries the oak flavor produced by long aging in new 50-gallon barrels is considered too strong. If the new barrels have been washed out with mild alkaline solutions, such as sodium carbonate (soda ash) and then hot water, the danger is less. Such barrels may be "broken in" by using them for a short period for aging wines to be blended into standard wines before use with premium wines. Aging in barrels (Figure 15) may also

FIG. 15. Fifty-gallon (190-liter) oak barrels used for aging varietal table wines. (Source: Paul Masson Vineyards.)

be for only a limited time and then the wine may be transferred to larger casks or tanks for further aging. The wines are carefully watched during the aging process. The ullage is made up as often as necessary (at about one- to three-week intervals), or the containers may be stored on the side so the bung is covered by wine and kept tight. Representative samples from each wine lot are carefully tasted and analyzed by the winemaker periodically—certainly twice a year, and preferably more often. The wine is ordinarily racked and as a result slightly aerated about twice a year, to promote clarification and aging. When the desired stage of aging in wood is reached and the wine is mature or ripe to bottle, it is given additional clarification and stabilization if needed. Often this consists only of a final polishing filtration as the wine is bottled.

Care should be taken during bottling (Figure 16) that the wine is not agitated in the presence of air or permitted to take up too much oxygen. The bottles should be stored for at least six months after being filled and corked; such binning, or case storage, is practiced by some wineries for two to four or more years for their premium red table wines. Many red wines, especially those of adequate tannin content, will improve for as long as ten to twenty years in bottles, and survive in good condition for much longer. Naturally such aging is expensive, involving hazards and tying up capital.

Again consumers can add much interest, save part of the cost, and probably raise the average quality of the red wine served at their tables by buying some well in advance of immediate needs. If long bottle-aging is practiced, some "crust" will probably form as tannins and pigments gradually precipitate with time. There are no known stabilization procedures which will prevent this and still retain the desirable features of the wine. The wine can be decanted clear for serving, and the crusted bottle placed on the table as a conversation piece. If you prefer the brighter red and more fruity, zestful, and hearty flavor of younger red wines, of course, they can be consumed as purchased. If the brick-red color and the more complex and mellow flavors appeal to you, buy older wine or age your own wine. And if you enjoy wine frequently with your

FIG. 16. Bottling table wine with automatic corking and labeling equipment. (Source: The Wine Institute.)

meals, you will probably learn to vary your menu by enjoying both. After a little experience with wines of various types and ages served with different dishes, you will be able to recognize the light simple wine that deteriorates rapidly with age and must be consumed young. You will also come to recognize the richer wine which may be too young, harsh, or strongly flavored for your taste now, and can profitably be aged longer.

Summary. —The production of table wines demands knowledge, skill, and attention, but not necessarily a large or expensive establishment. Most white table wines are produced from grape juice in such a manner as to emphasize a light color and delicate, fresh, grapy flavors. Red table wines are generally more intensely flavored and more astringent, owing to fermentation with the skins and extraction of certain materials from the crushed whole red or purple-skinned grapes. Rosé wines are intermediate in that a light, bright pink color, and usually a fresh, fruity flavor, result from brief fermentation on the skins of light red-colored grapes. The production methods outlined will give acceptable wines. Great table wines require an outstanding vintage of premium varieties grown in cooler regions and, besides good technology, much care, some art, and a little luck. Often the winemaker must exercise restraint—do no treatment unless it is necessary, because overtreatment can lower quality.

Table wines are traditionally dry, although some naturally sweet table wines, especially the white botrytised type, have a long and illustrious history. Slightly sweet wines have become rather popular on the United States market for moderate-priced standard white, rosé, and red table wines, but their sweetness is not uniform and might be disadvantageous in that quality defects can be masked by sugar. Furthermore, unless the sugar level is indicted by the label, those preferring dry wines may be disappointed.

Other important quality variables in table wines include the grape-varietal flavors (which may or may not be present) and the flavors resulting from age. Relatively few white table wines currently on the retail market exhibit much aged bottle-bouquet flavor; longer aging could bring a gain in complexity of flavor and only a small loss of their young-wine freshness. Red table wines exhibiting a reasonably wide range of the flavors developed by short or long aging in wood are available in the better wineshops. Some with additional bottle-aging are available at relatively higher prices. Since aging is costly, the inexpensive red wines receive less aging than the premium-priced wines.

While Champagne in close array,
Pride of Reims and Epernay,
Not in bottles but in dozens
(Think of that, ye country cousins!)
Stood, of every growth and price,
Peeping forth its tub of ice.
                    —HENRY LUTTRELL

Chapter 9

MAKING SPARKLING WINES

Wines which are not still, those which contain a high level of carbon dioxide, are called sparkling wines. A layman's definition would be that sparkling wines pop when opened and give off copious amounts of carbon dioxide bubbles when poured into a glass from a freshly opened bottle of the cool wine. The legal American definition for tax purposes is that wines containing more than 0.392 gram of carbon dioxide per 100 milliliters are subject to tax as sparkling wines. This amount is equivalent to about one atmosphere of carbon dioxide pressure. The level was originally chosen as about the maximum carbon dioxide content without appreciable visual or flavor effects in wine served cool (55° F., 12.8° C.). The level has been raised twice in the last ten years. It is possible for white table wines (if fermented very cool, or under pressure and bottled without much aging or other opportunity for the carbon dioxide of the original fermentation to escape) to retain small amounts of carbon dioxide. If a malo-lactic fermentation occurs in the bottles or just before bottling, as in the *vinho verde* wines of Portugal, considerable carbon dioxide may remain in the wine. If these wines do not exceed the legal limit, they, along with wines that have been stripped of air with carbon dioxide gas or have otherwise contacted carbon dioxide at low pressure during processing, would be classified as still wines. This is important, for the federal tax on still table wines is currently 17 cents per gallon, and the tax on sparkling wines $3.40 per gallon. It follows that sparkling wines cannot be inexpensive, since the federal tax alone is 68 cents per bottle on top of all the processing costs, distributing expenses, state and local taxes, and retailing costs.

Champagne and champagne-type wines are the classic and important group of effervescent or sparkling wines. The carbon dioxide pressure in these wines is high, about 4 atmospheres, or 60 pounds per square inch of bottle surface as found in the market. Wines of less than 2 atmospheres of carbon dioxide, sometimes called "pearl" wines, are popular in Germany, South Africa, Australia, and some other countries, but have not been marketed to any great extent in the United States. These high levels of carbon dioxide can be introduced into wine in two major ways: by yeast fermentation in a closed container to prevent loss of carbon dioxide, and by artificial carbonation, as for carbonated soft drinks.

Artificial carbonation is accomplished by passing the proper amount of carbon-dioxide gas under moderate pressure into the wine at about 24° F. (−4.4° C.) and then bottling it immediately. The carbon dioxide, like most gases, is much more soluble in the wine at low temperature and high pressure. Since the gas is not soluble in ice, maximum solubility occurs just above the freezing temperature for the wine. As the bottled wine warms up, the pressure, as determined by the amount of carbon dioxide taken up, increases: 2 atmospheres just above freezing becomes about 7 atmospheres at room temperature. This type of wine must be labeled as artificially carbonated, and is subject to a federal tax of $2.40 per gallon. In spite of its tax advantage over the fermented sparkling wines, this type of wine is low in sales in the United States. Several factors have contributed to the near-disappearance of carbonated wine from American usage. (Note that the term "carbonated" should be reserved for this relatively rare type of wine, and that still wines with nearly the permitted maximum carbon dioxide content cannot be labeled carbonated, even though it is, unless the higher tax is paid!) The consumer seems to feel that, since champagne is a luxury, he wants the best or none at all, and is repelled by the labeling requirements for artificially carbonated wine. Perhaps as a corollary to this, the carbonated-wine producer has tended to try to stay in the market by shaving costs and cutting prices. Although good wines can be made by artificial carbonation, generally the best base wines have not been used. Moreover, most artificially carbonated wines tend to lose their carbon dioxide more quickly than do effervescent wines produced by fermentation in a closed container. The prolonged display of bubbles and the tingling taste of sparkling wines are highly desirable parts of their appeal.

Several known factors, and perhaps some unknown ones, promote the desired retention of carbon dioxide with prolonged slow evolution of bubbles. One factor is the complete lack of haze or particles in the wine which would serve as nuclei for bubble formation; brilliantly clear sparkling wine is, therefore, important for this reason as well as appearance. The presence of nitrogen or other poorly soluble gases also initiates bubble formation and hastens the loss of carbon dioxide. Dispersion of headspace gas in the bottle by shaking it before opening produces gushing upon opening, for the same reason. Traces of surface active agents promote bubble emission and an undesirable persistent foam on the wine in the glass. This could conceivably result from the use of detergents without completely rinsing them from winery equipment. Winemakers are careful to avoid this, and the glasses in which the wine is served are the more likely source. The presence of agents such as glycerol, sugar, and soluble peptides appears to favor the formation of smaller bubbles and slower carbon dioxide loss. The peptides and amino acids arising from yeast autolysis seem to have this effect. Complexes or reaction products which slowly form during aging have been said to exist between the wine constituents and the dissolved carbon dioxide. These presumably revert to carbon dioxide more slowly than if carbon dioxide were merely in solution.

The production of artificially carbonated wine at home by using dry ice is a dangerous practice and should not be attempted. The gas will evolve from the solid carbon dioxide faster than it can dissolve in the wine. The resultant high pressure is likely to cause the closed container to explode. If an open container is used, little carbonation results, and oily or metallic off-flavors may be introduced by impurities in the dry ice. The flavor differences between the same base wine carbonated and naturally fermented can be considerable, and they have only the carbon dioxide in common.

The discovery of champagnization of wine by fermentation in a stoppered bottle is attributed to Dom Pérignon, who was cellarer in the Benedictine Abbey of Hautvillers in France near Reims from 1668 to 1715. He is also said to be one of the first to use corks from Spanish cork oak to close wine bottles. The better seal provided by natural cork must have been an important factor in the first accidental production of sparkling wines. Wines bottled too soon from a vintage which, owing to cold winter weather, had not completed fermentation of all the sugar could begin to ferment again in the spring. The bottles which survived the increased pressure may well have inspired the reported cry of the discoverer: "Come quickly! I'm drinking stars!" The details of the matter are obscured by time, and it is quite probable that the good monk would be horrified at the immodesty of the role attributed to him. Be that as it may, the district of France called Champagne gave its name to this sparkling wine. Through the art and technology of many winemakers, first in France and later elsewhere as well, the controlled process of fermented-in-the-bottle sparkling wine production has developed. It remains one of the prevalent methods of champagnization; the other common method is the bulk- or tank-fermentation method.

Making sparkling wine includes, first, careful making or selecting of the base wine. This is essentially a dry white table wine. It should have a moderate alcohol content (9.5 to 11.5 percent), a good acidity (0.7 to 0.9 percent titratable as tartaric acid), and no more than a light straw or low-yellow color. It must be "clean," meaning properly made, with no noticeable defects or off-flavors, and should have less than ten parts per million of free sulfur dioxide. This is an important consideration, because the evolution of the carbon dioxide bubbles when the wine is poured carries odors to the nose and enhances any defects in odor as well as the desirable aroma and bouquet. Excess addition of sulfur dioxide may show up as objectionable sulfur dioxide odors, or the yeast fermentation may cause the reduction of some forms of sulfur to hydrogen sulfide—the rotten-egg odor.

Sparkling-wine stock is ordinarily a blend, and varietal designations, with the exception of muscat, are not usually noted on the labels. Chardonnay and Pinot noir are used in Champagnes of France. The red or "black" Pinot noir is converted to white wine for this use by special selection of the clusters and berries used and immediate pressing of the grapes in shallow presses, usually without prior crushing. Sometimes "blanc de blancs" (white from white grapes) and "blanc de noirs" (white from "black" grapes) are label indications of which type of grapes was used.

Sparkling muscat wines are a famous product of Italy—the *spumante* of Asti, for example. California and other regions which produce sparkling wines make sparkling muscat wines as well as champagnes (the name is now considered generic in the United States when not capitalized) and pink or red sparkling wines by essentially the same processes. Pink champagne is a more common label than the equivalent champagne rosé. Sparkling red wines may be called sparkling burgundy or champagne rouge. Cold duck, a blend of red and white sparkling wine, often with a *labrusca* flavor, was intensely popular for a few years about 1970.

The base wines are frequently chosen for their rather neutral fruity-vinous quality rather than for pronounced varietal distinctiveness. However, many of the better varieties for white table wine, such as Sylvaner, Saint-Émilion, Folle blanche, Chenin blanc, Chardonnay, or French Colombard, are ordinarily included in the blend to achieve the necessary acidity, balance, and fruitiness for a good sparkling wine. When used for producing a sparkling wine, they are picked earlier than if used for a still table wine. Popular sparkling wines are made in New York, Ohio, and Canada by blends including some *labrusca*-flavored varieties, particularly Delaware and Catawba, and often also a neutral wine to prevent the flavor from being excessively strong. Since the escape of the carbon dioxide enhances the aroma of the wine, a light and delicately pleasant odor is desired in the base wine, and strong or heavy odors are avoided. An intense muscat grape aroma is not objectionable in sparkling muscat wines.

The wines prepared or selected for champagnization are racked, blended, clarified, stabilized, and fined beforehand. The descriptive terms used in sparkling wine production have come mostly from the French language, for obvious reasons, and the lot of stable, clear, blended wine for a particular run of sparkling-wine production is termed the *cuvée*, literally "tubful." The fermentation of this wine for the second time requires the addition of more yeast, more fermentable sugar, and (occasionally) yeast food in the form of ammonium phosphate (0.5 to 1.0 grams per liter). If the alcohol level is higher than 12 percent, or if the sulfur-dioxide level is appreciable, it may be difficult to referment the wine—an additional reason for holding these low. The yeast starter is grown up in the usual fashion in some of the *cuvée* wine, and the sugar and other additives, if any, are prepared as a concentrated solution in some of the same or very similar wine. Pressed yeasts are also now used. The yeast is specially selected for the purpose. Two desirable traits of such yeasts are the ability to ferment under these conditions (low temperature and high CO_2 particularly) and the production of an agglomerated "granular" sediment of yeast cells when the fermentation is finished. "Champagne" yeast is often a strain of *Saccharomyces bayanus*.

The yeast starter and the sugar solution are added in the proper amounts to the *cuvée*, and the whole is well mixed to ensure even distribution. Generally 2 to 3 percent by volume of active starter or pressed yeast is used. The *cuvée* wine is usually dry, but if fermentable sugar remains it must be taken into account, or excessive pressure will result. As a rule of thumb, 4 grams of sugar per liter of wine will produce one atmosphere of carbon-dioxide pressure upon fermentation. Therefore, for a total of about 6 atmospheres (about 90 pounds per square inch), 6 × 4 grams per liter = 24 grams of sugar per liter should be present at the start of the refermentation, or about 20 pounds of sugar per 100 gallons. It is usual to aerate the wine slightly to encourage yeast growth. The mixture, consisting essentially of base wine, yeast cells, and sugar, is then drawn off to the next stage, the *tirage*. Up to this point the process is essentially the same whether bottle or bulk fermentation is to be used.

FERMENTATION IN THE BOTTLE

For bottle-fermented sparkling wine, the wine is kept well mixed to prevent the settling out of the yeast, and is filled into strong champagne-type bottles. The bottles are closed with the large wired- or clamped-on corks, especially made for sparkling wines, or today often with cork-lined crown caps. The sealed bottles are then stacked horizontally in a cool place (not over 60° F., 15.6° C.) to ferment. The bottles are made of heavy glass, and the push-up or punt at the bottom gives added strength; but if the temperature is too high, fermentation too rapid, sugar addition incorrectly high, or the bottles defective, breakage and loss will be excessive. Since scratched bottles may burst, handling is careful and the bottles should not be reused ones.

Complete fermentation and pressure generation are slow and usually take several weeks. The *tirage* should then be stored at a lower temperature, traditionally 50° F.(10° C.), and remain undisturbed for at least a year, preferably three or four, to allow the yeast to settle and die (Figure 17). This is important because much of the special flavor and bouquet of bottle-fermented champagne develops as the wine ages at this stage. It is believed to result from the autolysis of the thin film of yeast cells on the walls of the bottle, followed by complex reactions of the liberated chemical compounds.

At the completion of aging on the yeast sediment, the bottles are placed neck down in racks and the riddling, or *remuage*, process begins. The yeast which has deposited on the walls of

FIG. 17. Champagne aging in a cellar. (Source: The Wine Institute.)

the bottle must be prepared for removal. Each lot, or *tirage*, behaves somewhat differently, and each person develops his own technique of riddling by experience, but the objective is to cause all the sediment to collect in a thin layer upon the cork, leaving the wine and the walls of the bottle absolutely clear. In order to break the "mask" of sediment loose, the bottle is given a short sharp spin of an eighth of a turn or so and then dropped back into the rack, neck down, with a jolt calculated to move the sediment toward the cork. A skillful riddler or "turner" can manipulate as many as 20,000 to 30,000 bottles a day. Each bottle is turned once a day (in opposite directions on alternate days), and if the wine is easily clarified a week may suffice for completion of the riddling operation. For another lot, a month or more may be needed to collect all the sediment. Various types of special riddling racks have been developed so that several bottles can be riddled together with less hand labor and more economy.

The next operation is *disgorging:* the removal of the collected yeast-cell sediment from the bottle. For this operation the bottles are handled carefully so as not to disturb the sediment. They are refrigerated to nearly the freezing point to lower the pressure, and a small plug of ice is then frozen in the neck by immersion of the cork and two or three inches of the neck in a subfreezing bath (about 5° F., -15° C.). All of the sediment is then included in the ice plug. Care is necessary in these operations to avoid an abrupt temperature change which would crack the thick glass. The bottle is then turned about 45° from upright and opened; the gas pressure pushes out the ice plug, and the sediment with it. Properly completed, these operations leave the bottle and its remaining contents brilliantly clear. Some carbon dioxide is lost during the time the bottle is open and, if the disgorging is not skillful or the wine foams out of the bottle when the pressure is released, considerable wine may be lost also. The wine must be cold (35–45° F., 1.7 -7.2° C.) to retain as much of the carbon dioxide as possible, and the work must be rapid and efficient. Only a few bottles are open at a time. Between operations they are held in an apparatus with a spring-loaded stopper to minimize escape of the sparkle-producing gas. The *dosage* is then added (Figure 18), the level of wine is replenished if necessary from another bottle, and the bottle is recorked with its final natural cork or plastic stopper, which is wired in place.

The *dosage* (like *tirage,* this rhymes with garage) operation consists of adding a syrup to adjust the sweetness of the wine. Although most people would say they liked their sparkling wine absolutely dry, the fact is that without a little sugar they would find it unpleasantly tart (or, as they might say, sour).

The designation of sweetness levels is by no means uniform, but the common terms and their approximate meaning in percentage of sugar are: *brut* 0.5–1.5 percent, *sec* 2.5–4.5 percent, *demi-sec* 5 percent, and *doux* 10 percent. The required amount of sugar to reach these levels is added to each bottle as a measured amount of concentrated syrup in the *dosage* operation. This *dosage* syrup usually consists of about 60 grams of cane sugar in 100 milliliters of a well-aged, high-quality white table wine. In some cases the mixture may include 10 percent of good quality brandy. The *dosage* solution itself may be aged for some time before use.

Why does this *dosage* sugar not ferment? Most of the yeast cells are dead and few remain in the wine after the aging and disgorging operations. Even though some carbon dioxide is lost, the pressure remains at about 2 to 4 atmospheres (30 to 60 pounds per square inch) and inhibits fermentation. Nutrients other than sugar are likely to be depleted by the first

FIG. 18. Champagne dosage machine.

two fermentations, and the alcohol is raised slightly by the second fermentation and by the brandy of the *dosage*. These and other factors combine to make a third fermentation unlikely. However, if the bottle fermentation is conducted at a relatively warm temperature and the aging in the bottle is less than six months, viable yeasts may be present. This routine speeds production and lowers costs, but there is a risk of fermentation of the *dosage*. To prevent this, sulfur dioxide may be added with the *dosage*. The quality of the resultant wine is reduced.

The bottles of finished wine are generally stored horizontally for a brief period before sale, during which the cork sets into the familiar mushroom shape. This also allows detection of leakers. Further aging at this stage appears to have no great advantage. The bottle is now dressed in its labels, foils, and furbelows and sent off to grace elegant occasions, launch ships and brides, and otherwise make all this trouble worthwhile. Since an estimated 120 hand operations go into each bottle of fermented-in-the-bottle champagne and its production requires skill, involves an appreciable risk of loss, and pays higher taxes, it will always be a costly product. The traditional production process is not particularly amenable to improvement or economy by large-scale operation, and therefore a few small family-type champagne cellars have competed successfully. Sparkling wine does have an advantage over other wines in that it can be made from the stock wine at any time of the year, and thus the use of equipment and labor can be spread more evenly and planned more efficiently.

Ways of saving labor and decreasing the cost of sparkling wine include the transfer process (Figure 19) for bottle-fermented wine, and the bulk or tank fermentation process, which is essentially the use of a large "bottle." In the transfer process, the wine is fermented and aged in individual bottles as just described. Instead of riddling and disgorging, however, the bottles are discharged by machinery into a large tank. The tank and the filtering system used to remove sediment and yeast from the wine are maintained under counterpressure to avoid loss of the carbon dioxide sparkle. Meanwhile, the

Fig. 19. California sparkling-wine cellar. The wine is fermented in the bottles, lower left, disgorged into the transfer tanks, and later filtered into new bottles. (Source: The Wine Institute.)

bottles are washed and after addition of the appropriate *dosage* the wine is filtered into the washed bottles, corked, and finished as for the hand-processed product.

The transfer process not only saves labor but gives a more uniform product, since the natural bottle-to-bottle variation even within a single *cuvée* of bottle-fermented wine can be noticeable. However, there can be some contact between the wine and air, and the highly reduced condition of the wine may be modified, with consequent darkening of color and change in flavor, in the direction of oxidation. Some sulfur dioxide may have to be added. Transfer-processed wines can be labeled as bottle-fermented. Producers using the more costly traditional process distinguish their product from transfer-processed wines by the label "fermented in *this* bottle."

BULK-PROCESS SPARKLING WINE

The wines produced by fermentation in bulk must so state on the label to prevent them from competing unfairly with the more costly bottle-fermented wines. These wines are also referred to as tank-fermented or Charmat-process sparkling wines, after the inventor of the widely used type of tank. The selection of the *cuvée* and its preparation for champagnization are nearly the same for bulk as for bottle fermenting. The fermentation tank is made of inert, nonreactive materials such as stainless or glass-coated steel. It is relatively small, as wine tanks go, holding from 500 to 25,000 gallons, so that temperature and pressure can be controlled more economically. The tank is constructed to withstand 200 to 250 pounds per square inch as a safety factor. It is outfitted with pressure and temperature gauges and safety pressure-release valves, and is equipped for temperature control by circulation of refrigerant in a jacket. Since excess pressure can be allowed to escape, the sugar control need not be as precise as with bottle fermenting. Since these tanks are expensive, reasonably rapid turnover is desired. About one to two months per cycle, or six to twelve per year, are typical.

A single tank is usual, but two or three may be arranged to accommodate different stages in the process. The fermentations are preferably conducted at about 55° F. (12.8° C.) and should be completed in about two weeks. The large volume of wine produces a relatively thick layer of yeast cells as they deposit after fermentation. If the wine is allowed to stay in contact with this thick sediment, off-flavors, particularly hydrogen sulfide, may be introduced as the yeast cells begin to decompose. This is ordinarily prevented by limiting the time of contact between the wine and the sedimented yeast. Some of the desirable features of bottle-fermented champagnes arise from the breakdown of yeast cells during the aging period. Thus a difference in flavor between the two types may result from the lesser aging with yeast in the bulk process. The degree of difference depends, of course, upon the aging received by the bottle-fermented wine being compared, and may be minimized by transferring the wine to another tank for aging with some but not all the yeast, or by agitating the bulk-process wine for a period to prevent the formation of a thick layer of sediment.

The bulk-processed sparkling wine is ordinarily given a cold-stabilizing treatment to remove the excess tartrates after the secondary fermentation, and is filtered cold and under pressure to remove the remaining yeast cells and precipitated tartrates. This filtration is an important step, because viable yeast cells remain which might re-ferment the *dosage*. Therefore this last polishing filtration should be under sterile conditions to render the product free of yeast cells. The wine is filled into bottles with the appropriate *dosage*, and the bottles are finished for marketing. It is still usual to include some sulfur dioxide in the *dosage*, to prevent growth of any viable yeast cells that may have escaped filtration.

Bottle-fermented wines have little chance of contacting air and picking up oxygen unless the transfer process is used. Sparkling wines fermented in bulk, however, are likely to absorb some oxygen in the course of transferring, bottling, and filtering. As a consequence, bulk-processed sparkling wine may darken in color and partially oxidize from contact with air. A small amount of sulfur dioxide at bottling may be added to counteract this problem, and incidentally to make more remote the possibility of yeast or other organisms growing in the finished wine. Free sulfur dioxide is very noticeable, however, even at relatively low levels in sparkling wine, and thus easily becomes objectionable. This is a further reason that dry sparkling wines "fermented in this bottle" *may* have a quality advantage over transfer or bulk-processed wines—but they are, of course, more costly.

Red and pink sparkling wines are processed in a manner very similar to the methods described for the white. The higher tannin content and frequently higher alcohol of these wines make them more difficult to re-ferment. To start the yeast, more aeration of the *tirage* wine may be necessary, and a slightly warmer fermentation temperature may be helpful. The red wines are more difficult to clarify completely and hence are more likely to gush, that is, foam over explosively when the pressure is released. For these reasons, bulk fermentation, with its greater opportunity for correction of difficulties, is more commonly used than bottle fermentation for pink champagne and sparkling burgundy. The relatively strong flavor of these wines also makes the delicate bouquet of bottle-aging less important than in white sparkling wines.

Summary.—Sparkling wines are relatively expensive, owing to high taxation as well as processing costs. High quality cannot be attained without care in the selection of the table wine to be champagnized. Directly carbonated wine has not achieved wide acceptance by the public, and sparkling wine is produced by secondary fermentation either directly in the bottle or by the bulk process.

The bottle-fermented sparkling wine is usually clarified by expensive and tedious hand processing, whereas in the bulk process the methods of production and filtration are less costly. The bulk processor usually achieves high quality in his sparkling wines by emphasizing fruity-grapy qualities. The bottle-fermented sparkling wines may be produced so as to emphasize age-derived flavors by allowing time for yeast autolysis and aging reactions. The transfer process involves bulk filtration and consequent cost reduction for bottle-fermented champagnes, but may produce a slightly different product owing to such effects as air pick-up during this process.

The sparkle—carbon dioxide—of wines in this class constitutes an important part of their appearance and flavor. They are properly served very cool to prolong the bubble display and to retain the dissolved gas. Although, owing to the low temperature and the sting of carbon dioxide in the nose, these wines are not "sniffed" in the glass, the evolution of the gas tends to make more pronounced both good and bad odors.

Considering the difficulty and expense of learning to judge and appreciate sparkling wines, it is not surprising that the full range of their qualities and variations is fully appreciated by relatively few consumers. Sparkling wines can, of course, display all the range of dry table wines, which are their base, plus the character produced by the secondary fermentation and augmented by more or less aging before disgorging.

O for a beaker full of the warm South,
Full of the true, the blushful Hippocrene,
With beaded bubbles winking at the brim,
And purple-stainèd mouth;
—JOHN KEATS

Chapter 10

MAKING DESSERT WINES

In this chapter we consider the making of wines which require the addition of ethanol distilled from wine. These are often referred to as fortified wines, and may be defined as that group of wines produced by the addition of wine spirits. As a rule, those produced in the United States have a final alcohol content of 18 to 21 percent by volume, except sherries, which may be as low as 17 percent. Certain special wines such as altar wines and wines in this class imported from other countries may have 14 to 17 percent alcohol. The term "fortified" is avoided by the industry, because it suggests that the extra ethanol serves no special purpose other than raising the alcoholic potency of the wine. This is not true. The level of 17 to 18 percent alcohol is about the minimum that will reliably make the wine microbiologically stable. If a yeast fermentation is coaxed along by gradual addition of sugar ("syruped fermentation") or by other means, it is possible to produce maximum alcohol levels of 16, 18, or even as high as 20 percent by volume, depending upon the yeast strain. Fortification is not only more convenient than syruped fermentation, but also the latter process creates special tax problems and often the wines develop a "mousy" or bacterial flavor.

Fermentation by all yeasts and growth of nearly all other organisms are either nonexistent or too slow to be much of a

150

problem at 18 percent or more alcohol. Thus the wines containing 18 percent alcohol by spirits addition are barely above the limit for biological stability, and can be aged, shipped, and left in half-finished bottles with much less danger of spoilage from microbial action than table wines with their legal (tax-bracket) limit of 14 percent alcohol. Addition of wine spirits before the sugar is all fermented arrests the fermentation and preserves the remaining sugar, giving a stable sweet wine. Although residual sugar in wines of lower alcohol is now commercially possible, it requires special treatment and care to prevent yeast spoilages avoided in fortified wines.

The third and perhaps most important reason for the addition of wine spirits to wine is that it makes possible special types of wine. These wines owe a good part of their special and distinctive flavors to the type of wine spirit used, the manner of its addition, and the special properties and reactions resulting from or made possible by its presence. These wines include a broad spectrum from sweet (dessert) wines to dry (appetizer) types, typified by the extremes available in port and sherry. For convenience we shall refer to the entire group as dessert wines, to avoid the cumbersome term "wines produced by the addition of wine spirits" or the connotations of "fortified wines."

In some wine-producing areas of the world famous for dessert wines, the winegrower is still a small vineyardist-winemaker. Even in highly developed winegrowing regions such as California, there are a few small but well-known producers of dessert wines. However, the necessity for the production of neutral wine spirits for addition to these wines places a special burden of expense for equipment and operational skill on the small operator. This may be avoided if the small operator obtains the wine spirit from a central distiller rather than producing it himself. However, the typical California dessert-wine plant is a large operation (Figure 20). In some countries beverage alcohol is produced by or for a governmental agency which then controls its distribution and use in dessert-wine production. The more usual development in our free-enterprise system has been that the wineries which produce dessert wines have become large (in terms of gallons processed) in order to benefit from the efficiency and economy of a centralized, integrated operation.

The dessert winery operation to be described is typical of several of the large organizations with nationwide distribution of their brands. In modern agricultural business vernacular, these companies are integrated both vertically and horizontally. They have multiple facilities to produce wines in various regions, and thereby have a broader-based business and product line. They may, for example, develop some of their wineries to produce premium table wines, others for standard table wines, still others for standard dessert wines and distilled brandy, and so on. They may then collect and blend wines from these different wineries for a quality and price range as well as a wide range of types under their various labeled brands. These larger wine cooperatives and companies may tie together under one management vineyards, wineries, distilleries, aging cellars, bottling plants, distributors, and even glass factories, trucking companies, and cooperage works.

FIG. 20. Aerial view of dessert wineries; still tower and water cooler in center. (Source: The Wine Institute.)

By no means all the dessert-wine producers are as large or diversified as this, but even the smaller producers are very efficient and cost-conscious because of the equipment and facilities required. In the 1970s there has been renewed purchase of wineries by national and international companies, particularly those with other food or beverage products.

The production of dessert wines is more adapted than that of table wines to the relatively hot regions where grapes are grown. Ripe grapes with more sugar are desired for dessert wines, and moderately low acidity is not as detrimental for these wines. Varietal flavors are less in demand for dessert wines (except muscatel), and high-yielding standard varieties are often used. Since about half of the total sugar of the grapes processed is diverted to the production of the spirits used for fortification, grapes and residues unsuitable for direct use as wine may be utilized. The best juice from the best available grapes may be used for the base wine to which the spirit will be added, and the spirit may be prepared from the grapes with too many raisins, too low acidity, little sugar, or browned juice. In this country the spirit used for dessert-wine production must come from grapes and is prepared by distillation at 185 proof or higher. Since 1 percent ethanol by volume measured at 60° F. (15.6° C.) is two degrees proof, 185 proof is $185 \div 2 = 92.5$ percent ethanol. The remaining 7.5 percent or less is mostly water which distills with the ethanol. The high-proof spirit for addition to wine is usually neutral or "silent," in that it is so purified that very little flavor-bearing congeneric substances are present, and it contributes relatively little direct flavor other than ethanol. The indirect effects on flavor are great, however, and the typical dessert-wine flavor does not develop in low-alcohol wines. A few American-made wines and several imported dessert wines are made with fortifying brandies which do contain appreciable amounts of flavoring substances in addition to ethanol. Pot-distilled brandy in particular may give a characteristic flavor which can be a quality feature of some wines.

The operations of winemaking described in Chapter 7 are applicable to dessert wines, with emphasis on the scale of the operation. The grapes are usually crushed in a Garolla-type crusher-stemmer. These large units crush 150 tons or more of grapes per hour, and a large winery may have as many as four in one installation. During the six weeks or so of the crushing season, such an installation may produce a million gallons of crushed grapes per nine-hour working day and process 25,000 tons of grapes in a five-and-a-half-day work-week. Each day's million gallons of crushed grapes must be processed to make room for the next day's million gallons. A million gallons would fill about thirty family-sized swimming pools!

The preferred method of collecting white juice or red wine is by settling and draining off the free-run, followed by processing of the wet pomace to recover the remaining sugar or wine for blending or distilling. The total volume of wine is reduced by the distillation of part to be added back to the rest. The yield of finished dessert wine will be 135 or less gallons per ton of grapes processed, depending upon the alcohol-recovery procedures, sweetness of the grapes, and type of wine being produced.

WHITE SWEET WINES

The white sweet wines include muscatel, white port, and angelica. Angelica, a product which originated in the early days in California, is a medium golden-colored, fruity, very sweet dessert wine. White port as made for the United States market is rather similar to angelica, but is typically somewhat lower in sugar, has less color, and possibly is more neutral in flavor. Both are marketed as such, but also are useful as blending wines to adjust sweetness (e.g., of sherry) or as base wines for flavored specialty wines. Most of the wine marketed as angelica is selected from stocks carried on the inventory as white port.

Muscatel is a white sweet wine made from muscat-flavored white grapes, predominantly Muscat of Alexandria and Muscat blanc, and is full-flavored, with the typical muscat aroma and a light to medium golden-brown color. Muscat of Alexandria is also used to make sun-dried raisins. Most of the muscat varieties tend to raisin easily. Raisin flavors are undesirable, however, in muscatel, and so should be avoided by early and selective harvesting. Muscat varieties tend to be pulpy and difficult to convert to a high juice yield.

White port and angelica may be made of any of the standard varieties of light-colored wine grapes. Thompson Seedless and other viniferous table-grape varieties are often used also. A few varieties such as Fernão Pires and Verdelho produce more distinctively flavored white dessert wines, but are not widely planted in California.

Low-colored red varieties such as Mission may be used for white dessert wine production, but the musts tend to be darker even under the best conditions; considering the present standards for white port, they are more suitable for darker wines such as sherry.

Grapes for sweet wines are usually harvested at about 23–25° Brix. If it is necessary to make use of less sweet grapes, such as rejects from table-grape shipments, they are diverted to wines for distilling.

Sulfur dioxide is almost always added, in the proportion of about 100 parts per million, at or immediately after crushing. It is preferable to inoculate with 1 to 3 percent of a separately grown yeast starter or an equivalent amount of pressed yeast; but if the fermentations are clean and progressing well, a portion of the preceding lot of wine may be used. The free-run juice is separated before inoculation and fermentation when making angelica and white port. For muscatel it is not uncommon to ferment for a short period (24 to 28 hours) on the skins to extract more of the characteristic flavor. A short period of heating by passing through a heat exchanger (2 or 3 minutes at 180° F., 82.2° C.) may be used to produce the same effect, but tends to give darker and cloudy wines. In order to achieve the desired light color for white port, low-colored grapes with no raisins and little enzymic browning, a low contact with air, the use of sulfur dioxide, and fermentations not over 80° F. (26.7° C.), and preferably lower, are emphasized. Dessert wines are made in hot areas, at the hot time of the year (100° F., 37.8° C., in the shade is common);

large-capacity refrigeration systems are needed to cool the musts and fermenting wines. Angelica is usually handled similarly. Angelica can be essentially fortified grape juice, and color control is less of a problem, although it is required by law that the must be fermented to at least 0.5 percent alcohol before angelica is fortified.

White port and muscatel ordinarily receive their addition of wine spirit after fermentation has lowered the temperature-corrected hydrometer reading to about 15° Brix (Figure 21). Addition of neutral high-proof spirit at this point to 18 percent ethanol by volume gives a new corrected hydrometer reading of about 5° Brix after the wine has been well mixed. Thus a typical wine may be spoken of as 18 × 5, meaning 5° Brix by the hydrometer stem and 18 percent alcohol by volume determined by distillation of a sample. Dessert wines as marketed generally range from 5° to 7° Brix, or about 9 to 14 percent sugar, with angelica and muscatel on the high side, and ports on the low, of this range.

To avoid complications, the wine spirits are added after pomace separation for muscatels and, of course, for the other white sweet wines. The addition of the spirits is carefully controlled by government regulations to protect the tax and legal interests of the federal government. The fermentation stops as soon as the alcohol is mixed in, but it is necessary to allow for the small degree of fermentation that occurs during the addition and mixing with large, rapidly fermenting lots. The wine is allowed to settle for as little as one day to as long as thirty days to allow the precipitation of lees and initial clarification to occur. Early racking may prevent development of off-flavors if the lees are copious. The wine is usually fined with bentonite at about 5 pounds per thousand gallons, settled, racked, and filtered. Wines may be blended at this point to adjust the composition. The blend may then be passed through heat and cold treatments for stabilization. The heating (usually one minute at 180–185° F., 82.2–85° C.) pasteurizes the wine, aids clarification by coagulation of proteins and other colloids, and helps mature the wine. Refrigeration to 16–18° F. (−8.9 to −7.8° C.) for about a month, with at least

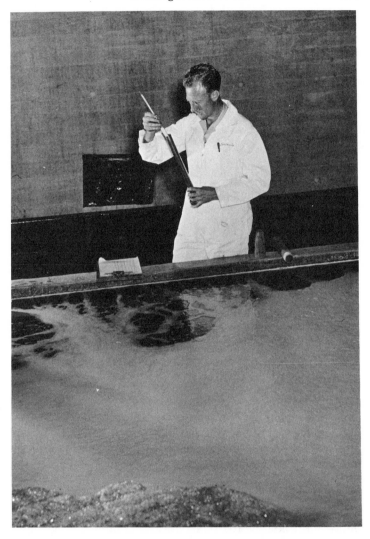

FIG. 21. The consumption of sugar during rapid fermentation of a white dessert-wine must is followed by testing frequently with a hydrometer. Note concrete storage tank in background. (Source: The Wine Institute.)

one filtration while cold and perhaps cycling of the temperature between 16° and 32° F. (−8.9 and 0° C.), promotes the complete removal of the precipitable tartrates and colloids.

White port is not usually placed in wooden tanks, and has been treated with activated charcoal to keep its color low. It is ready to market after these treatments and sufficient storage to allow the harsh taste of the freshly added spirits to mellow and marry with the wine. Marrying is a term used by flavorists and perfumers to describe the poorly understood but observed effect of increasing harmony of a blended mixture of flavors after they have been allowed to react together for a time. Any further haze development, etc., following blending can be then corrected before bottling.

Dessert wines are not immune to bacterial spoilage, particularly by *Lactobacillus trichodes,* also called cottony "mold" (incorrectly) because of the fluffy tufts of cells which it produces by growing in dessert wines. Therefore white port and most other dessert wines are given about 50 to 70 parts per million of sulfur dioxide at bottling. The use of sulfur dioxide in white port is more important for antioxidant effects and color control than for its antibacterial action. Hot bottling (pasteurization) is not often used.

White dessert wines do not improve much after bottling and may become sherry-like after a long time, so bottle-aging is not practiced. These wines are intended for reasonably immediate consumption and are usually marketed in easily resealed bottles with metal screw caps or occasionally wooden-topped replaceable cork stoppers. The relatively small amount of white port produced in Portugal is aged in the manner of red port, and is a somewhat different product from that usually produced in America. Angelica formerly was aged for a period in well-seasoned wooden tanks, and still may be found slightly more colored than the typical very light-colored white port. However, the final processing of the two is essentially the same. Muscatel, on the other hand, should be aged for three years or longer in puncheons or tanks of wood, preferably oak. These should be "topped" at least every few months to make up the ullage and prevent excessive oxidation. The muscat-grape aroma will persist during this aging, and the wine will become more smooth and mellow as the yeasty, new-wine flavor and harsh rawness of the freshly added high-proof brandy disappear.

PINK DESSERT WINES

California tokay is a pink dessert wine prepared by blending to the winemaker's taste. Approximately equal parts of ruby port, California sherry, and angelica are often used. It has no relationship to Hungarian Tokay, which is not fortified and has a golden or amber color. Other dessert wines may be prepared from grapes with a low red color content incapable of giving a red wine. Aleatico, a muscat-flavored variety, has been used to produce a pink muscatel. However, production practices for such wines do not differ appreciably for those for red dessert wines, and they are not common products. Dessert wines which might be considered pink, based upon their red color content, but which have an appreciable brown or orange hue arising from color modification of red wines, are called tawny. Tawny port arises from either long aging (four to six years) of port in barrels with occasional racking and aeration or from a quick-aging treatment involving baking at 120–140° F. (48.9–60° C.) for a few days to weeks. The latter treatment tends to develop a more pronounced caramel flavor than does the former, and is therefore forbidden in Portugal and is not used by the better American producers.

RED SWEET WINES

The classic red sweet wine is port, and unless qualified by other terms (i.e., tawny or white) it is red. Ruby port implies port which is bright red and relatively young and fruity, as distinct from aged ports of more complex but less fruity flavor. The port of Portugal was developed by Englishmen for the English trade. It is interesting to consider the production of this rich, full-flavored, generous wine in a hot climate for consumption in a chilly, clammy one. This warming, comforting, sweet beverage serves as a sort of shippable "bottled sunshine" to transfer some of Portugal's (or California's) excess to wintry areas. With energy shortages and lowered thermostats, such wine is expected to regain some of its popularity. The only other California red dessert wine of importance, red (or "black") muscatel, is made using Muscat Hamburg or Aleatico grapes and combining the techniques of port and ordinary muscatel production.

The grapes used for port production in California naturally include all red varieties widely planted in the warmer regions of the state. Since the red-color content of the grapes is reduced by growing them in a warmer climate, some light-red varieties (e.g., Mission and Grenache) are too light-colored for conversion to port without blending, and in fact may be made into sherry or even white port. Other varieties, such as Carignane and Zinfandel, can be made into good port, but red-pigment content may be a problem. Some varieties can produce high-quality port with distinctive odors and flavors which deserve varietal labeling. These include Tinta Madeira, Touriga, and Souzão. To bring the red color up to desired levels, the red-pulped varieties Salvador and Alicante Bouschet may be used. Since these two do not have very desirable characteristics other than high color, it is hoped that newer varieties, such as the recently introduced Royalty and Rubired, can replace them and give better quality as well as high anthocyanin pigment content.

Grapes picked for port should have a moderately high sugar content (23–25° Brix) but few raisined berries. The presence of many raisins will give their characteristic flavor to the wine, which is undesirable and off-type in port. The grapes should not be allowed to become overripe, because of the excessive loss of acid and the danger of raisining. The increase in pH resulting from too low acidity in overripe grapes gives a bluish shade to the wine and a flat flavor, whereas normal acidity helps keep the color a brighter red and improves the flavor. The anthocyanin (red pigment) content is relatively low for grapes grown in warm, port-producing regions. Care in picking and handling the grapes to prevent damage and loss of the red color by sunburn, raisining, and enzymic changes after bruising is important, and harvesting too late is likely to give less rather than more red pigment in the finished wine.

The grapes are stemmed, crushed, and sulfur dioxide added as for white port, but the starter yeast is added to the whole crushed mass. From this point on, the port-maker is racing to get the red pigment extracted from the skins and the fermenting wine pressed off the skins before it must be fortified to retain the desired sugar. Even if the musts are refrigerated and the fermentation conducted below ambient temperature, say at 75–85° F. (23.9–29.4° C.), the Brix will usually drop from 24 to 15° Brix in 24 to 48 hours, and the wine must be separated from the skins and the wine spirits added. The winemaker is probably using low-colored grapes, and must make the best use possible of this time to ensure the transfer of all the extractable color from the skins to the wine. He is likely to have crews working almost continuously punching down the cap in these large installations or, more probably, continuously pumping the wine over the cap. In so doing, the disintegration of the pulp, the death of the grapeskin cells, and the release of the pigments to the wine are hastened. The same purpose was formerly accomplished in Portugal by the process of treading the grapes. Although this is effective, it does not appeal to modern producers or consumers.

Even continuous pumping over may not be efficient enough in recovering the red color from the skins, and other procedures are in use or under test for improving this process. Storage of the grapes for a few days under carbon-dioxide pressure before fermenting has been used in Europe. The grapeskin cells die and then the anthocyanin pigment readily diffuses out. This process, carbonic maceration, has mostly been applied to making "nouveaux" table wines, not ports. Another procedure has been to add the fortifying spirits or a completely fermented wine to the freshly crushed grapes. The alcohol serves to kill the cells and extract the color. This leads to either loss or more reprocessing of the alcohol, however, and complicates the excise supervision. The most common practice is short-term, high-temperature treatment. Properly done, the color is quickly released and little "cooked" flavor introduced. An example might be pumping the must through a heat exchanger at 180° F. (82.2° C.) for two or three minutes, followed immediately by cooling back to fermentation temperature. This also pasteurizes the must, so that the necessary yeast starter provides a clean fermentation. The use of 100 parts per million of sulfur dioxide in the freshly crushed must aids in releasing the red color and helps avoid loss of it by enzymic browning reactions.

As soon as the maximum color has been extracted by fermentation, preferably while the wine tests about 15–17° Brix, the free-run is drained off and the pomace pressed. One of the gentler presses (basket, Willmes-type, etc.) is preferred, but speed and capacity dictate the use of screw presses. The pressed wine is usually more highly colored than the free-run, and may be blended back to raise the color and tannin level. These fluid-recovery processes take time and the Brix will continue to drop as fermentation goes on. A drop of 2° Brix during draining and pressing is common. At about 15° by Brix hydrometer, the wine spirits are added and the fermentation is halted.

The California port cellar must be balanced so that the wine may be marketed as a standard port, perhaps 18 × 6, with the desired color level. This poses a problem, and a different one each vintage season, because of variation in the composition of the grapes and of the wine, lot by lot and season by season. To achieve the desired blends, the winemaker adjusts his production practices for each lot accordingly. If he has several very sweet lots, he may ferment some lots nearly to dryness on the skins, as if they were to be table wines, before adding the wine spirits. If several lots have been low in sugar, he may produce red juice by heat treatment, ferment only slightly, and fortify. He may use concentrated red juice for sweetening. Some lots of Salvador or other very highly colored grapes can be made into dark-red port. By judicious combining of these products, he can produce the main lot or lots of young port wine to be further processed for sale as the type or types of port his winery markets.

If the winery is marketing an early-maturing ruby port, the wine is passed through the usual cold or ion-exchange tartrate stabilization, bentonite fining, pasteurization, and so on, and bottled. Such wines are stored in large stainless-steel or lined concrete tanks (Figure 22), and can be on the market within a few months of their production. If the company desires to market a more "aged" type of port, it may give the wine one or more cycles of heating (either similar to pasteurization or more prolonged, at temperatures of about 120° F., 48.9° C.), followed by refrigeration. This process and the related rackings and pumping give definite but limited oxidation which

FIG. 22. Part of an outside "tank farm" at a large winery. (Source: The Wine Institute.)

modifies the wine's flavor, color and quality. Sometimes a period of contact with small chips of seasoned white-oak heartwood may be used to give a portion of the wine a slight oaky taste, reminiscent of the barrel flavor.

These quick-aging procedures give to the wine many of the same attributes of prolonged aging—a richer, more harmonious, and more complex flavor. However, the preferred practice is still considered to be the traditional type of storage in wooden cooperage for four to six years. The wine is ordinarily blended and stabilized before filling into the aging barrels. Some producers, especially the large port shippers, have developed into a fine art the preparation of complex fractional blends of young wines plus some very old wines to produce a range of standardized, distinctive, port-type wines for their own and their wholesale customers' brands. "Vintage" or "crusty" port, a type produced with limited age in wood, but six to twenty or more years in bottles, is not so common on the market today. Rich ports may improve considerably with age in the corked bottle, but this practice is prohibitively costly for most wineries, and few wine merchants take the time. By choosing his wine carefully and "laying down" a stock, the consumer can experiment with this effect himself. At one time a proud father would store away some port when his son was born, to be used at the son's coming-of-age celebration. Certainly this is a pleasant custom worthy of revival.

SHERRIES AND RELATED WINES

We have previously emphasized the prevention or control of even limited oxidation. In the preparation of wines now to be described, oxidation is produced deliberately, but still in a controlled manner. Whether one starts with a red wine or a white wine, the final product of oxidation by air contact is a rather dark, slightly reddish-brown or amber wine with a characteristic flavor. Because of the loss of red color, red wines are seldom used as starting materials. Oxidation reactions in wine are of more than one kind, and produce different types and degrees of flavor and compositional change. The major overall flavor change has been described as maderized (purists insist on the spelling "madeirized," since the word derives from Madeira Islands, but the first syllable is accented and the spelling given is comparable to that used in French, Italian, etc.), *rancio,* sherry-like, and plain oxidized wine. Nutty, raisin-like, or caramel flavors may be associated with the maderized flavor, but are not the same. *Rancio* (incorrectly translated as "rancid") is reserved by some for the maderized flavor when it arises in old red wines aged in the presence of air. Maderization, per se, may be produced by prolonged aging or by heating.

The wines in this group are all of somewhat elevated alcohol, produced in the United States in the 17 to 21 percent range. A fairly high level of alcohol (over 15 percent) is necessary for the wine to survive oxidative processing without becoming vinegar through the action of acetic acid bacteria. Since these bacteria are inhibited by alcohol more easily than are yeasts, some wines in this class from other countries are marketed at only 16 percent alcohol. Other microbes, partly because of the high alcohol content, are also seldom a problem.

The three types of product we are to discuss are prepared by spirit addition to white base wine and production of oxidized flavors either by heating, by prolonged aging in the presence of air, or by growing yeasts aerobically on or in them —the *flor* yeast process.

Some method of heating is used for most of this type of wine sold on the American market. The three M's—Malaga, Marsala, and Madeira—are grouped in this class. Malaga is traditionally a muscat-raisin, caramel-flavored, very sweet fortified wine. It can be prepared by making an angelica-type sweet wine from partly raisined grapes. Very little is so produced in the United States at present. Marsala has a cooked-caramel flavor which has occasionally been produced in the United States by concentrating white grape juice through boiling it down to a syrup over steam. The flavor is not the same as boiling down over fire, but little is so produced outside Sicily. This syrup is used in blending with baked sweet wine to produce the approximate effect.

Madeira-type wines include a range of sweetness, and are also produced today by heating or baking the wine. Little wine made in the United States is labeled madeira, but actually a great deal of such madeira-like wine is produced. A large part of the wine produced in California, New York, and other states which is labeled sherry has more in common with imported Madeira than with Spanish sherry. It is interesting to note that baked wines are called "madera" in the Soviet Union. American-produced baked sherry is made by "baking" the fortified wine at 120–140° F. (48.9–60° C.) for 45 to 120 days. During this period some contact with oxygen is allowed. The only contact may be between the surface of the wine and the air above it in the tank during heating, or bubbles of air or oxygen gas may be passed into the wine during heating. The term "baking" should not be taken too seriously, since the temperature inside a room used to bake sherry is livable, even if uncomfortably like standing in the sun in Death Valley. The best product results from the lower temperature and longer time of treatment in the range given.

The origin of this process in the United States and the reason why the product is called sherry rather than madeira are obscure. It may have represented originally a quick-aging procedure. A few producers combine heating with aging by placing the barrels of sherry wine in the sun. For a time greenhouse-type glass structures were used for heating the wine with better control, and this developed rapidly into the present system. Today such wines are baked in wood, concrete, or metal tanks. The high temperature may be maintained by placing the tanks in a heated, temperature-controlled room. Alternatively, coils heated by circulating hot water may be placed in the tank, or the wine may be pumped through a heat exchanger and back to the tank. A large body of fluid does not heat up or cool off rapidly, and one must avoid excessive localized heating at the heated coil or other surface. If the heating surface gets too far above the desired temperature, true cooking, scorching, or charring will produce undesirable harsh flavors.

The wine to be converted to sherry is called sherry material, or shermat. This is usually produced as a white wine fermented "dry" $-1°$ to $0°$ Brix) and then adjusted by addition of wine spirits to the desired alcohol content. Since the characteristic flavor results from the processing, varietal-flavored grapes have no advantage. In fact, a varietal flavor is usually not desired in the product. Eastern producers use *labrusca* varieties, but the processing (often by the oxygen process of Tressler) removes the "foxy" flavors completely or nearly so. Other varieties in use include most of the common white and low red-colored standard dessert-wine varieties such as Mission, Thompson Seedless, Emperor, Malaga, Flame Tokay, and Palomino. The Palomino and Pedro Ximenes varieties are the most common of several grown in Spain for sherry. The Palomino is a pulpy grape difficult to crush and press, and is noted for a low acidity and high pH. A moderate total acidity and rather low pH are desirable features of must for sherry, and better varieties should be developed.

One way of lowering the pH of the must for shermat is to "plaster" it. The addition of the mineral gypsum (calcium sulfate), or in Spain "yeso"—an earth with a high gypsum content—will lower the pH and increase the apparent acidity. Two molecules of potassium bitartrate of the wine and one of calcium sulfate react to produce calcium tartrate, which precipitates out of the solution and leaves one molecule of potassium sulfate and one of free tartaric acid. This process is permitted in the United States only for *flor* sherry. The residual potassium sulfate may contribute a slight salty taste to the product. If most of the potassium bitartrate has already precipitated, as in an aged or stabilized wine, calcium sulfate will not have much effect, and it may be necessary to add tartaric acid or citric acid to lower the pH.

The preparation of the base wine, shermat, except for the more complete fermentation, is essentially as described for white port. The wine may be settled and racked to separate the yeast lees before adding the wine spirits, and again afterward. Usually a small amount (1.0 to 2.5 percent) of residual sugar is desired during baking; if not present in the initial shermat, it can be added by blending in the appropriate amount of angelica or white port. The "cream" (7.5 to 10 percent sugar) and medium (2.4 to 3.5 percent) sweet baked sherry may be brought up to their final sugar level by the same method, preferably after baking. Some aging of the shermat in wood cooperage before baking would be desirable, but for economic reasons is seldom done. Treatment with white-oak heartwood chips at about 5 pounds per 1000 gallons may accomplish part of the same effect and may be applied before or during baking. It is usual to fine the shermat with bentonite and rough-filter it before baking. It may be fined again with bentonite or with gelatin or casein and tannin after baking.

During baking the progress is followed by critical tasting and by analyzing color development (it darkens), aldehyde content (it rises), and furfural-derivative production (they increase as sugars react) to determine the desirable point for termination. For premium quality, the baked wine may be aged for one or two years more in wooden containers. In some cases a fractional blending system is used (Chapter 15). The wine is stabilized to prevent tartrate precipitation in the bottle by refrigeration to about 17° F. (−8.3° C.) for two to three weeks and then filtration, or possibly by ion-exchange treatment. It may receive a small amount of activated charcoal to lighten the color, in view of the preference today for paler sherry. After a final polishing filtration, the wine is bottled and is ready for sale. Sherry of most types may be kept for a long time in the sealed bottle with no appreciable improvement or deterioration, although some of the lighter types, particularly *fino* or *flor* sherries (see below), do seem to lose quality after a few years in sealed bottles, and rather quickly in opened bottles.

Sherry may be produced by long aging of the shermat in wooden cooperage (Figure 23) without any baking. The smaller the container, the more rapid is the change. If well conditioned white-oak 50-gallon barrels are used, two to four years is probably long enough. In some wine cellars, the barrels

Fig. 23. Imported barrels for aging sherry in a California cellar. (Source: The Wine Institute.)

of sherry are not filled full and the ullage is not replenished, to hasten oxidative changes. This type of aging is costly, but can produce distinctive, high-quality wines or wines very useful for blending. Much care and art must go into the blending of any wine, and sherries are particularly suitable for improving quality and uniformity by fractional blending. A series of trial blends should be made up and adjusted by critical tasting and evaluation, in comparison with samples from previous lots under the same label, before the commercial-sized lot is blended.

Flor sherry is produced by a very different process. The dry shermat for *flor* (Spanish for flower) sherry is initially fortified only to 14.5 to 15.5 percent alcohol by volume. If it is lower, acetic spoilage may occur, and if higher the *flor* yeast will grow poorly. The wine is then inoculated with yeast for the "flowering" process, in which the aerobic growth of yeast produces a special flavor and the *flor* or *fino* odor. This involves the production of acetaldehyde by the oxidation of part of the ethanol and other complex changes. The aldehyde content is increased in most sherries to some degree, but may reach 300 parts per million or more in *flor* sherry. This aerobic yeast growth is accomplished in two ways: surface growth of a film of yeast cells, or submerged growth with aeration and agitation of the solution. A film-forming yeast such as *Saccharomyces fermentati* appears to constitute a physical modification which can form a floating film, rather than a metabolically special organism, for the *flor* aroma can be produced by aerobic submerged culture with several fermenting yeasts.

If the surface-film method is used, the wine is kept in a fairly shallow layer with access to air, as in a half-empty barrel. The film-forming yeast grows and develops a rather heavy, wrinkled, creamy-white film on the surface. The film is aerobic, but the wine under the film is actually at a rather low oxidation-reduction potential and remains rather light in color. With time, the film occasionally breaks (especially if allowed to get too hot in the summer or too cold in the winter) and falls to the bottom. Autolysis of some of the yeast occurs, but the film usually regrows over the surface when the temperature becomes suitable. This process may be allowed to continue for several years. In dry climates the relative loss of moisture through the side of the cask, and perhaps via the film, slowly increases the concentration of the alcohol and of the nonvolatile constituents of the wine until eventually the *flor* is unable to grow. It is obvious that withdrawing part of the wine at different stages can give a whole range of products with more or less wood-age, yeast autolysis, and *flor* contributions to their flavor. Submerged-culture *flor* production in modern controlled fermentors has the advantage of speed and controllability, but does not give sherry with the wood-aged, yeast-autolysate complexities of the film process. It is a useful blending material and can be used to impart a *fino*-type aroma to a lightly baked sherry base, giving a very interesting yet inexpensively produced wine. The *flor* sherry or *flor* blend is finished by further fortification if necessary to bring it to the desired final alcohol content (17 to 18 percent in this country), and is finished in essentially the same manner as are the other sherry types.

Summary.—Production of dessert wines and sherries lends itself well to the economics of large-scale operation. Grape varieties capable of moderate to high production are used for these wines, and the vineyards are characteristically in the warmer grape-growing districts. Many of the products emphasize flavors developed by processing and aging, rather than the distinctive flavors of specific grape varieties, although this is not true of muscatels and need not be true of ports.

The spirits used in fortifying these wines contribute directly to their quality and composition. By arresting fermentations with fermentable sugar remaining, stabilizing wines against microbial and other changes, and making possible special reactions during aging, the added spirits indirectly modify the wine's quality. In the United States, most producers use highly purified neutral spirits to avoid heavy, hot, or harsh flavors requiring long aging to become smooth. The resultant wines can be very bright or light-colored and have a fruity flavor. If less purified, richer, or stronger-flavored brandy is used—pot-distilled, for example—longer aging may be required, and a different type of wine is produced. Long aging in wooden containers can be an important quality factor in some muscatels, ports, and sherries, giving a richness, complexity, and smoothness to the product. Bottle-aging seems less important in these wines than in the lighter wines, but certain types of port benefit from bottle-aging for a long time.

Sherries are prepared in three major ways: by the *flor* process, by baking, and by long aging in partly full containers. All these processes involve oxidative changes which largely determine the final flavor of the wine. Many styles and flavor gradations of sherry are available on the market, and anyone who "does not like sherry" is betraying the fact that he is not aware of or has not tried the wide range of available sherries. The same is probably true of the rest of the dessert wines described in this chapter, though all the others are sweet, whereas sherry need not be.

The production of dessert and appetizer wines has been declining worldwide, in response to their declining sales and the shift to table wines. There is a faint but logical and hopeful trend toward rejuvenated interest in wines of this broad group, particularly in higher-quality products with more distinctiveness and age, led by the drier types of sherry. A few producers of premium sherries, varietally distinct ports, and well-aged angelicas or muscatels have increased their sales rather steadily in the face of declining markets for the standard products.

The Spirit of Wine
Sang in my glass, and I listened
With love to his odorous music,
His flushed and magnificent song.
—WILLIAM ERNEST HENLEY

Chapter 11

DISTILLATION AND BRANDY

Distillation, the technique of boiling off volatile constituents and collecting them in concentrated or purified form by cooling the vapor, is too old to be of certain origin. It was used as early as 1500 B.C. by the Egyptians in preparing wood distillates during charcoal making. The ancient Persians used it to make rosewater, and its use is very old in India and China. Aristotle mentions making pure water by evaporation from sea-water about 320 B.C. Its application to the production of alcohol and various other uses in alchemy appeared in Western Europe before the end of the Middle Ages. Several scholars attribute its arrival in Europe to contacts with the Arabs during the Crusades. It is probably significant that the word *alcohol* is of Arabic origin.

From the alchemist's laboratory, distillation probably first "graduated" to commercial production of spirits from wines by the sixteenth century. The equipment used was primitive but effective: a pot to which heat could be applied, an enclosed air-cooled space above the pot where some volatile materials condensed, and a cooled delivery pipe where condensation of the remaining vapors to liquid occurred. It is obvious that the more volatile constituents of the wine are found in increased concentration in the condensate from the vapor, and

173

the less volatile in increased concentration in the liquid residue. Nonvolatile substances such as sugar or tartaric acid remain completely in the residue in a properly operated still. Ethanol (ethyl alcohol) and water are soluble in each other in all proportions. Ethanol is lighter than water (specific gravity 0.79384 *in vacuo* at 60° F. 15.6° C.) and boils at 173° F. (78.5° C.) at sea level (760 mm. pressure). When ethanol is added to water, a rise in temperature and an increase in volume occur. When the mixture is returned to the original temperature, the volume decreases and becomes slightly less than the sum of the water and alcohol volumes alone. The maximum contraction occurs when eight molecules of water and one of alcohol are mixed. At about 97.3 percent ethanol and 2.7 percent water by volume, a constant boiling-point mixture (an azeotropic mixture) is formed. Since this mixture boils at a slightly lower temperature than does pure ethanol, it is not possible to raise the alcoholic content of the condensate above this percentage by simple distillation.

Ethyl alcohol, the 2-carbon alcohol, is by far the most important volatile constituent of wines as far as brandy production is concerned. Methyl alcohol (1-carbon atom) is present in small amounts in wines made from grapes: a little less from varieties of *Vitis vinifera* than from *V. labrusca,* and more in spirits from fruit wines or in brandies distilled from the pomace (skins and seeds). Methyl alcohol is highest in wines from high-pectin fruits, because it comes from pectin ester hydrolysis. It may be important in the formation of odorous constituents. In spirits distilled from grape wines, it is present in too small quantities for toxic effects, but increased content indicates a mixture of spirits from other sources.

Alcohols containing more than 2 carbon atoms are present in small amounts in wines and other fermented beverages. These include *n*-propyl and isopropyl (3 carbon atoms), *n*-butyl and isobutyl (4), 2-methylbutyl and isoamyl (5), and *n*-hexyl (6). In normal brandies produced from wines, the sum of the higher alcohols (also called fusel oils) does not exceed 1 percent of the total alcohol present. The total amount of higher alcohols present in the brandy depends on the composition of the wine and on the method of distillation. The volatility of the higher alcohols varies with the alcohol content. Thus iso-amyl alcohol (one of the chief components of fusel oil) is less volatile than ethyl alcohol if the ethyl alcohol content is above 40 to 45 percent by volume, and more volatile if below. In the first case, the higher alcohols tend to concentrate in the later or higher temperature fractions (tails, or "feints"); in the second case, in the "foreshots," or heads.

The higher alcohols all have very pronounced odors, and if present in too high a concentration are definitely undesirable. Up to a certain point they may contribute to the desirable odor of the product. As products of yeast fermentation, they are present in all alcoholic beverages.

Acetaldehyde, the most important aldehyde produced by fermentation, is always present in wines and brandies. Being more volatile than water or ethyl alcohol, it distills off first and is concentrated in the heads fraction. If present in too high a concentration in the distillate, it has undesirable sensory properties, but normally the amount is too small to detect. It may be important in reactions with alcohol to produce acetals.

When wines are heated, especially those containing yeast cells and distilled in direct-fired stills, some furfural may be produced by decomposition of pentose sugars. Although furfural boils at 324° F. (162° C.), small amounts are found in the distillates because it "steam distills" (carries over in the vapor stream). In larger amounts its odor is undesirable.

Wines and brandies contain a number of ethyl and some methyl esters with fruity odors. Fermentations with certain undesirable yeasts may produce excessive amounts of some esters. Distillation of wines containing higher amounts of yeast cells also seems to result in a higher ester content in the distillate. Ethyl acetate is present in detectable amounts only in spoiled wines. It appears in the heads during distillation.

Acetic and, to a lesser extent, lactic acids are volatile, but insufficient amounts are present in normal distillates to give an odor to the product.

Other volatile materials include those found in the grapes or those produced by fermentation of defective musts. Varieties of the *V. labrusca* type contain the very distinctive ester methyl anthranilate, but little distills over. Musts containing free sulfur (from that dusted on the grapes to control powdery mildew, *oïdium*) often result in wines containing hydrogen sulfide or mercaptans—both undesirable and possible distillate contaminants if present in sufficient amounts. Musts or wines to which excessive sulfur dioxide has been added are also less desirable for distillation since the gas is both volatile and corrosive and the wine will be higher in acetaldehyde. Moldy musts are usually settled prior to fermentation, and special care is taken in distillation of their wine to avoid carryover of off odors.

STILLS AND DISTILLATION

When the temperature of a liquid is gradually raised, one reaches a temperature when the liquid boils, i.e., molecules escape from the surface as vapor. In an alcohol-water mixture (of below 97.3 percent ethanol), the vapor leaving the surface contains a higher percentage of alcohol than the original liquid. This is the basis of fractional distillation, which permits brandy production from wine. As the distillation of an alcohol-water mixture continues, the alcohol content of the residual liquid is gradually lowered and finally approaches zero.

If the wine is placed in a closed pot provided with an outlet arranged to cool the vapors, one has a pot still (Figure 24). Heat may be applied by direct fire (as usually in Cognac) or with steam (as in California and elsewhere). The simple pot still has been greatly modified. A simple or more complex system of partially cooling the vapors is usually provided. This partial condensation is called rectification, or reflux. The wine to be distilled is often used to partially cool the vapors. This is a desirable economy measure recovering heat that would be wasted.

The more volatile constituents tend to be present in higher percentages in the first fractions that come off (heads). When distilling wine, the non-alcohol components of the distillate are high early in the distillation, when the alcohol content of

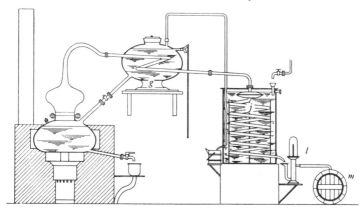

FIG. 24. A pot still: *g*, preheater; *j*, worm condenser; *l*, simple proof-measuring try box; *m*, barrel for receiving the brandy.

the distillate is over 50 percent. Furfural starts to distill over when the alcohol content of the distillate reaches approximately 40 percent, and continues down to about 25 percent. The higher alcohols are essentially completely distilled over by the time the alcohol content of the distillate from a pot still has fallen below about 30 percent.

When distilling not from wine but from previously distilled distillate (as in Cognac), somewhat different results are obtained. The aldehydes are then still primarily found in the heads, but the esters, at this higher alcohol percentage, distill over a wide range of alcohol content, even a small amount during the distillation of the tails fraction. Increasing the speed of distillation increases the rate of distillation of the volatile acids and esters. It is believed that a slow distillation gives a product of higher quality.

However, the quality of the product of a pot-still distillation is partially (if not largely) controlled by the sensory examination of the distillate which is made during distillation. As the character of the distillate changes during a run, the receiver is changed at least at the end of the heads "cut" and at the transition from the main cut to the tails. Intermediate fractions may be separated as the distiller desires. Depending on the quality of the distilling material and the quality of product desired, more or less heads or tails are removed by the distiller. The percentages removed and the amount of heads or tails returned before and after secondary distillations obviously greatly influence the quality of the final product.

The advantage of the pot-still procedure for production of brandy may be assigned primarily to this control over the composition and quality of the product by the distiller. Even when the raw product is of poor quality, the distiller, by controlling the amount of heads and tails retained and by the double distillation technique, influences the quality of the product. The disadvantage of the pot-still procedure is primarily its higher cost of operation. This is true whether the product is brandy or whiskey.

Because of the high cost of operation of pot stills, the continuous procedure was introduced in the nineteenth century —first for industrial alcohol and whiskey and later for brandy. The continuous still is essentially a series of interconnected pot stills (Figure 25). The column type of continuous still is a cylindrical tube divided into sections by a series of plates. Each plate functions as a separate pot still. Holes arranged in the plates allow vapor to rise through each plate and its covering liquid. Down-pipes between plates provide for return of liquid from one plate to another. The upper part of each down-pipe extends above the plate to maintain a liquid layer on the plate. The lower end of the down-pipe is inserted in a cup in the lower plate to form a liquid seal. As a result, each chamber between plates is isolated, so that the vapor and liquid in each equilibrate before the excess distills on as vapor or refluxes back as liquid. In the typical column still, the wine is introduced at some intermediate plate on the column. Heat is supplied from steam introduced at the bottom of the column. The alcohol percentage decreases as the wine flows down the column, and increases at each plate above as the more volatile alcohol vapors rise up the column. To conserve heat, as with the pot still, the dealcoholized liquid (*stillage,* or *bottoms*) from

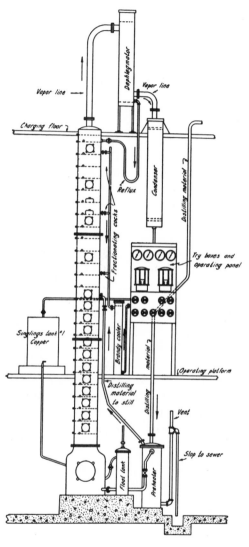

Fɪɢ. 25. A column still. (Source: Joslyn and Amerine, 1941.)

the bottom of the still is used to heat the wine which is to be introduced into the still. The lowest temperature and highest percentage of alcohol are found at the top of the column still. The holes or perforations on the lower plates of the column are more open to permit distilling materials with a larger percentage of suspended solids to pass. The upper plates function as the rectifying (i.e., purification) part of the column, and the perforations are usually covered by bubble caps to force the rising vapor to bubble through the liquid layer.

The product from the top of a column still, like that from a pot still, must be cooled to condense the vapor to a liquid and lower it to room temperature. Column stills function continuously, but eventually the plates need to be cleaned. In normal practice the column still is shut down and washed out once a week.

Two special problems of column-still operation are the removal of higher alcohols and of aldehydes. The higher alcohols gradually accumulate on an intermediate plate of the column—usually at a plate with an alcohol content of about 135° proof.* It is possible to draw off a higher alcohol fraction from a plate on which it accumulates if the column is operating to produce high-proof (over 170° proof) spirits.

To remove aldehydes, a special heads column may be attached to the still. The aldehydes removed are best utilized by introducing them into a rapidly fermenting must where the yeast enzymes reduce the acetaldehyde to ethyl alcohol.

Continuous stills, like pot stills, must have condensers to

Proof is an old English term for measuring the alcoholic strength of distilled beverages. Black powder and the beverage were mixed, and a flame applied. If the mixture burned well, the beverage was "proof"; if it did not it was too high in water. When physical methods for determining alcohol percentage were developed, "proof" was found to be slightly over 50 percent alcohol. Legally, English 100-percent-proof spirit contains 57.1 percent by volume of alcohol, and alcoholic strength is usually expressed as under or over proof. In the United States, proof (or 100 proof) spirits contain 50 percent by volume of alcohol measured at 60° F. (15.56° C.). Hence 200 proof spirit is absolute alcohol. Most brandies, whiskeys, rums, and liqueurs are sold at between 80 and 102 proof—i.e., between 40 and 51 percent alcohol by volume.

condense the vapor and to reduce the temperature to normal. Two condensers are usually used: a dephlegmator which condenses only part of the vapor and returns this fraction to the column, and another which condenses the remaining vapor. The product brandy is drawn from the appropriate plate to give the desired proof or, particularly for high proof for use in wines, it may be distilled "over the top" and caught at the main condenser.

In California, the column still is used both for the production of beverage brandy and for fortifying brandy for dessert-wine production. The fortifying (high-proof) brandy is usually distilled at 185° to 189° proof. Brandy for beverage purposes must be distilled at 140° to 170° proof.

Separation of fusel oils is difficult when using a column still to produce beverage brandy, for the plates on which the higher alcohols accumulate are only one or two plates lower on the column than those from which the 160° to 165° proof brandy is to be withdrawn.

Continuous stills are not only more efficient than pot stills in their energy utilization, but also their operation can be automated. Automatic controls for feed, product flow, and temperature control of the condensers are easily applied to continuous stills (Figure 26). These lead to more uniform distillates and less expensive operations. However, pot-still brandies are generally different in flavor and higher in non-ethanol flavor constituents, and may be preferred by some producers for fortification or beverage brandy.

Many modifications of the simple pot and column stills described above are being used. In California, specially adapted column stills, sometimes with mechanical movement of fermented pomace in the still, are used to remove the residual alcohol from the pomace. Distillation under vacuum seems to result in fruitier products, but the equipment is expensive and whether the product justifies the expense has not been determined.

Aging of brandy for beverage purposes is an expensive operation. Not only is the product tied up for two to ten or more years, but there are considerable losses of alcohol during aging. In this country the federal government estimates a certain amount of evaporation for each year of aging, and within this allowance taxes are paid only on the aged product remaining for bottling. The present tax on brandy and other distilled alcoholic beverages is $10.50 per 100° proof gallon ($2.77 per liter), more than $2.00 per bottle if sold at 100° proof. In order to protect this revenue, the production of distilled spirits is very closely supervised and controlled by B.A.T.F. agents.

TYPES OF BRANDY

Brandies are usually classified by region of production. This may to a small degree be due to the influence of soil conditions or the variety of grapes used. However, the biggest differences in quality appear to originate from the method of distillation and the aging practices.

The most important French brandies are produced in the Charente district north of Bordeaux. The product is called Cognac, from the town of the same name. The soil of the district is highly calcareous, and the best brandies are produced in the district containing the highest calcium carbonate content in the soil, called the Grande Champagne. A neighboring district with less soil calcium carbonate is Petite Champagne. Other districts are Borderies, Fins Bois, Bons Bois, and Bois Ordinaires. The product of the first two districts is usually sold as Grande Fine Champagne or Fine Champagne Cognac. The word "Champagne" in this usage has nothing to do with the sparkling wine of this name.

Brandies of different parts of the Charente district and of different ages are used to produce the other commercial types of Cognac. Traditionally these were sold as "3" or "5" star (for the cheapest), VSOP (for a better quality), and under proprietary brands of varying quality and price. VSOP is supposed to stand for "very superior old pale." Today, many Cognacs on the world market are given just the proprietary brand designation.

FIG. 26. Control panel for a brandy distillery. (Source: The Wine Institute.)

The predominant grape variety of the Charente is Saint-Émilion (called Trebbiano in Italy and Ugni blanc in the south of France). In the cool Charente it ripens poorly, in most years producing a wine of only about 8 to 9 percent alcohol and 1.0 to 1.5 percent total acidity. The composition of the wine that makes the best beverage brandy here as elsewhere is: white grape source, low alcohol, high acid, preferably no added sulfur dioxide, and no damaged or moldy fruit.

Immediately after the vintage, distillation of the wines is begun. The wines are not clarified; indeed, distillation of the yeast deposit with the wine is one of the factors favorably influencing quality. The traditional pot still is exclusively used for the distillation. The stills are usually direct-fired. Two distillations are made, the first at only about 54 proof. Heads and tails fractions are often not collected separately at this stage. The still is then emptied, and a new charge is made. The initial distillates are combined and redistilled to give a product at about 140 proof. Heads and tails fractions are separated in the second distillation, and usually are recycled back to the first distillation of another batch.

The product is cut to about 100 proof with distilled water, and aged in new oak casks. These are made of Limousin oak, and vary in size from 50 to 200 gallons. During aging the Cognac decreases in alcoholic strength but improves in quality for a number of years; some are aged for as long as 25 years. Eventually, aging in the wood must be discontinued because too much woody flavor is extracted and the alcohol content becomes too low. The older brandies are especially useful for blending purposes. Some brandies are transferred after a year or so from the new small cooperage to used or large cooperage, to reduce the extraction of oak tannin.

Most of the younger Cognacs (the "3"-star quality, for example) are slightly sweetened before sale. Connoisseurs prefer drier Cognacs with a moderate but clean aged odor. One should beware of imported brandies which are offered for sale in odd bottles implying long aging. Napoleon brandies (whether of Napoleon I or III) have long since disappeared from the market, and if bottled would be no better now than when bottled; if left in the wood for more than about 25 years before bottling, they would be of lesser quality. The regulations of the Treasury Department require honest labeling as far as age is concerned, and since about 1960 most of the exaggerated claims of excessive aging on imported brandies have disappeared. The best Cognacs are sold as Grande Fine Champagne, though the blended Cognacs of some firms are very fine—and expensive.

Armagnac is produced in much smaller quantities than Cognac, and is less exported and less well known. It is produced in a delimited district in southwestern France. The wines are distilled in a semicontinuous fashion at only about 126° proof in pot stills with a small rectifying column. Only one distillation is made. The product is aged in oak casks. The odor of Armagnac is considered by some experts to be less elegant and fine than that of Cognac, even when well aged. Armagnac criteria of quality are certainly less standardized than those of Cognac, and commercial products of very variable quality are found on the market—some in fancy bottles which obviously have nothing to do with the quality of the contents.

Much cheap brandy is produced in pot and column stills in the south of France. Some of this, at highly competitive prices, may be found on the American market as "French brandy." We have perhaps been unlucky in finding many of these to be newly distilled brandies with added color, sugar, and flavor.

If the pressed skins and seeds from the fermentation are placed in a pile and aged for one to several months, they undergo changes in flavor—anaerobic changes which have not been well studied or elucidated. If the surface of this pile of pomace (or *marc*) is then removed, and the remainder placed in a pot still, very pungent distillates will be obtained. These are usually not aged, and reach the market as clear liquids. In France these are called *eaux-de-vie-de-marc*, or marc brandy. The best are produced in small amounts in Burgundy. They are expensive, and the odor is so pungent that one must cultivate a taste for them—which, truthfully, hardly seems worth the effort. Some people use them in coffee, but their cost hardly recommends this use. Grappa, an Italian pomace brandy, has a similar odor, as it is produced in the same fashion. During World War II some Portuguese brandy was exported to this country. It was often excessively sweetened and flavored and was sometimes noticeably high in higher alcohols. After the war these importations decreased and show little sign of again increasing.

In contrast there is a continuing modest (about a tenth of the French importations) demand for Italian and Spanish brandies in this country. This is surprising to us, because they have tended to be rather hot-tasting and lack a fruity or winelike odor. Some of the cheaper products are clearly sweet. Some Spanish brandies are aged by a fractional-blending system (or in a *solera*) and sell at premium prices. Aging alone, however, cannot produce a high-quality product. Use of wines of better quality would improve the product and give a better result after aging. One clear test of the lack of quality of some of these brandies is their harshness when consumed straight, or even in a highball.

Some French wine is imported into Germany for brandy production, and French oak casks have even been used for aging brandy in Germany. In spite of this and excellent stills, highly trained operators, and skillful blending, the products usually are of only moderate quality.

Greek brandy has enjoyed popularity in the United States; we wish that we could recommend it. We have found it often sweet and hot. South African brandy has been found to be more interesting. It has a cleaner grape (not raisin) odor and is less sweetened. It is pot-distilled and well aged. Unfortunately, it is apparently available in few localities. The younger brandies made in the Soviet Union are frankly hot in taste, but the more expensive have obviously been aged for a considerable time and have complex flavors.

Peruvian *pisco* brandies are sold as clear brandies, so obviously they have little true wood aging. They and similar brandies made in Chile usually have some muscat-grape aroma. Their almost exclusive use in sweet fruit-flavored punch seems appropriate and significant. The Mexican brandies tasted here and in Mexico have not been memorable, except for a noticeable added flavor of "oil of cognac" in some. "Oil of cognac" is a highly flavored product produced by distilling a yeast suspension in a pot still. It is usually high in ethyl laurate and other esters.

California brandy has enjoyed increasing popularity since World War II. Virtually all of it is produced by column stills. After distillation at nearly 170° proof it is cut with water to about 120° proof, a small amount of caramel syrup is added, and it is aged in barrels (50 gallons) made of American oak. The cheaper sorts are aged from two to four years, two being the legal minimum, but some eight-year-old California brandy is now available. California brandy is carefully distilled, so that excess higher alcohol content is rare. In fact, some seem to be so highly rectified in distillation that they lack grapiness.

Two general types of California brandy are found on the market: those containing sweetening and flavoring materials (rectified brandy) and those without (straight brandy). If the latter are aged for four years or more at over 100° proof and are not reduced below 100° proof when bottled, they may be labeled "bottled in bond" (identifiable by a green tax stamp across the top of the bottle; the date of distillation and bottling is given on the stamp). Only a small amount of California brandy is bottled in bond.

Most California brandies are therefore reduced (cut) to 80° to 88° proof with water before bottling. The best brandies can be enjoyable without further dilution, but many are served in highballs with soda or, preferably, water. A good California brandy has an unmistakable wine-like odor, a distinct oak or vanillin-like smell, and a clean, nonhot dry taste. It should be light amber in color with no greenish tint (due to excessive iron).

Some pomace brandy, produced by distilling fermented pomace in a pot still, has been produced in this state. It has been called grappa and is sold as a colorless beverage. It is often used in coffee, which seems as good a use as any.

The use of gigantic snifters for serving brandy (California or imported) is almost pure affectation. The snifter tends to volatilize too much of the brandy. Where an off-odor is suspected, a snifter may be useful to professionals. When the snifters are ostentatiously warmed, it is positively offensive. The warmth of the hand on the bowl of a small glass is sufficient to bring out the odor of a fine brandy.

Judging brandies requires experience. However, the defects of sweetness, higher alcohols, hotness, and added flavor are relatively easy to identify and avoid. For the best comparison, the brandies should be examined both straight and diluted 50 percent with water. The great desideratum is a complex but balanced odor and a clean and soft taste. Cognacs should have the characteristic Cognac odor involving pot distillation and European oak, but not too concentrated. Marc brandies should have a pungent odor, but not an offensive one. California brandies are usually light in color and flavor and should have a pleasant or vanillin odor. They—as well as most other brandies, including the cheaper cognacs—are best served as highballs. Only the very finest and oldest brandies can be appreciated pleasurably when served undiluted.

Summary. —Distillation separates and concentrates ethanol and other volatile materials from wine. Pot stills have certain advantages, particularly the possibility of controlling the quality by sensory examination of the product during distillation. Continuous stills are cheaper to operate and are now used for brandy production in most countries.

The most important single type of brandy worldwide is Cognac. It is a pot-distilled product which is produced in a variety of types and qualities. Armagnac is the second most important type of French brandy. The increasing popularity of California brandy seems to be due to its careful distillation and to the aging in oak barrels. Other countries produce brandy, some of which is sweet or hot in taste, or flavored.

The sensory qualities and proper use of brandy are outlined. Brandy, particularly California brandy, appears to appeal particularly to the consumer interested in a lighter, more fruity product than traditional whiskies, but not one so simple as the nearly pure alcohol of vodka.

There are people who have been known to prefer bad wine to good, just as there are men who are fascinated by bad women. —ANDRÉ L. SIMON

Chapter 12

SPECIALTY WINERY PRODUCTS

BYPRODUCTS OF THE WINERY

The residues obtained in winery operation may be converted to byproducts. These include the fusel oil recovered incidental to large-scale wine distillation for eventual use in lacquer solvents, and tartrates recovered from pomace, lees, and distillery wastes to give cream of tartar for baking, tartaric acid salts for use in photography, and tartaric acid for acidification of wines and other foods. Although it was done in this country during the two world wars and is sometimes practiced now with tank argols, tartrate recovery from winery wastes has not been economically attractive here in normal times, because of the low price of tartrates imported from countries with larger wine production and lower production costs. Grape residues are, however, the major world source of tartaric acid, and more interest is being displayed in recovering this useful acid as labor costs rise in other countries and wine production in the United States becomes more centralized in few and larger modern wineries.

In general, the same situation prevails for the other three potential processed byproducts—red pigment from skins and tannin and oil from the seeds in winery pomace. Concentrated anthocyanin extracts from red grapeskins have been prepared and dried for use in meat stamping and other food and beverage coloring, especially in Italy in recent years. With the shift to natural food dyes this may become more important, but as a rule the winemaker prefers to transfer the pigment as completely as possible to his red wine and is unwilling to divert much to byproducts. Grape-seed tannin has been produced in Australia and Europe and sold worldwide, primarily for use in adding to and fining wines. It has been used successfully during wartime shortages in tanning a good quality leather. The production and demand are small compared to the total possible production. Grape-seed oil is a good semidrying oil suitable for food uses as well as for paints. Beyond a small amount produced for special uses, particularly raisin "polishing" to decrease sticking and give improved appearance, this oil is not usually recovered except under wartime or food emergency conditions. The nonprocessed residues such as pomace and still bottoms usually constitute more of a disposal problem than valuable byproducts. The value of winery wastes for cattle feed and soil-improvement agents is minimal, but they may be so used owing to availability, low cost, and need for disposal.

Some other products of wineries are more properly termed accessory products. Juice from wine grapes is sold to home winemakers and to be used in production of grape juice drinks, jellies, and as a sweetener in baby foods and many other food products. This may be white or red juice. If it is to be red, the color must be released from the skins by appropriate short heat treatment or other means. The juice is clarified and processed at low temperature with minimal air contact to avoid browning and flavor changes. High sulfur dioxide levels (1,000 parts per million or so) may be used to prevent fermentation, and the free sulfur dioxide may be removed later by treatments such as stripping under vacuum. Such unfermented sulfited juice is called *muté* in the winery. Today it is more common to process the juice by concentration under vacuum to a high sugar level (60–70° Brix); this red or white concentrate is stored under refrigeration until needed. The extremely high sugar content deters fermentation, and cold storage away from air contact helps prevent browning and other changes. Of course, the decreased volume lowers storage and shipping costs.

Concentrated juice is not only a product marketed to other food processors, but also is useful in the winery for sweetening wines, and may even be diluted and fermented to wine after the usual vintage season. With the modern type of high-vacuum, low-temperature, and perhaps essence-recovering concentrator, a very high quality product can be obtained. Dealcoholized, concentrated wine to be used for flavoring can be prepared by similar processes as an accessory product. The alcohol is recovered for other uses. Wine vinegar may be another accessory product of wineries. Unlike the situation in former times, it is seldom produced accidentally. Usually aerated tanks are used for vinegar production.

In addition to these byproducts, accessory products, and the primary products of table wine, sparkling wine, dessert wine, and distilled wine spirits, there are numerous specialty wine products. Some are made by only one producer by a secret process. These are considered proprietary products—the copyrighted brand name and secret process are owned by a proprietor. Two classes of these specialty wines—flavored wines and fruit wines—are worthy of discussion of the general principles of their production.

VERMOUTHS AND OTHER FLAVORED WINES

The production of flavored wines is a very ancient practice which appears to have gained historical impetus primarily from two directions. The ancients' wine was often poorly flavored or partly spoiled owing to acetification and other contaminations. It often kept poorly owing to low alcohol, lack of sulfur dioxide, and ignorance of the process of making and keeping good wine. The addition to wine of substances to correct, cover up, or resist such spoilage was a matter of trial and error. The addition of sea water to wine, particularly that for slaves, was a Greek and Roman practice. Besides preventing excessive intake and brightening the color of the red wine, no doubt this helped cover the off flavors of low quality wine. Addition of pine resin, as still practiced to some degree in Greece to produce retsina, may have arisen similarly. From the effort to cover bad odors and tastes, it is a short step to the practice of adding desirable flavors and letting the wine serve as the vehicle, and to some extent the preservative, for the added flavor. Just as spices and perfumes developed originally to cover food spoilage and body odors, and then evolved to give extra interest and pleasure after conditions improved, so did spiced, perfumed, and flavored wines develop and survive.

The second line of development of flavored wines was medicinal and mystical. The medicines, narcotics, and love potions of the day were mostly botanicals chosen for known or supposed efficacy. Potions were prepared partly on the basis that any plant with an unusual or strong odor or taste must be good for something, and a little bit of everything should make a fine cure-all. Formulas were ritualistic and complicated. Wine was the solvent of choice for the ancient would-be pharmacist, because the alcohol made it a better solvent and lent its own euphoric talents. It was a happy marriage, because the mild antibacterial and preservative value of the essential oils and other materials extracted from these herbal medicaments helped keep the low-alcohol, more-or-less sweet wine from spoilage, and the alcohol of the wine in turn helped preserve the medicine, tonic, or magic potion. Many of the botanical medicines which have real value are bitter: those containing quinine, for example. A bitter taste came to be desired and preferred in these products. This acquired taste for bitterness survives today, and many of the traditional types of flavored wine have a noticeably bitter aftertaste.

After the development of distillation, fortified wines and brandy became the base chosen for flavored wines and liqueurs. The extra alcohol improved the solvent power and the ease of preservation, particularly after opening. It is interesting that the traditional class of flavored wines—the vermouths—retains much of the ancient character, even though few people still believe that vermouths have medicinal value or magical properties.

The name vermouth derives from German *Wermut* (literally, "man's strength"), and is related to wormwood, a common herb, *Artemisia absinthium,* used in many formulations. The name of the herb derives not from any infestation of its stem, but rather because one of its medical uses was as a vermifuge —which may or may not make it seem more attractive to you. Vermouths today are prepared with familiar flavors and spices such as allspice, anise, bitter orange peel, cinnamon, clove, coriander, fenugreek, ginger, marjoram, nutmeg, rosemary, sage, savory, thyme, and vanilla. Exotic botanicals are also used: angostura, blessed thistle, cascarilla, cinchona bark, horehound, hyssop, dittany of Crete, European centaury, galingale, hart's-tongue, hops, lemon balm, rhubarb, saffron, valerian, yarrow, and zeodary. The list of materials which have been used is very long, and the ingredients and amounts employed by any one producer are seldom made public. Although there are class similarities, the flavoring specialist strives to produce a blend of flavors which is so complex and harmonious that his product is distinctive and yet not readily "analyzable" by either tasters or chemists. The use of fifteen or more different ingredients in one formulation is usual, and more than fifty not unknown.

There are two general types of vermouth, the French and Italian styles, sometimes referred to as dry vermouth and sweet vermouth. The dry or French type is characterized on the American market by a very light straw color, about 4 percent sugar, a light but definite aromatic herbal flavor, and a slightly bitter aftertaste. The traditional level of herb addition is about 0.5 to 0.75 ounce of the mixture of dry herbs per gallon of wine. This type of wine served cold, or perhaps over ice or with soda, is a delightful preprandial libation for social gatherings. Unfortunately, Americans generally have not learned this, although vermouth is so used in Europe. A major portion of American vermouth is used in mixed concoctions such as the martini (dry vermouth) and the manhattan (sweet vermouth). Since it has become fashionable to make the martini almost straight gin, and yet economics (and in our opinion, desirable flavor) dictates a sizable portion of vermouth, the market has favored almost colorless and lightly flavored dry vermouths.

Italian style or sweet vermouth has a much darker color and richer flavor. It usually is prepared with from 0.75 to 1.5

ounces of dry herb mixture per gallon. Caramel coloring may be used to give the typical medium dark-brown color. The base wine is or includes some muscatel, and citrus, anise, or vanilla as well as herbal notes are often recognizable in it. The after-taste is still basically bitter, but the sugar level (about 15 percent) contributes sweetness and body to Italian style vermouth.

The base wine for dry vermouth is prepared by blending white port or angelica, white wine, and high-proof spirits to the proper sugar and alcohol content. It may be treated to a limited extent with activated charcoal to ensure low color and a neutral odor. Angelica, white port, muscatel, and, rarely, sherry are blended in California for the sweet vermouth base. The alcohol content of American-made vermouths is in the dessert wine range, 18–20 percent by volume. Those made in Europe are often lower, 16–18 percent. The base wine is usu-ally colored with caramel or decolorized with carbon, as the type of vermouth requires; clarified; and stabilized before addition of the flavoring substances. The base wine may be aged in wooden cooperage before and again after flavoring for a total of three to five years; however, this is no longer gene-rally done for sweet vermouths, and dry vermouths are usually finished and marketed within a year of production.

The preparation and use of the flavoring mixture is a critical part of the production of these wines. The whole plants, fruits, seeds, barks, roots, flowers, and other botanicals that make up the herbs and spices to be used are often expensive materials which must be collected from many parts of the world. Like all natural products, they are variable by source and season and are subject to damage and deterioration. The vermouth producer must depend upon reputable suppliers and must be selective for genuineness, quality, and freshness in his purchases. To compensate for unavoidable variation in the strength and characteristics, he must adjust his formulas to maintain a uniform flavor in the finished wine.

The dry herbs may be added to the wine and steeped there-in, perhaps at slightly elevated temperature, for some weeks or a few months. This is termed the infusion process. Small trial lots are prepared for comparison with the previous production of the winery, and the selected proportions are carefully weighed out for the production lot. The materials are preferred whole or only coarsely ground. They must be dry, clean, and mold-free, and are stored carefully to retain their odors—usually in a refrigerated room. The herbs are not left in the wine too long, lest undesirable flavors or clarification problems result from excessive extraction. For the same reason, the herbs are not pressed when removed from the wine. As long as stirring and circulation of the wine are provided, a convenient method is to submerge the flavoring materials in the wine in an open-mesh cotton cloth bag.

A second method of adding the flavoring to the wine is to prepare a concentrated extract of the herbs in wine spirits, water, or wine, which is then added to the production lot of vermouth. It is possible to buy such concentrated flavoring from supply houses, as extracts of individual flavoring substances or the total mixture for standard or selected vermouth specifications. Producers with large sales of vermouth are believed to prefer some modification of the extract process, but often prepare their own extracts, wholly or in part.

After the wine has been flavored, it is filtered. Fining with bentonite, refrigeration, filtration while cold, and pasteurization may be necessary to achieve stable clarity, but excessive processing is avoided to prevent loss of the added flavors. The flavors are usually allowed to "marry"—stabilize and harmonize their flavor values—for a few months, and then the wine is bottled for sale. A final polishing filtration and a small sulfur dioxide addition, 25 parts per million or so, to maintain some free sulfur dioxide and a low color in dry vermouth, are usual precautions at bottling.

In addition to the traditional vermouth types, there are many proprietary flavored wines. Byrrh, a product from France, is a "secret formula" branded wine which is quite bitter and made from red wine. Dubonnet, both red and white, is another which is made under license in other countries as well. There are many others, both native and imported (e.g., mint flavored wine, coffee flavored wine, etc.), but most of them are not widely distributed in this country.

Owing to a reinterpretation of the laws on flavored wines, a new class of wines has appeared on the American market. The prototype of these "special natural wines" was given the proprietary brand name of Thunderbird and was first marketed in 1957. This and a number of similar products have recently accounted for about 20 percent of the total wine consumed in the United States. They are called "special" because each individual named brand has a specific formula of added flavors which is approved by and filed with the Internal Revenue Service (but not made public). They are "natural" in that the flavoring substances must all be isolated or prepared directly from natural sources and not chemically synthesized. Most of these wines were at first prepared from a neutral white port base wine, but a few are made from red dessert wines, and now many are being made with a table wine alcohol level. Some of the latter also contain a small amount of added carbon dioxide, as do some fruit wines. The extracts and essential oils for these wines are purchased from flavor supply houses, added to the base wine in the proportions called for by the formula, and finished for marketing as are other dessert and also sweet table wines.

FRUIT WINES

A special natural wine could be prepared from a neutral white grape wine base by adding flavor concentrated from raspberries, except for the legal restriction that fruit juices cannot be used to give wine from one fruit the flavor of another, without clear labeling at least. Ignoring a few other legal and labeling requirements, it would be possible to prepare a similar wine by adding neutral spirit to raspberry juice. Still a third wine-like beverage could be prepared by direct fermentation of raspberry juice. The first type could not be labeled raspberry wine; the second type could be so labeled, if the added alcohol was derived from raspberries. The wines labeled with raspberry or other specific fruit names are usually made by a modification of the third process.

The wines made from fruits and similar products other than the wine grape—cider (apples), perry (pears), blackberry wine, mead (honey), plum wine, and a host of others—are important home products and some are important commercially, especially in colder climates where wine grapes cannot be grown. North-central Europe and Scandinavia are noted producers and consumers of such wines and wine-like alcoholic fruit beverages. England and northern France also have important cider and perry production. Fruit wines and mead have a long history and are worthy of study in their own right, but their commercial production is relatively limited and their perishability such that most of them are not stored long or distributed widely. This group would include products of the home winemaker (rhubarb wine, dandelion wine, etc.) which involve steeping or fermenting the named material in "wine" resulting from sugar syrup, yeast, and yeast nutrients.

The wine grape is virtually the only fruit which commonly reaches a high enough sugar and the proper acid balance for a good-flavored and stable wine. Other fruits, including *Vitis labrusca* grapes and many fermentable substances such as honey, require adjustment of either sugar or acid or both to produce a satisfactory wine-like product. Most fresh fruits such as berries, cherries, Concord grapes, citrus fruit, and so on, are rather high in acidity; so if all the sugar is fermented, the dry wine is unpleasantly sour. The law permits, for such wines, the reduction of the concentration of acid by dilution with water and sugar to a minimum of 0.5 percent (calculated as malic acid for apples, tartaric acid for grapes, and citric acid for other fruits) if the volume added is not more than 35 percent of the total ameliorated volume of juice or wine. Wine from loganberries, currants, or gooseberries, owing to the very high natural acidity, may receive additions to 60 percent of the diluted total volume. If the fruit to be used is below 0.5 percent acid, citric or other approved food acid may be added to that level. Acid may also be added at the discretion of the winemaker, if the total added is not greater than 0.2 percent and if the juice or wine is not then diluted with water.

The sugar content of most of these fresh fruits is too low for stable wine, and is lowered still further if the acidity is ameliorated by addition of water. It is therefore permitted to add sugar (sucrose, glucose, invert syrups, simple syrup, etc.) under strict control. The rules are complex, but in general the juice before fermentation may not exceed 25° Brix. After fermentation and perhaps sweetening for sale, the alcohol should not exceed 14 percent (after final sweetening, etc., unless wine spirits from the same kind of fruit have been added) or the solids content of the wine exceed 21 percent by weight. The permitted practices with respect to wines from dried fruit (raisins, dates, etc.), honey, and other fruit products are similar to those just described for fruit wines, except that those with high sugar content may be adjusted with water to not less than 22° Brix before fermentation, in most cases.

These fruit-type wines are subject to the same considerations as are table wines. They are marketed as fresh fruity products with as much as possible of the characteristic flavor and color of the specific fruit. Furthermore, they not only lose their characteristic flavor with time, but also tend to develop harsh or bitter flavors as they age or oxidize. Thus dry wines from labrusca or other American grape species are more difficult to improve by aging than are those from vinifera.

The fermentation may take place in the presence of the whole macerated fruit mass; but if so, the pulp is pressed off and removed within two or three days. Since the presence of berry seeds and such parts in the later stages of fermentation may allow the extraction of bitter or haze-producing substances by the alcohol, such contact should be limited as much as possible. The release of the juice before fermentation by pressing, usually after heating for a short time to disrupt the cells, is often practiced. Addition of pectin-splitting enzymes to increase juice yield and to help clarify the juice is helpful, especially for high-pectin fruits such as plums. It is usually necessary to add an inoculum of wine yeasts, and—particularly with highly ameliorated (sugar and water added) fruit musts—yeast nutrients such as ammonium phosphate, and yeast extract are likely to be beneficial. Since the juices of most of these fruits are highly susceptible to oxidative browning reactions and other deterioration, moderately high levels of sulfur dioxide (100 to 200 parts per million) and minimal contact with air are employed.

Most of these wines are marketed with residual fermentable

sugar, and therefore require a final pasteurization or sterile filtration to maintain them biologically stable after bottling, unless they are fortified. The tannin level is ordinarily low in fruit wines, and they are not as stable to air or as easily fined or clarified as the wines from wine grapes. Bentonite fining is used. These wines are seldom aged; they are finished and marketed young, with essentially the same techniques and considerations as for any sweet white or rosé table wine, except that only *V. labrusca* wines in this group require stabilization with respect to potassium bitartrate, for fruits other than grapes rarely contain it.

Considerable amounts of apple wines have been used in recent years in this country—some flavored, of less than 11 percent alcohol, and with low carbonation.

Summary.—Byproducts of the winery such as tartrates, red pigment, seed tannin, or seed oil are usually of marginal profitability and recovered only in special situations or war emergencies. Accessory products such as concentrated grape juice are important both for sale to other food processors and for use within the winery, as a means of prolonging the fermentation season or making other products.

A major class of the specialty wines are the flavored wines, both vermouths and others with specially formulated natural-flavor mixtures. The formulas used for these wines can be generalized to some degree, but for specific products are seldom revealed. The taste of the blender and of the consumer can have free rein. Wines with both dessert-wine and table-wine alcohol levels are so produced.

Fruit wines and other nongrape wine products are often subject to special production problems, such as dilution to lower the acid concentration and addition of sugar and yeast foods to make proper fermentation possible. The products are at their best when they resemble an alcoholic fresh juice of the fruit concerned. Some flavored and lightly carbonated fruit wines are being produced. Such wines are currently quite popular as party beverages, especially among younger consumers in this country. They were not designed as an accompaniment for meals.

. . . offered a glass of Chambertin 1945 . . . I would consider I had acquitted myself very creditably, if I were able to say, "It is a Burgundy. I think it is a good one, but I think it is a little old." —ALEC WAUGH

Chapter 13

THE WINES OF FRANCE

France has been the most important wine country in the world, not because of the amount of its production (in recent years Italy has often produced more grapes and wine than France) but for the following reasons: French per capita consumption is higher than any other country; France produces more kinds of important wine types; and aesthetic production and appreciation of wine have been brought to a higher degree in France than in any other country. This may not continue to be true in the future, as wine appreciation and consumption increase in other countries.

Vines are grown in all except the northern departments of France. The most important wine districts (see Figure 27) are those of Alsace, Burgundy, the Rhone, Provence and the Midi, Bordeaux, the Loire, and Champagne. In discussing each of these and their wines, we shall emphasize the factors which influence the quality of the wine produced, the types of wine made, and the use of the wine.

Some French wines are "classified," and certain wine-producing regions are "delimited." In France the *appellations contrôllées* wines (often abbreviated A.C.) are the most respected. However, *vins delimités de qualité supérieure* (usually abbreviated V.D.Q.S.) are of distinctive character. Since this subject is important in most European wine-producing

200

countries and is a constant bone of contention between the European and some non-European countries, it deserves consideration.

Certain regions in Europe (e.g., Burgundy) have been famous for the quality of their wines for centuries—so famous that when new areas started to produce wines (e.g., California), they labeled their wines after the famous wine districts of Europe. The exclusive right to an appellation of origin based on geographical names has been officially claimed since the Madrid agreement of 1891. The Lisbon agreement of 1958 also reaffirmed this right, but some countries, including the United States, were not signatories to these agreements. Although the right has most often been expressed against for-

Fig. 27. The main wine and brandy districts of France.

eign countries in the twentieth century, it also is exercised against wines incorrectly labeled within a single country. The best example of this was in the Champagne region of France, where importation of white wines from the south of France so lowered the price of Champagne grapes as to threaten economic ruin. This led to the Champagne riots of 1910 and the promulgation of an early type of *appleLlations d'origine* for Champagne in 1911. Wines from the south of France could no longer be used to produce "Champagne" wine.

This, and all later such laws, assume that the climate, soil, variety (or varieties), and local methods of wine production result in a unique wine type which deserves to be protected by the government. Gradually most of the important wine-producing districts of France have been classified and de-limited, and the practice now extends to the Douro and other regions in Portugal, to the sherry district of Spain near Jerez de la Frontera (with perhaps less rigidity), to many regions in Germany, and, recently, to certain Italian districts. It is now being applied in all the countries of the European Economic Community as well as in South Africa and other countries. It also applies in part to geographical appellations in the United States.

In general, the laws first delimit the district, sometimes on the basis of soil types and geological formation, and sometimes on historical precedents. The variety or varieties which may be used are specified and often their maximum production is fixed, the theory being that when a grapevine of a certain variety is overcropped, it no longer has the typical flavor. Restrictions may also be placed on minimum percentage of alcohol, methods of wine production used, sensory quality, and so on.

It would be naive to believe that this had solved the problem of authenticity for all wines labeled Burgundy, port, and so forth. The extensive enforcement organizations which have had to be set up, and the plethora of lawsuits, would indicate that legislating vinous honesty is no easier than legislating any other kind of honesty.

Nevertheless, these laws constitute an answer to the non-

French "burgundy" producer as to how it should be done, theoretically at least, in France—and, of course, make a quasi-legal case that, since it is not so done elsewhere, the wines do not have the right to the appellation. Our own Federal Alcohol Administration Regulation No. 4 expressly prohibits American wines and brandies from using appellations such as Château d'Yquem, Saint-Julien, Saint-Estèphe, and Cognac. It permits generic use of foreign geographical names such as burgundy and rhine—unfortunately (or not, depending on one's point of view). The whole subject of *appellations d'origine* is certainly in a state of evolution. There is an obvious disadvantage from the prestige point of view for a California wine to be labeled "burgundy." If California producers developed unique local names, protected by proprietary or regional regulations, and eschewed all foreign appellations, perhaps the public might soon forget the foreign appellations. According to this theory, the label "California burgundy" simply advertises that the "real thing" is produced in France. There have been some efforts to use regional and coined names in California; but except for the increasing use of varietal appellations, most California table wines are still sold with generic names.

Californian (and Australian and other) producers do not believe that the problem is this simple, and have officially resisted any limitations on the right of non-European producers to use whatever foreign appellations they please. Even the limitations of Federal Alcohol Administration Regulation No. 4 were vigorously fought by the official representatives of the California wine industry when they were proposed nearly forty years ago.

In view of the intransigent positions of both protagonists, we will not go into the matter further here. However, it does weaken the position of all producers of *quality* wines to say that geographical appellations are without meaning.

ALSACE

From 1870 to 1918 Alsace was a part of Germany, and most of its wines were shipped from Alsace to eastern Germany to blend with German wines. They were sold as ordinary table wines without any indication of origin. Consequently there was very little demand for quality wines from Alsace, and only a small amount of the wine was bottled. When Alsace was returned to France after World War I, some decision had to be made in regard to the viticultural industry. Since 1870 the great Algerian wine industry had developed to supply blending wines for the low-alcohol wines of France. There was thus very little demand for cheap blending wine in France; in fact, France had a surplus of wine in the late 1920s. Consequently, with their higher cost of production, there was very little place for ordinary Alsatian wines in the French wine economy. The decision was made in 1920 that Alsace should produce better-quality wines, wines worthy of being bottled, which would command a sufficiently high price to adequately recompense the growers for planting better varieties. The district then had no regional designations that were important enough to use as the basis of labeling. Consequently, Alsace is the only district of France in which varietal labeling is widely practiced, since the variety of grape used constituted a method of distinguishing wines from each other.

Alsace is a cool viticultural area mainly in Region I. White varieties are used primarily; the most important traditional variety was Chasselas doré, but since 1920 it has gradually been supplanted by White Riesling, Sylvaner, Gewürztraminer, and small amounts of Chardonnay and other varieties. The wines are fermented in the normal manner for white table wines, but after the fermentation they may require a malolactic fermentation to reduce excessive total acidity. The best wines are probably those of Gewürztraminer, although a number of fine Rieslings are produced in the warmer years, and Sylvaner is the favorite of some growers and producers in the northern part of Alsace. The particular vintage is not as critical as in Germany, but the best wines are produced in the warmest years.

The wines of Alsace are thus pleasant to drink and have a fruity flavor with characteristic grapy varietal flavors. They are perhaps not as crisp and as distinctive as similar wines made in Germany, but they are very good drinking wines for all that and are, we think, particularly adapted to being served at luncheon.

Alsace is a good example of how a wine district can improve the quality of its wines and achieve consumer recognition. The wines of Alsace are now distributed throughout the world, and are a tribute to the attention which the French have been able to give to the creation and production of a quality wine in a relatively short time.

BURGUNDY

Although the Burgundy region proper is confined to the slopes of the Côte d'Or, it is customary to include Chablis and the districts to the south of the Côte d'Or in the "Burgundy" classification (see Figure 28). This is especially true as far as listings in wine lists are concerned.

Chablis is one of the smallest classified wine regions of France, and it may be a disappearing wine district. The reason is that vines are grown in a chalk soil in Chablis, and the culture of the vine at best is difficult. A series of poor years owing to frost and hail has made the growing of vines in this region more expensive. The primary variety grown is Chardonnay, and it ripens only moderately well in Chablis. Exceptions to this were in 1949 and 1959, when the vines of Chablis ripened their fruit so well that their wines resembled those of Burgundy more than the traditional Chablis.

Characteristically, the wines of Chablis are high in total acidity, with a fruity tart flavor. They are what the French call "fish wines" and are properly served with fish, for their high acidity helps to reduce the fishy odor. The best wines of Chablis are always labeled with the name of the vineyard following the word Chablis. However, such wines are expensive and are found less and less on the market. Wines labeled simply "Chablis" are of markedly lower quality.

The Côte d'Or is one of the most famous wine districts of the world, and its fame is an ancient one. Vines were certainly planted in this region during the Roman period, and many famous monasteries had vineyards here during the Middle

Ages. It is properly divided into three parts: the Côte de Dijon, the Côte de Nuits, and the Côte de Beaune; the Côte de Dijon is the smallest and least important of the three. The whole area extends about 30 miles from Dijon to just south of Beaune. The Côte d'Or is a gentle slope facing to the east, and the soil is generally calcareous. The climate is about equal to that of Region I, and consequently only early-ripening varieties can be grown here. The grapes ripen best on the well-drained warmer slopes facing east.

There is little reason to believe that the calcium content of the soil per se has anything directly to do with the quality of the wine. More likely the higher quality is related to the fact that calcareous soils are well drained, and the temperature of the soil (and of the microclimate directly above the soil) is higher in well-drained soils. Grapes grown in a similar soil on the lower slopes or in the valley do not ripen as well as those on the well-drained slopes above. Since this is a cool region, the extra ripening of the warmer soils is of particular importance so far as the composition of the musts and the quality of the wines are concerned.

The best red wines are all made from the variety Pinot noir or from selections (clones) thereof. On the lower slopes some Gamay is grown. There are many different clones of the Pinot noir variety in use, some of them differing appreciably in the amount of color in the skins. The wines of Burgundy thus vary considerably in color. They also vary in color because more attention is given to the extraction of color from the skins during alcoholic fermentation in some cellars. In several cellars the musts are warmed after crushing and before fermentation, and in others the cap is manipulated so that more color is extracted from the skins. The use of sugar, which is legal, also influences the amount of color and flavor extraction. There is considerable variation from producer to producer in these processing variables.

The sole variety planted for the best white wines is Chardonnay, but on the lower slopes there are some vineyards with plantings of the variety Aligoté. Aligoté makes a pleasant wine, but the climate of Burgundy is often too cool for it and it rare-

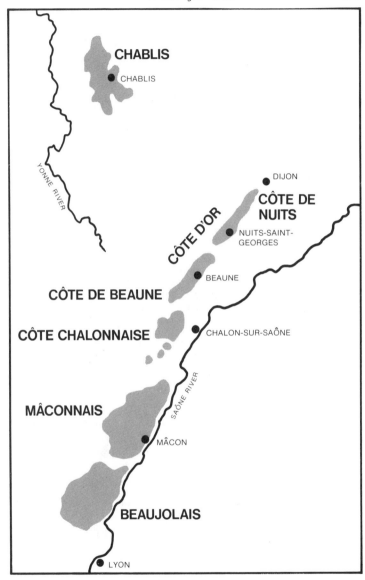

FIG. 28. The Burgundian Côte d'Or and related districts in France.

ly ripens sufficiently to show its best quality. Because of the cool climate it is often necessary to add sugar to the musts of Aligoté, to those of Chardonnay occasionally, and to those of Pinot noir about two or three years in five. Some producers, unfortunately, add sugar almost every year.

After pressing of the whites, the fermentation is carried out in relatively small cooperage of 50 to 1,000 gallons. The reds are fermented in 500- to 2,000-gallon open vats. Following pressing, the final fermentation and aging take place in relatively small cooperage: 50- to 500-gallon oak containers.

The nomenclature of Burgundy wines can be rather complicated. The best wines come from small vineyards and are usually given the name of the vineyard. Thus we have Clos de Vougeot, in the Côte de Nuits, and in the Côte de Beaune, Pommard. However, many of the vineyards have been subdivided. The famous vineyard Romanée has been subdivided into La Romanée, Romanée-Conti, and Romanée-SaintVivant. The same is true of Pommard, which has the vineyards Les Épenots, Les Rugiens, and others.

Sometimes a village appropriates the name of its most famous vineyard, and the wines of the village are sold with this hyphenated name: for example, from the towns of Chassagne and Vosne we have Chassagne-Montrachet and Vosne-Romanée. In the case of Montrachet, which lies between two villages, both have attached the vineyard name: Chassagne-Montrachet and Puligny-Montrachet. Some wines are sold just as Bourgogne, without village or vineyard appellation. These are certainly of lesser quality and are sold at a lower price. Occasionally one finds Burgundy labeled Hospices de Beaune, with a donor's name. The Hospices, a charity hospital in Beaune which owns a number of fine vineyards, makes these wines and usually bottles them with the name of the person who gave the vineyard to the Hospices. Many of these Hospices vineyards are in the Côte de Beaune.

Most experts consider the red wines of the Côte de Nuits to be the best wines of Burgundy. The great white wines generally come from the southern part of the Côte de Beaune — Meursault and Montrachet.

The red wines contain considerable alcohol, frequently as much as 13 percent or more. They are soft in texture, not high in acid or in tannin, and they have a most intriguing ripe-grape odor from the Pinot noir grapes. The reds may be sugared too much (to raise their alcohol content and to increase color extraction). Such wines are alcoholic without the ripe-grape flavor of Pinot noir. In some instances the musts have been heated too much, to facilitate color extraction, and the wines have acquired a special odor (undesirable, but not always so recognized in the trade). Occasionally the wines have undergone too prolonged a malo-lactic fermentation; so we find bottles on the market which are gassy. Formerly some old Burgundies developed a bitter taste with aging, but in recent years this seems to be rare, possibly owing to the discreet use of sulfur dioxide. Good recent vintage years have been 1959, 1961, 1962, 1964, 1967, 1969 to 1971, and 1974.

The whites likewise are high in alcohol. Many of the 1959s had about 14 percent, and some did not ferment completely dry. In any year they are very rich wines with the characteristic ripe, almost apple- or fig-like odor of Chardonnay grapes. This is particularly noticeable in the warmer years.

The red Burgundies may age for five to ten or more years. In recent years the white Burgundies have shown a tendency to go "off" in three to five years. This is usually evidenced by darkening of the color and the development of a distinct oxidized odor. Whether this is a permanent development involving changes in winery practice or only reflects the climatic conditions of the last few years we do not yet know. Some white Burgundies have begun to appear on the market with noticeable sulfur dioxide.

South of the Côte d'Or there are a few Pinot noir vineyards producing good wines under Region II climatic conditions. The slopes are not as definite to the east, and the soil is not as highly calcareous as in the Côte d'Or. For this reason the grapes do not ripen quite as well and the wines do not have as distinctive a quality. A little farther south, in Beaujolais (Figure 29), the main red variety is Gamay, not Pinot noir. Here it makes an early-maturing, very fruity red wine which is one of

FIG. 29. Partial crushing of the grapes in a Beaujolais vineyard—
a scene less common now than formerly. (Source: Institut
National des Appellations d'Origine des Vins et Eaux-
de-Víe, Paris.)

the most popular early-maturing wines of France. Carbonic
maceration, suffocation of the picked grapes in a closed
container prior to pressing and yeast fermentation, lends a
characteristic flavor to some Beaujolais Nouveau wines. Some
Chardonnay has been planted at Pouilly-Fuissé. A Pouilly-
Fuissé used to be a very good bargain indeed, because it did
not have the snob appeal and exaggerated price of the high-
quality white Burgundies of Montrachet or Meursault. Alas,
this cannot be said to be true today. Moreover, it must be admitted that it does not have the vinosity or overall quality of
a fine Meursault, much less a Montrachet.

THE RHONE

A number of important red and pink wines are produced in the viticultural districts south of Lyon. The climate becomes progressively warmer toward the south of the Rhone Valley. Conditions in the northern vineyards are as cold as in Region II, but many of the southern vineyards are in Region III and in certain years as warm as in Region IV. Starting from the north, the first district with an *appellation contrôlée* is the Côte Rôtie. The vineyards of the Côte Rôtie are planted to Viognier (a white variety) and Petite Sirah (a red). These are blended in the vineyard as well as during fermentation. The wines can be high in color and rather tannic, and age slowly in the cask for three or four years and in the bottle for several years. Formerly, wines fifteen or twenty years old from the Côte Rôtie might just be coming to their peak maturity; this is seldom true today. The wines may throw considerable sediment during aging in the bottle, but it is not difficult to decant the wine off from the sediment prior to serving.

The Hermitage district farther south is likewise a red-wine district, although a small amount of white wine is produced. The variety used for the red, Petite Sirah, produces a wine of fine color and marked tannin. Old red wines twenty and thirty years of age from this district have been tasted at their peak quality. The tannin obviously acts as an antioxidant during the aging of these wines and helps to maintain them free of excessive oxidation for long periods of time. However, the aging potential of recent vintages seems to be much less. Usually the wines are decanted and rebottled before shipment if they have thrown much sediment; occasionally it is necessary to decant them before serving. The whites are from the grape varieties Marsanne and La Roussette, a variety of Marsanne which is replacing the old variety Roussane.

The region near Avignon called Châteauneuf-du-Pape has an ancient viticultural reputation, but the district fell into bad planting practices after the invasion of phylloxera. By 1911 it was no longer considered one of the better wines of France.

Thanks to the efforts of the growers, the varietal planting has been greatly improved and the wines of Châteauneuf-du-Pape have again achieved a sound reputation for quality. Among the important varieties are Grenache, Mourvedre, and Cinsaut, although several other varieties are permitted by the regulations of *appellations d'origine*. Other varieties include Clairette blanche, Terret noir, Picpoule, and Carignane. The apparent reason for continuing the mixed planting is that Grenache does not have a high color, and to produce a good red wine some better-colored varieties are necessary. Although the wines of Châteauneuf-du-Pape are not high in color or in tannin, they do age well, although perhaps not quite so long as the wines of the Côte Rôtie and Hermitage districts. A little white Châteauneuf-du-Pape is also produced. The wines of this region have considerable robustness and alcoholicity, and can be very good when they are about ten years of age. Recently some have appeared on the market with too little barrel- or bottle-aging. Good wines were produced along the Rhone in 1961, 1962, 1964, 1966, 1967, and 1969 to 1973.

Across the Rhone River from Châteauneuf-du-Pape, near the town of Tavel, Grenache is grown by itself and is used to produce a pink wine. It is well known in France and occasionally exported to the United States. Unfortunately, some Tavels are rather highly sulfured to reach the American market in good condition, and they have a tendency to oxidation and development of a slight bitter aftertaste. They are better drunk in France than in this country, and even there tend to be a little alcoholic for a rosé and of orange-brown rather than pink color.

PROVENCE AND THE MIDI

In spite of the contrary opinion of local enthusiasts, the wines of Provence barely rate mention as quality wines. The varieties are undistinguished, the climate hot, and the rosé wines (the chief product exported) only passable. There are exceptions to most rules, and a few better wines can be found, but the scarcity of wines entitled to an *appellation contrôlée* indicates the moderate opinion of French enologists regarding the quality of the wines produced in Provence.

Quantitatively, the Midi is by far the most important grape-growing district of France and probably the most intensely cultivated large grape-producing area of the world, with the possible exception of Fresno County in California. Over one-third of the wine produced in France comes from the four Midi departments of Aude, Hérault, Gard, and Pyrénées-Orientales. From Marseilles west to the Spanish border, one sees vast vineyards of Aramon, Carignane, Alicante Bouschet, and other heavy-producing varieties. It is a district of over-cropped grapes and high yields—8, 10, and 12 tons to the acre—of low alcohol content (7, 8, and 9 percent are common), and generally undistinguished wines. Only a few of the vineyards in the whole of the south of France are allowed a geographical *appellation contrôlée*. Among these are the muscatel from Frontignan and the various red sweet wines from the Pyrénées-Orientales department, especially Banyuls from the region near the Spanish border. Minervois and Corbières are examples of wines entitled to the lesser *vins delimités de qualité supérieure* appellation, and in the Aude and Pyrénées-Orientales departments a fair amount of such are produced. But these are only a drop in the bucket to the ocean of ordinary red, pink, and white wines produced in the departments of Hérault and Gard.

The economic importance of Algeria to France was that the high-alcohol wines of Algeria were imported specifically to blend with the low-alcohol wines of the Midi in order to produce the 9, 10, and 11 percent alcohol wines which the French worker drinks every day with his lunch and dinner. Recently there have been efforts to improve the quality of wines of local sections of the Midi, but few of these have yet appeared on the American market. Because of the moderating influence of the Mediterranean, it is a region of warm climates. The exposure is to the south, so the vineyards on the upper slopes often develop a higher percentage of sugar, and the warm conditions reduce the acidity.

BORDEAUX

When Eleanor of Aquitaine married the Duke of Normandy and Count of Anjou (later Henry II of England) in 1152, she brought with her as her dowry all the southwestern third of France. For 300 years the British crown ruled Bordeaux and left many imprints on the region. A large and important wine trade developed between Bordeaux and the British Isles. The British taste for clarets has thus dominated the Bordeaux wine picture for many centuries. The English law of inheritance by the eldest son has been applied in Bordeaux, and many of the large vineyards have been maintained more or less intact. It is not a small region viticulturally, with over 250,000 acres of grapes and a production which varies from about 50 million to 130 million gallons per year.

Locations of the important districts are indicated in Figure 30: Médoc, Graves, Sauternes, Saint-Émilion, and Pomerol are the most important for quality. These are all entitled to an *appellation contrôlée,* and the names of the districts are found on the labels on the French as well as the American market.

The Médoc is the most important red wine-producing district of the Bordeaux region, and one of the most important in the world. It has rolling hills, and the exposure and soil conditions are not critical, although there are local prejudices in favor of some vineyard areas and against others. The unique feature of the Bordeaux region is the relatively large size of the vineyards—many of 15 to 50 acres and some of 100 and even 200 acres. Whether large or small, the vineyards are commonly called "châteaux."

The Médoc is divided into a number of communes—Saint-Julien, Saint-Estèphe, Pauillac, Margaux, etc.—and wines produced within these communes are also entitled to an *appellation contrôlée.* Many wines are bottled under the label of the commune. Saint-Julien was so well known in California before Prohibition that some California producers actually called their wine St. Julien because of a fancied resemblance to wine of the Bordeaux district.

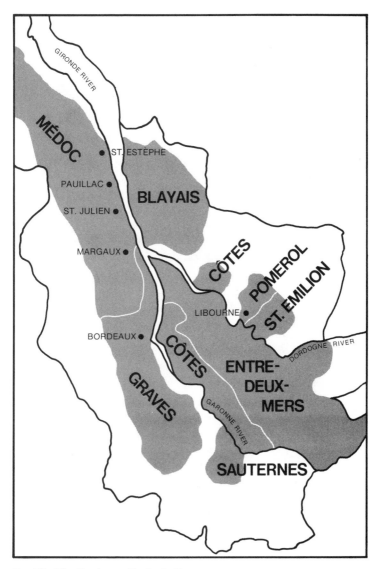

FIG. 30. The Bordeaux district in France.

Within the communes there are many individual vineyards; in Bordeaux the *appellation contrôlée* applies to the commune, *not* to the vineyard, name. In 1855 the wines of the Médoc were classified officially, and this classification is still often quoted. It divided the best vineyards into five categories: first, second, third, fourth, and fifth growths, or *crus.* The classification obviously was related to the prices paid on the Bordeaux market for the wines prior to 1855.

Since that time some of the châteaux have increased their plantings and changed their boundaries, phylloxera has caused many changes in the percentages of varieties used *(encépagement),* the owners have changed (several times in some cases), winemaking procedures have been greatly modified (especially in some châteaux), and the skill of the winemakers of the châteaux has certainly varied. Wines of certain châteaux which may have achieved a relatively high price in 1855 sell today at a lesser relative price, and thus are not really entitled to a rank above wines of other châteaux of the district. The wine merchants in Bordeaux would probably like to change the classification, but châteaux which now have a high classification are not willing to see any change made. Certainly the classification of 1855 is only a very rough guide to the quality of the wines of Bordeaux, and the wine merchants' current prices more clearly reflect the quality of the wines than the classification of 1855. Nevertheless, the first five big growths of that classification, Château Latour (largely English-owned), Château Margaux (to be distinguished from the wines from the commune of Margaux), Château Lafite-Rothschild, Château Mouton-Rothschild (only recently officially promoted), and Château Haut-Brion still produce some of the best wines. Strictly speaking, the latter château is in the Graves district, but was classified with the Médocs because of its high quality. It is now American-owned.

Formerly, the major châteaux bottled their wine at the château only in the best years. Recently the demand for these wines has been so great that they are bottled at many of the châteaux in poor as well as in good years. The cult of château-bottling may have been desirable when the quality of the wines differed so much from each other and from year to year. Even then, a certain amount of sound château wine was exported for bottling abroad. Finally, a few châteaux do not bottle at the château and are thus not entitled to the magical *mis en bouteilles au château* or *mise du château*. What "label drinkers" forget is that it is the quality of the wine that counts: as long as the Bordeaux châteaux insist on bottling their wine at the château in good and poor years, the practice is meaningless. We recommend buying Bordeaux wines on the basis of their quality, not on the basis of the 1855 classification.

Graves is best known for its white wine, but actually more red than white is produced in this region. The reds are usually sold as Graves, or sometimes with the château name. The district-named wines are not of exceptional quality, but some château wines are certainly as good a buy as the wines of the Médoc. The white wines of the Graves are widely distributed simply as Graves, although many château-bottled white wines are sold. The whites are produced from Sémillon and Sauvignon blanc, in the ratio of about one to two. These are dry to slightly sweet white wines which tend to be rather high in sulfur dioxide. Formerly one could find better bargains in white wines from elsewhere in France than from Graves. The enological practices of Graves will probably continue to improve, to reduce the sulfur dioxide and to improve clarity.

Sauternes is the most famous sweet white table wine of France. It is probably best exemplified by the wine of its premier vineyard, Château d'Yquem. However, in recent years it has sold at such a high price that wines of other vineyards represented a better bargain. In Sauternes the same varieties as in Graves are planted, Sémillon and Sauvignon blanc, but the ratio here is about two to one in favor of Sémillon, because it is somewhat more subject to a fungus, *Botrytis cinerea,* which is necessary for the production of the sweet wines (see Chapter 4).

The effect of *Botrytis* is to loosen the skin and hasten moisture loss from the berry; this results in a decrease in the volume of the berry, and hence in an increase in the concentration of the sugar. The shriveled berries also have a high concentration of odor and tannin because of the larger surface-to-volume relationship of the shriveled berry. A special flavor also results from the *Botrytis*. From these musts, wines of 12 to 14 percent alcohol and from 5 to 15 percent sugar are produced. The production of Sauternes is a climatological phenomenon, because the growth of *Botrytis* depends upon having a high humidity for short periods of time, to secure infection; these periods of high humidity must be followed by dry periods, so that moisture loss will be encouraged and the berries can shrivel. Similar conditions exist in many years in vineyards on the Loire and in Germany.

Saint-Émilion is a wine district which has only recently been classified. Its wines have markedly improved their quality in the twentieth century. The two best vineyards, Château Cheval Blanc and Château Ausone, are now as well known and as expensive as any of the premier châteaux of the Médoc. The same varieties are planted here as in the Médoc, namely, Cabernet Sauvignon, Cabernet franc, Malbec, and Merlot. But these varieties are of the Cabernet family and have somewhat similar varietal aromas. The Cabernet franc, planted more here than in the Médoc, tends to make the wines a little softer, but the difference in tannin content is not great. The wines of Saint-Émilion are a little softer in flavor than those of the Médoc since the grapes are more protected from the cool Atlantic breezes which reach the Médoc. But it is not correct, as is frequently claimed, that the wines of Saint-Émilion resemble those of Burgundy. If they resemble any other French red wines, it is the wines of the Médoc or the other red wines of Bordeaux!

Next door to Saint-Émilion is Pomerol, a region whose production of quality wines also seems to be on the increase. The wines resemble those of Saint-Émilion, but because they are less well-known they are sometimes better buys than those of Saint-Émilion. Château Petrus, however, is by no means inexpensive. Merlot is extensively planted.

Large amounts of ordinary red and white wine wine are produced throughout the Bordeaux district. If sold inexpensively

—say at about two dollars per bottle—they may be worth investigating. Good quality red wines were produced in 1961, 1962, 1964 (care is needed in selecting), 1966, 1967, 1970, 1971, and 1975. Good white wines were produced in Bordeaux in the same years except for 1964 and 1966.

THE LOIRE

All along this river there are many vineyards, some of considerable extent and vinous importance. To the east near Sancerre and Pouilly-sur-Loire, vineyards are planted to Sauvignon, which may be the same as Savignin blanc of the Jura, but is the same as or very similar to the Sauvignon blanc of Graves and Sauternes. These are white wines of moderate quality and are usually dry. When they are not too highly sulfited and in years when their alcohol content gets as high as 11 or 12 percent they can be nice wines. But by no stretch of the imagination can they be considered great wines.

A little farther west are the vineyards near Vouvray, which are the best-known vineyards of the Loire. They were planted to Chenin blanc, which here is often called Pineau blanc de la Loire.* The wines of Vouvray can be either dry or sweet; some are slightly but naturally sparkling, called *pétillant;* others are made sparkling by fermentation in the bottle (and are sold as Vouvray *mousseux).* The *pétillant* wines are said not to travel well, for they lose this gassiness when they are shipped through warm regions or held under warm conditions. It is thus probably true that the best wines of Vouvray are to be drunk in Vouvray. In the very best years, when it is humid and then dry and warm, a considerable amount of *Botrytis* will cause the berries to reach high sugar, and naturally sweet Vouvrays are produced. Some of these age very well and reach qualities which approach those of Sauternes—but alas, there are few such wines produced.

---

*This is the origin of the mistaken idea in California of labeling the Chenin blanc as White Pinot, and the justification for the recent use in California of Pineau de la Loire instead of the preferred Chenin blanc.

Still farther west are the Anjou vineyards around Saumur and Angers. Here again the Chenin blanc is the predominant variety and the wines are generally dry and white, but occasionally one finds a sweet white wine in the best years.

A little to the south are the Touraine wines of Chinon and Bourgueil, where some rather light red wines are produced from Cabernet Sauvignon or Cabernet franc. They are seldom as good as even the wines of the lesser districts of Bordeaux.

Finally, at the very end of the Loire near Nantes, are the wines produced from the variety Melon and known as Muscadet. They have no connection, however, with muscat wines, as they are dry and white and have a very pleasant non-muscat character. They are high enough in acidity to go well with fish, and have recently increased considerably in both popularity and price.

CHAMPAGNE

The Champagne district south of Reims is the coldest area where grapes are grown in France. It is also one of the most famous single wine regions in the world. The wines originally produced in this district were dry white and red wines of no particular merit. However, about 150 years ago the commercialization of the wines of the district began, and the present type of sparkling wine gradually developed in the nineteenth century.

The industry was an extremely hazardous one in the early years until methods of determining sugar were developed, and it was not until the latter part of the nineteenth century that the industry entered into its prosperous period. Before this, many of the wines had been bottled with too much sugar, and the bottles broke during fermentation in the bottle. However, the development of accurate methods of determining the sugar content made it possible to add the exact amount of sugar, and breakage was reduced to only 1 to 3 percent. At present, breakage is due more to defects in bottles than to excessive pressure.

At present about two-thirds of the vineyards are planted to Pinot noir (red) and one-third to Chardonnay (white). The district is strictly delimited; in fact, it is the prototype of the classification of districts under *appellation d'origine*. This delimitation took place following the Champagne riots of 1910, when growers rebelled against the importation of white wines from the south of France for the production of wines to be sold as Champagne.

Because it is necessary to produce a white wine from red grapes, the grapes must be completely free of damaged or moldy fruit, for in such fruit the pigments from the skin will get into the juice and it will not be possible to produce a white wine. The red grapes must thus be hand sorted to remove the undesirable berries. Also, it is not possible to crush the fruit in the usual type of crusher, since excessive contact of the crushed fruit with the juice will lead to an increase in the color of the juice. Therefore, the red grapes are pressed in large flat presses directly without crushing. The Pinot noir variety is used only because it ripens a little before the Chardonnay and thus gives the wine a little more alcohol than if it were made completely from white grapes. This balancing of wines of the white and the red grapes is one of the secrets in preparation of Champagne. Nowadays the primary fermentation is carried on in large temperature-controlled containers and the wines are clarified by fining and filtration so that they are ready for the secondary fermentation by the spring of the year following the vintage.

The Champagne companies produce two basic types of wine. The so-called vintage Champagne must be at least 80 percent from the wines of the given year. The blending involves more or less wine from white grapes and the blending of wines from vineyards in different parts of the Champagne district. Each company has its own blending formulas for assembling the *cuvée* of a vintage Champagne. It should be emphasized that a vintage wine is not made every year but only in the years when at least 80 percent of wine of superior quality can be assembled from that particular year. The other 20 percent is wine blended in from other years to increase the alcohol or adjust the acidity, or for balancing the flavor.

The second main type of Champagne produced today is the

nonvintage type, a blend of wines of both white and red grapes from various parts of the Champagne district and from different years. Here the wines are not, of course, of as high a quality as the vintage Champagnes, but they are assembled with great care so that the nonvintage Champagne of a given company will have a characteristic and uniform flavor from one year to the next. Recently a certain amount of *blanc de blancs* wine exclusively from Chardonnay has been produced —usually at high prices.

Whichever type of wine is being produced, the appropriate amounts of sugar and multiplying yeast are added, and the wines are then bottled and properly corked. The secret of making high-quality Champagne is that the wine should remain in the bottle in contact with the yeast for at least one year. The development of the so-called "Champagne nose" depends on the autolysis of the yeast cells and the development of new types of odorous materials from the products of autolysis. It is believed that the amino acids account in part for the development of these new nuances of odor. The wines are then placed on racks to bring the sediment down onto the cork and are later disgorged, and the appropriate amount of *dosage* is made in order to produce the various types of Champagne: *brut, sec, demi-sec, doux.* The *dosage* is prepared from a sweetened wine and often some Cognac (see Chapter 9).

Champagne, then, is a blended wine produced by careful secondary fermentation in the bottle and finally given its proper sweetness level by the addition of the appropriate amount of *dosage.*

The appeal of Champagne is partly psychological—Champagnes are almost synonymous with the *nouveaux riches,* with high society, and perhaps with engagements, weddings, christenings, and anniversary celebrations. However, the appeal of Champagne is not merely psychological, but involves the special character of the Champagne nose referred to above. It is not difficult to detect the difference between a Champagne wine and sparkling wines produced from other districts where the varieties of grapes, the climate, and the processes used are different.

Summary.—The reputation for the high quality of some French wines is certainly justified. The important factors contributing to quality include variety of grape, exposure of vineyards, soil temperature, specific winemaking procedures, and proper aging of the wines. The maintenance of this reputation for quality depends on the honesty and idealism of individual producers and on the strict French laws which authenticate labels, delimit the grape-growing regions, control the varieties which may be planted (and their maximum production), determine the minimum percentage of alcohol, and to a certain extent standardize wine production and quality.

Among the external forces which have greatly influenced the French wine industry is the export market, particularly of Great Britain, Belgium, Switzerland, and increasingly for the last 40 years, the United States. The standards of the English market have been particularly influential in the Bordeaux wine industry. Unfortunately, the recent increase in demand has forced prices upward, a trend which moderated from 1974 for a number of reasons.

But the greatest factor influencing the quality of French wines has probably been the French people, who consume over thirty gallons per capita and whose pride in the quality of French wines helps immeasurably in maintaining high quality. Many poor wines are, of course, produced in France, and some are even exported. But France also produces some of the finest —wines whose fame have made them the prototype for similar wines produced in other countries.

Wine, true begetter of all arts that be;
Wine, privilege of the completely free;
Wine, the foundation; wine, the sagely strong;
Wine, bright avenger of sly-dealing wrong.
—HILAIRE BELLOC

Chapter 14

THE WINES OF NORTHERN AND EASTERN EUROPE

Most of the wines of Germany, Switzerland, Czechoslovakia, Austria, and Hungary are white wines, and they bear a family resemblance to each other because of the cool climate under which they are produced and, to a lesser extent, the varieties used. Other countries included in this chapter are Rumania, Bulgaria and the Soviet Union.

GERMANY

Germany is not a large grape-growing or wine-producing country, but it is important because of the high quality of some of its wines. A large percentage of the wines of Germany are prepared for bottling, a much larger percentage than in Italy or France. This is all the more remarkable when we consider that in nearly every year most of the musts of Germany need to be sugared so that the wines will contain an adequate amount of alcohol. The alcohol content of German wines tends to be low—usually only 9 to 11 percent—even with sugaring. Because of the cool climate, the natural acidity is usually excessive, and some form of acid reduction is almost invariably practiced to reduce the excessive tartness.

224

The most important wine districts of Germany are along the Rhine River (Figure 31). In the south, opposite Alsace, are the vineyards and wines of Baden. In spite of local enthusiasm they are not often of memorable quality, with occasional notable exceptions. Much Chasselas doré is still planted here,

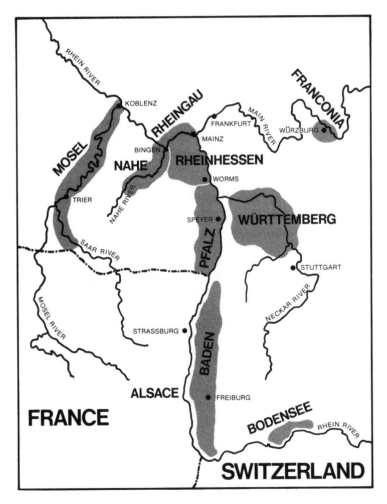

FIG. 31. Main wine districts of Germany.

which limits the quality obtainable. Very modern technology, however, is used to good effect.

Slightly to the north, in the Pfalz (Palatinate), many good wines and occasionally great wines are produced. In this district Sylvaner predominates, but White Riesling is also planted. Most of the vineyards face to the east.

Farther north, still on the Rhine, is the Rheinhessen, a district of many common wines, but occasionally a better quality of white wine is produced. Again Sylvaner is the predominant variety, but White Riesling is also planted, and from it in the best years and locations the better wines are produced. Grapes are grown in Würtemberg, across the river from Pfalz and Rheinhessen, but the wines are of moderate quality, with some few exceptions. At the northwestern corner of the Rheinhessen is the small Nahe River wine district; some of its wines from favorable exposures are excellent.

The most famous and according to many experts the finest wine district of Germany, the Rheingau, extends from Wiesbaden directly west to Rudesheim. Here the vineyards are growing on the north bank of the river, facing south, where the exposure to the sun is most favorable. In contrast to the districts noted above, here White Riesling is the predominant variety. The wines of the Rheingau are by far the biggest and most flavorful wines of Germany. These are among the finest wines of Germany, particularly in certain years.

From Wiesbaden the River Main leads south and east, and near Würzburg is the important district of Franconia, where some very good wines are produced. Here the Sylvaner predominates, but the soil and climatic conditions are somewhat different and the wines have a different flavor and a lower acidity than those of the other German districts. These wines are bottled in stubby bottles called *Boxbeutel* (or *Bocksbeutel*) rather than in the tall and graceful brown and green bottles which predominate on the Rhine and the Moselle, respectively.

The last important wine district in Germany is along the Moselle River, and its tributaries the Ruwer and the Saar. Vines are grown where they will get the best drainage, hence warmer soils, and the best exposure to the sun (Figures 32 and 33). The White Riesling is the predominant variety, and in the opinion of many connoisseurs the wines of the Moselle are equal to, and sometimes better than, those of the Rheingau. In general, the wines of the Moselle are a little more tart and perhaps have a more flowery aroma than those of the other German districts.

The present nomenclature of German wines is governed by the new wine regulations which apply to all wines sold since 1971. These provide for a new three-level quality system: *Deutscher Tafelwein, Deutscher Qualitätswein,* and *Deutscher Qualitätswein mit Prädikat.* These mean, roughly, that any wine sold as *Deutscher Tafelwein* is table wine, and is usually made from sugared musts in good years and always in bad years. If sugar is added, the volume increase in the wine from the must cannot be *more* than 15 percent. Regional and village names may be used, e.g., *Rhein, Mosel, Meckar, Main* and *Oberrhein.* for the regions. One should not expect much from a wine labeled *Deutscher Tafelwein.* German wines so labeled, whether in the German or American market, should be *very* reasonably priced as befitting their very modest quality (poor years, regions, or varieties). It is significant that no official tasting number is required on *Tafelwein.*

The appellation *Qualitätswein* fixes a minimum alcohol of 8.5 percent. It may be labeled after a region (e.g., Rheingau and ten others) or by subregion (there are 32), or as a newly instituted collective vineyard (about 300 *Grosslages*), or by the village *and* vineyard) (about 3000 named vineyards). If the vineyard is given on the label, only 75 percent need come from the specific vineyard named. There are restrictions on the varieties approved for various regions, and the amount of sugar that may be added is conditioned on the ripeness of the grapes. If more than a certain amount of sugar is required to bring the must to a sugar level to produce 8.5 percent alcohol, the right to the appellation *Qualitätswein* may be lost. (There is a zone A with a minimum Brix of 14° and a zone B with a minimum Brix of 15.4°.) If sugar is added, the volume

Fig. 32. Terraced vineyards on the Moselle. (Source: Presse- und
Informationsamt der Bundesregierung, Bonn.)

of *Qualitätswein* may not be increased more than 10 percent
(in contrast to 15 percent allowed for *Tafelwein*). The final
alcohol content for *Qualitätswein* cannot be more than 11.5
(zone A) or 12 (zone B) percent. The only district labels that

FIG. 33. Hoeing and spraying in a terraced vineyard on the Moselle. (Source: Presse- und Informationsamt der Bundesregierung, Bonn.)

are approved are Ahr, Hessische Bergstrasse, Mittelrhein, Mosel-Saar-Ruwer, Nahe, Rheingau, Rheinhessen, Rheinpfalz (Platinate), Franken (Franconia), Württemberg, and Baden.

However, the use of village plus vineyard appellations is approved for *Qualitätswein,* providing at least 75 percent of the wine comes from the vineyard named. Additionally, only 75 percent need be from the year given on the label.

Any wine entitled to a *Qualitätswein* appellation must be tested by an official committee of the government. The tasting number P.R. (for *Prüfungsnummer)* appears on the label.

The best German wines under the new regulations will appear with the appellation *Qualitätswein mit Prädikat,* which can be translated as "quality wine with special attributes." The district appellations are the same as those indicated for *Qualitätswein.* The must sugar has to be capable of producing at least 10 percent alcohol; sugar may not be added prior to the fermentation. The richness of the must and wine sugar is indicated by various designations. In increasing order these are: *Kabinet* (also Cabinet), minimum natural alcohol 7 percent; *Spätlese* (late-harvested grapes), more maturity; *Auslese* (selected harvested fruit), more mature clusters selected— usually *botrytis* (here called *Edelfäule*) will be present; *Beerenauslese* (wines made of selected fruit more or less dried by *botrytis;* colloquially called BA; and *Trockenbeerenauslese* (only dried, botrytised berries are used; called TBA).

Naturally as the sugar and harvesting requirements get higher, the price gets higher. *Trockenbeerenauslese* and *Beerenauslese* wines are produced only in the most favorable years. They represent a sacrifice of quantity to quality and hence are expensive (often $20 to $50 or more per bottle).

German wines labeled *Qualitätswein mit Prädikat* also have to pass a sensory examination, and the tasting control number will appear on the label. Each of the five subclasses *(Kabinet* through *Trockenbeerenauslese)* indicated above theoretically has individual quality standards.

The new features of the current regulations are that *Tafelwein* may not have vineyard names. For vineyards to be named on the label, the minimum vineyard size will be 12.5 acres (about 10,000 vineyard names will disappear as this regulation is applied). Special new names will be created to handle the larger vineyard combinations. This feature of the new regulations (that names of many small vineyards will no longer be used) will cause regret among connoisseurs of German wines. From the point of view of the German wine trade, though, this will simplify commercial transactions. The actual names to be approved for vineyard appellations are still under litigation, especially in the Mosel and Rhine areas where many vineyard areas have historical antecedents.

Both the producer and the bottler should be listed on the labels of the upper two categories. If the producer is also the bottler, the label may carry the estate bottling appellations *Erzeugerabfullung* or *aus eigenem Lesegut.* Old names such as *feine* or *feinste, Natur, Rein, Natureein,* etc., which supposedly indicated quality, may no longer be used.

Eiswein (wine produced from late-picked, frozen grapes) may still be used. We do not find this type of wine to be of such exceptional quality as the price would indicate. Liebfraumilch and Moselblümchen are commercial appellations which may still be used, but whether they represent *Tafelwein* or *Qualitätswein* is not clear.

An especially disturbing feature of the new regulations is that they provide for the addition of grape juice to the *wines.* Whether this will be used to give low-quality wines a sugar content similar to that of wines made of botrytised grapes is not yet clear. The commercial demand for German wines with residual sugar (to cover their natural high acidity?) is an ostensible reason for this new provision. The tendency engendered by the *Kabinet* to *Trockenbeerenauslese* system for increasing wine sweetness to be equated with increasing quality in German wines is to some degree unfortunate.

German technology has made it possible to put these wines through filters that remove most microorganisms, so they need not be too high in sulfur dioxide. However, some German wines are still high in sulfur dioxide, and this reduces their quality. Owing to the high standards of enological technology, the wines are often clarified and bottled within six months of the vintage. Except for the richest or sweeter types, they are best within five years of the vintage.

A few red wines are produced in Germany, chiefly from Pinot noir grapes, but their quality is only moderate. A good deal of sparkling wine, called *Sekt,* is produced, both by the tank and bottle process. It is well made and reasonable in price, but seldom notable in quality. The best dry German wines for everyday drinking are those made from unsugared musts and made and bottled by the producer of the wine, with the name of the village and the vineyard. Shippers' wines are commonly sold with regional or proprietary labels. They are often inexpensive and are usually of ordinary quality; they should, therefore, be modestly priced. Germany again illustrates the importance of variety, soil temperature, and exposure. It also indicates how modern technology can be applied to an old industry without reduction in quality, in fact with a general enhancement of quality. The best bargains in German wines are usually not the shippers' wines but those of individual growers, particularly those made without sugaring. Often the lesser-known wines of the Nahe or Pfalz districts are of comparable quality and more reasonably priced than the better-known Moselles and Rheingaus.

SWITZERLAND

It is surprising that wines are made at all in Switzerland, for the climate is unfavorable for grapes. Most of the vineyards are planted around lakes where the drainage, favorable exposure, and moderating influence of the lake on temperature help to ripen the grapes. Even so, to get reasonably ripe grapes it is necessary to use very early-ripening varieties. In western Switzerland, where most of the wine is made, the table grape variety Chasselas doré (Fendant) is widely used for winemaking. This is not a very satisfactory grape because it is too neutral in flavor for a good wine grape. However, it does ripen sufficiently to reduce the musts' acidity to manageable levels in most years. Nevertheless, its musts usually have to be sweetened to produce a 10 to 12 percent alcohol wine. In the very best years it makes a pleasant enough wine which is sometimes bottled with a little carbon dioxide to freshen up its flavor. In eastern Switzerland the Pinot noir, there called Clevner, is used. The prevalence of fungus diseases necessitates early harvesting but often adds undesirable color-destroying enzymes to the must. In the southern region, Tessin, red grapes are also grown, some of the best from Merlot.

In spite of all these problems, the wines of Switzerland are technically well made. The rational use of the malo-lactic fermentation is an important factor in their quality. Switzerland illustrates the limitation in quality which a cool climate can impose and the improvement in quality which improved viticultural and enological technology makes possible.

CZECHOSLOVAKIA

The wines of Czechoslovakia are mainly white and are made of a number of western European varieties such as White Riesling, Sylvaner, Traminer, Chardonnay, Veltliner, etc. Eastern or southern European varieties such as Ezerjó, Walschriesling, and Leányka are also grown. They tend to be rather light in character and low in alcohol, which is what we would expect from the cool climate. It is a small industry, however, and exports little wine.

AUSTRIA

The wines of Austria are primarily white, although a few reds are produced. The most important vineyards are along the Danube, but appreciable acreage is found in several other parts of Austria. The wines are frequently sold with the name of the grape variety: Traminer, Rotgipfler, Green and Red Veltliner, Muscat Ottonel, Blue Portuguese, Walschriesling, etc. On the Danube there are a number of important viticultural areas near Dürnstein, Krems, and Rohrendorf, among others. Near Vienna, Baden and Gumpoldskirchen and Bad Voslau are noted for their wines. In southern Austria, the Steirmark region produces low-alcohol, high-acid white wines. In eastern Austria, Burgenland produces red and white wines. Many Austrian wines are sold directly from the barrel to the consumer as soon as they become brilliantly clear, most often in restaurants. There is a small export market of Austrian wines to the United States. These are reasonable in price, but are often rather neutral in character, lacking the crisp, tart, and flavorful characteristics of German wines.

Because of Austria's cool climate, the major possibilities for the future appear to be in white wines. The varieties are not so standardized as in Germany, nor are the regions so highly classified. One seldom finds a poor Austrian wine, and less often a truly great wine: These are everyday drinking wines. Technically they are well handled, with cool fermentations, controlled malo-lactic fermentations, and proper clarification. The viticultural standards are exemplary, with perhaps some tendency to overcrop.

HUNGARY

The wines of Hungary are of very ancient renown, and Tokay (or more correctly, Tokaj) was considered one of the great white wines of Europe before World War I. There are about 500,000 acres of vineyard in Hungary, slightly less than in the United States. Both red and white table wines are produced, and the present government has sponsored the expansion of the industry, particularly on the sandy soils where, unfortunately, lesser quality wines are frequently produced. The government has also officially classified 17 wine-producing districts.

In the traditional wine district producing Tokay, the most important varieties are Hárslevelü and Furmint. Both dry and sweet Tokays were produced, but the best were those which retained a certain degree of sugar. Two factors account for the high sugar content: the natural drying of the grapes, allowed to hang on the vines until late October; and in some years a considerable amount of *Botrytis* infection, which helps to raise the sugar concentration. In the very finest years, the more shriveled grapes were piled up and the free-run juice produced by the weight of the berries on each other was kept separate and used to make Tokay *Essenz*. This was a very sweet wine of low alcohol content. It was very expensive, comparable in price to the *Trockenbeerenauslese* wines of Germany. Little, if any, *Essenz* has been produced since World War II.

The sweet Tokays currently produced have more or less of these crushed sweet grapes added to the must from less shriveled fruit to raise the sugar content. They are then fermented in small (less than 50-gallon) containers. These are sold as two, four, or six *puttonyos* (the *puttonyo* being a bucketful of the sweet juice added to the regular must), and now refer to increasing sweetness as defined by the government. These are usually sold under the appellation Aszu Tokay; a drier type without the must from the shriveled grapes is called Szamorodni. They are bottled in a graceful long-necked bottle holding about 500 milliliters (compared to the usual bottle of 750 milliliters).

Since the Second World War some of the Tokays on the markets in Western Europe have been found to contain hydroxymethylfurfural, which indicates that some heated grape concentrate may have been used to sweeten the must, contrary to earlier and better practices.

In the other districts, a wide variety of Western European and local varieties are planted. Ezerjó is a well-known local white variety and Kadarka a local red. Walschriesling (white) is extensively planted. The climate varies markedly from season to season, but tends to be cool; the white wines are thus usually better than the reds. The best districts are Mór, Badacsony-Balatonfüred-Csopak, Balatonmellek, Debrö, Villany-Pecser, Eger, and Somlö. The districts around Lake Balaton are considered especially good. Some Hungarian red and white wines reach the American market. They sell at reasonable prices and make an interesting comparison with similar types from other countries. Some of the reds, particularly those from Eger, would improve with additional bottle-aging.

RUMANIA

The various wine types produced in Rumania have never achieved much fame outside the country. In the past, use of table grapes, direct-producers *(V. vinifera* × non-*V. vinifera* hybrids), and ordinary local varieties have been handicaps to making high-quality wines. However, there is now a good technological background for both viticulture and enology, and marked improvements can be expected. Many fine non-Rumanian varieties have been planted: Walschriesling, Furmint, Pinot gris, Aligoté, Pinot noir, and Cabernet Sauvignon. Among the best local varieties are Fetească alba, Băbească neagră, and Fetească neagră. All types of wine are produced under both varietal and regional names. The best are said to be the whites, which indicates rather cool growing conditions. Recently we have tasted some well-made and a few outstanding dry white and red table wines from Rumania.

BULGARIA

This is primarily a table-grape-producing region (much of these are shipped to other countries). Many table and dessert wines are made for local consumption, and an export market is being developed. Local varieties (Pamid, Mavrud, Gamsa, and Sartschin) are employed as well as non-Bulgarian varieties (Cabernet Sauvignon, Aligoté, Saperavi, and Rkatsiteli). The dessert wines are often only 16 to 18 percent alcohol but with 10 to 18 percent sugar. The use of table grapes for producing table wine is a negative quality factor. Brandy is also produced.

U.S.S.R.

The vineyard acreage of the Soviet Union has been increasing very rapidly and is now nearly 3,000,000 acres. Production per acre is only moderate, since the vines in many areas must be covered during the winter to prevent winterkilling. This practice often weakens the vines and reduces production.

The main areas where grapes are grown are Moldavia, an important district next to Rumania; the Ukraine, which includes the Crimea; the Federal Republic, in the region of Krasnodar and Rostov; Georgia, in the Caucasus; Armenia, to the south of the Caucasus; Azerbaidzhan, east of Georgia along the Caspian Sea; and Uzbekistan, to the east of the Caspian. A small amount of grapes is grown in other of the Asiatic republics, but they are not very important as yet. Some raisins are made in Uzbekistan, and table grapes are important in several areas of the Soviet Union.

All types of wines are produced in Russia, but the best to our taste are the dessert wines: wines of moderate alcohol content, usually from 14 to 16 percent, but of high sugar content, from 16 to 22 percent. This means that the musts are fortified very soon after pressing and have undergone little alcoholic fermentation. The high sugar content gives the wines some protection against yeast and bacterial contamination, and they tend to remain stable in spite of their moderate alcohol content. The muscats made from Muscat blanc are flavorful wines, and some are of excellent quality. A number of red sweet wines are also made, as are many baked wines, which are called "madera." Russia is also producing some excellent film-yeast sherries.

The table wines are made from a large number of European varieties such as Aligoté, White Riesling, Sylvaner, and Cabernet Sauvignon. There are also many native varieties such as Rkatsiteli (white) and Saperavi (red). In some cases these are sold with varietal labels, but a number of local or trade names are also in use. While many of the table wines are pleasant, they are not as distinctive or of as high quality, to our palate, as the dessert wines. The appearance (clarity) of some Russian wines could be improved. Some table wines recently tasted from Georgia were tart, with 4 percent sugar and 11 percent alcohol.

The Russians have had a keen interest in sparkling wines since early in the century. They have increased their production at a very rapid rate since the Revolution. The tank process is mainly used, but it is being modified for continuous operation. The wines are of moderate quality, but have good clarity. As would be expected from the preference of Russian consumers for sweet wines, most of them are distinctly on the sweet side. The Russians are also increasing their brandy production. The best brandies are said to come from Georgia and Armenia; however, brandies are produced in Moldavia and other districts as well. They are generally aged in the wood, although new processes of treatment and aging of brandies are being introduced.

Summary. —In all the countries discussed in this chapter, the white wines are far more important than the reds, primarily because of the difficulty of producing high-quality, mold-free, ripe red grapes in regions of high humidity and low temperatures. The exceptions may be some of the red wines of Hungary, Rumania, Bulgaria, and the Soviet Union. Widespread use in the Communist countries of grape varieties not grown elsewhere has not yet led to new premium varietals recognized in world markets, perhaps because of lack of attention to quality and standards from an export point of view.

The cool climatic conditions restrict the whites to varieties ripening early or in midseason, grown on well-drained and south-facing slopes or near bodies of water. Nevertheless, by taking advantage of the action of *Botrytis cinerea,* a number of sweet wines are produced. In the Soviet Union, Rumania, and Bulgaria, fortified sweet wines are also made.

Improved technology is being increasingly applied to grape- and wine-production problems in all these countries.

There's none of these demure boys come to any proof; for thin drink doth so overcool their blood . . . that they fall into a kind of male greensickness; and then when they marry, they get wenches. . . . If I had a thousand sons, the first human principle I would teach them should be, to forswear thin potations and addict themselves to sack. —WILLIAM SHAKESPEARE

Falstaff, in *Henry IV, Part Two*

Chapter 15

THE WINES OF SOUTHERN EUROPE AND ASIA

Portugal, Spain, Italy, Yugoslavia, Greece, Cyprus, and Asia Minor produce wines which are often of distinctly different types from those of the northern countries. Some of the wines of southern France and of Russia, Rumania, and Bulgaria could have been considered here rather than in the preceding chapters. The main distinction differentiating the southern from northern European wines is the longer, warmer growing season of the south, with its resultant viticultural and enological consequences.

PORTUGAL

Portugal is one of the important wine-producing regions of Europe, with an annual production of over 300 million gallons. Most of this is table wine produced in the Estremadura region. It is consumed with meals by the working people of Portugal. Only a few of the table wines of Portugal are above standard quality. One of these, from the Dão region in north-central Portugal, is a soft red wine which responds well to aging. The red wine from the Colares district on the Atlantic coast near Lisbon has some reputation, but production is low.

239

The wine, however, is interesting because of its high salt content (from ocean breezes). Individual producers produce good wines in a number of other regions, including sparkling, sweet table, and dessert types.

Owing to the intelligent activity of the semigovernmental Junta Nacional do Vinho, the quality of table-wine production has been improved greatly. Even higher standards of wine quality could be established if the varietal complement of the vineyards could be changed and standards developed for different types of wines.

The wines of the Minho region north of Oporto are well known in Portugal. These unique wines are called *vinhos verdes*, literally green wines, from their tart (acidic) taste. Grapevines are grown on trees and pergolas. They are thus difficult to prune properly and tend to overproduce. The result is that the grapes do not ripen and are high in total acidity and low in sugar. During and after the alcoholic fermentation a malo-lactic fermentation occurs, and the acidity is somewhat reduced. The wines are bottled at a high total acidity, and in many cases the malo-lactic fermentation continues in the bottled wine so that the wines are very gassy when opened. They are thus naturally sparkling red and white wines, but the sparkle has been produced from the malo-lactic rather than from an alcoholic fermentation. The alcoholic content is usually below 10 percent. Though interesting, they are not high-quality wines in the classical sense— being often turbid, too low in body, alcohol, and varietal character, and some have unusual flavors of bacterial origin. Some of these *verdes* wines are now produced by carbonation. The wines are less likely to be defective but may be losing some of their unique character.

Many other still and carbonated rosé wines are also produced in northern Portugal. In our opinion, their chief claim to fame is their low price.

The production of two fine dessert wines makes Portugal especially important enologically. Red sweet wines are produced in the valley of the Douro River, which runs in an easterly direction from Oporto into Spain. Here the grapes are planted on steeply terraced slopes in a delimited geological area starting about forty miles inland. A wide variety of grapes are grown here; among the most important are Touriga, Tinta Roriz, Mourisco, Bastardo, and Souzão. A reason for the mixture of varieties is that climatic conditions vary rather widely from one year to the next, and it is desirable to have grapes which have high color in the warmer years to blend with grapes which have lesser amounts of color. It is doubtful, however, whether the ideal variety or varieties have yet been determined for this region.

The grapes are crushed, formerly by treading, into rather shallow stone or concrete *lagares*. The reason for the treading was more for economy than for quality, since labor was cheap in this region. As the cost of labor increased, mechanical equipment for crushing was introduced. The stems are usually not removed. The fermenting liquid is circulated over the cap to increase color extraction. During the fermentation, when the sugar content is reduced from 22–25 percent to about 12 percent, the juice is drawn off and fortified with brandy. The fortification is made to about 18 or 19 percent alcohol. Later in the year the wines are shipped from the Douro to the lodges (storage cellars) at Vila Nova da Gaia (opposite Oporto) for aging. More brandy is added when needed, particularly to the best wines. The typical Douro cask is the port pipe, which holds about 145 gallons (550 l).

Three different types of wines are produced in the Douro. The very best wines of the best years, which generally means in the cooler years, are shipped to London in casks and are declared a "vintage" port. There they remain for two years and are then bottled. These wines are high in flavor and color and are fortified up to about 21 percent alcohol. They age very slowly in the bottle, but after ten to twenty years achieve a distinctive bottle bouquet, the tannin content decreases, and the wines acquire a remarkably soft character. Vintage ports are the epitome of port quality and are always expensive because of the long aging required and the limited quantities available. Some are now bottled in Portugal. Dated ports which have been aged in the cask for many years before bottling never have the same quality as those which are aged in the classical way in bottles.

Standard red ports are aged in the cask for three or four years before bottling. They have a full red color and are sold as ruby ports. These are the standard drinking wines which are used as a before- or after-meal drink in the English and Scottish pubs or after dinner in middle-class homes.

A considerable amount of wine with a tawny red color is produced in the Douro. The tawny red color results from the use of the lesser-colored varieties, such as the Bastardo, and also from longer aging of normal red wines or by blending in of white port. These tawny wines are often lower in sugar than the ruby port wines, and have been used as an apéritif wine. However, they are usually served after the meal. Some people prefer the tawny to the ruby ports. A smaller amount of white port is produced in the Douro, but it has not achieved great popularity. Some of the drier white ports have also been used as an appetizer, but most are still much too sweet for a proper apéritif.

Port is a "manufactured" wine in the sense that a variety of different styles and qualities of ruby and tawny port are produced by the shipping firms. Large stocks of young and old wines are stored by the shippers in their lodges at Vila Nova da Gaia. The original wines coming down from the Douro are often blended from one *quinta* (the Portuguese equivalent of the French château) to another to achieve the standard types that are necessary. From these different basic types, blends are made to achieve exactly the style and quality of wine which a given consumer might wish. Thus wines differing slightly in color, sugar content, flavor, age, and, of course, price and quality are produced.

Port is one of the great classical types of wines. Soil, climate, and varietal components are undoubtedly important. However, the classification of the wines according to type and quality and the careful blending to produce distinctive types seem equally important. The treading was apparently not a unique factor. The demands of the English market for a standard high-quality wine have been paramount in the production of fine port. The English obviously developed the type concept and have insisted on high standards of quality.

Production of port has declined, however, owing mainly to decreased consumption in Great Britain. This is related not to any change in port quality but to changes in English drinking habits. The decrease may be due to the more general use of central heating in the home and hence to a reduction in after-dinner drinking. Calories (particularly in relation to obesity) may also be a factor. With energy crises and lowered room temperatures, perhaps ports will regain the popularity deserved by their unique and varied qualities.

Another dessert wine produced by the Portuguese is Madeira, from the main island of the Madeiras on which Funchal is located. This region, 600 miles off the coast of North Africa, has a semitropical climate. Because of the high humidity it is difficult to grow grapes without fungus infection. Before these fungus diseases were introduced from America, in the mid-nineteenth century, grape growing was apparently less difficult. A considerable amount of Jacquez grapes, a direct-producer variety of American parentage, is grown. It is believed by the shippers to account, in part, for the merely moderate quality of some of the modern Madeiras. Some of the old *V. vinifera* varieties such as Boal (Bual in Portuguese) and Verdelho are still grown also. Little Sercial remains, however, although some Sercial wine is sold. The musts are generally fermented dry and are then baked in concrete tanks at about 140° F. (60° C.) for three or four months. The wines are sweetened with fortified grape juice, called *vinho surdo,* and (if this was not done earlier) fortified to about 18 percent with alcohol (formerly from sugar cane molasses but now, because of the regulations of the European Economic Community, presumably with wine spirits).

The driest Madeiras (often not very dry) are sold as Sercial; the medium sweet wines, as Boal; and the sweetest wines, as Malmsey. Originally, these referred to the varieties of grapes from which they were produced, but for the standard Madeiras that are shipped today, these refer more to the sugar content than to their varietal complement, although more or less of the variety named may have been used. All these wines have an amber color and a slight caramel flavor from the baking.

Again, blending is very important, as wines of different ages and different characteristics are blended to make different styles and qualities of Madeira.

Occasionally, very old Madeiras reach the market. These are wines which have been, so it is claimed, kept in a single barrel for a long time and finally bottled, or in some cases have been bottled for many years. When they are authentic they can be of high quality, but some of them seem to be overpriced and of doubtful antiquity. One of the common negative quality factors to look for in Madeiras is their tendency to have rather high volatile acidity, an indication of poor winemaking practices. This is an undesirable characteristic, and if the consumer recognizes the volatile acidity he should avoid it.

Madeiras were much appreciated in the colonies and in the late eighteenth and early nineteenth century in the United States. Their rather high alcohol content, 19 to 20 percent, recommended them to the colonists; also the fact that they could be bought rather cheaply from the ships which were trading with Madeira; and finally, they could be and were aged for long periods of time. A number of American and English firms imported large quantities of Madeiras and gave their own names to these wines. However, it is no longer possible to obtain high quality Madeiras which have been aged and bottled in this country. The demand for Madeira has been decreasing, and probably one of the reasons has been a decline in quality. The baneful influence of the Jacquez variety should also be recognized. The early development of fungus diseases forces early harvesting and prevents the development of the ripe-grape aroma. As better methods of fungus control are developed, this may lead to abandonment of Jacquez and the planting of better-flavored *V. vinifera* varieties.

SPAIN

Vineyards were probably planted in Spain by the Phoenicians, or at least by the early Greek colonists. A thriving wine industry was in existence at the time of the Roman occupation. A number of table grape varieties were imported into Spain during the Moorish domination, but apparently many of the original wine grape varieties were still planted. Today Spain has nearly four million acres in grapes, the largest acreage in the world, but production per acre is low. About half a billion gallons of wine are produced annually, mainly table wine—far less than in France or Italy.

The best table wine areas are those of the delimited region of Rioja, where Mazuela, Grenache, Graciano, and Tempranilla are the leading varieties. This region was developed to its present high standards mainly through the French colonists who settled here when phylloxera invaded the vineyards of France—this is another example of the tremendous economic effects which phylloxera had in that country. The Rioja wines are mainly reds which are usually aged in the Bordeaux fashion, that is, in 50-gallon containers. Some fractional blending (see Chapter 10) was formerly done here, and the date on the label simply reflected the vintage of the oldest wine. Nowadays the date on the wine bottle (particularly since 1960) usually reflects its actual vintage.

Many red and white table wines are made in the regions around Barcelona, near Valencia, and especially in La Mancha. The latter is the largest and most concentrated vineyard area of Spain. It is planted primarily to white grapes. These wines are rather low in alcohol—11 to 12 percent—and are not high in acidity. They are the usual bar drink in Spain. They frequently are not very well standardized or stabilized, but they sell at a very low price, only a few cents per glass. The increasing standard of living and the quality of the beer and whiskey available, together with the lack of quality of many of these La Manchan whites, has sharply reduced wine consumption in Spain. The reds from Valencia are often high in alcohol, and some are exported as blending wines. Good standard table and sparkling wines are produced near Barcelona, plus a number of dessert wines. Of these, the best are those of Sitges (white) and *rancio* types from the Priorato region.

Spain is important as a wine-producing country on the international market primarily because of two dessert wine types: the sherry and the sherry-like types of wines of Jerez de la

Frontera and Montilla and the Málaga type of wines produced in or near the town of Málaga. Tarragona and Priorato dessert wines were formerly exported and presumably could be again if they were standardized in quality and if a demand could be developed. Recently a number of table and citrus-flavored wines have been exported in fairly large volume and at generally inexpensive prices.

The wines of Jerez de la Frontera have been known in England for many centuries, and were mentioned by Shakespeare as "sack" or "sherris sack." Up until the middle of the nineteenth century they seem to have been white wines of 15 or 16 percent alcohol, both dry and sweet, aged by rather normal processes in large *bodegas*. However, the process of developing a yeast film on the wine seems to have achieved wide acceptance in the district in the nineteenth century, and since that time many of the best-known wines of the sherry district have been produced by this interesting process.

A number of white varieties are grown, but the Palomino is the most important. It is planted mainly in highly calcareous, nearly white *(albariza)* soils. The importance of the soil is generally admitted, possibly owing to a higher sugar in grapes grown on these soils. To get the sugar content higher, grapes were formerly left on trays for two or three days before crushing. The crushing was traditionally done by walking on the grapes, and the pressing was done in primitive hydraulic presses. Nowadays modern crushers and continuous or Willmes (bag or bladder) presses are used. This is another reflection of the increasing cost of labor.

Palomino may not be the ideal grape for sherry production because of its moderate normal sugar content, the pulpy nature of the fruit, and the low total acidity of its musts. For this reason, calcium sulfate—gypsum—is often added to lower the pH; this is called "plastering." Tartaric acid has also been used to raise the acidity.

After fermentation the new wines are allowed to remain in the same containers in which the must fermented. At this time the containers are only about three-quarters full. A secondary stage of the wine yeast which causes the alcoholic fermentation, in this case *Saccharomyces fermentati,* forms a film (called *flor* in Spain) stage on the surface of the wine. This film stage utilizes alcohol and acetic acid as a carbon source and produces aldehydes as one of several important ordorous products. The film process may continue for a number of years. The film is not present on the surface of the wine continuously throughout the year. Usually it forms on the surface during the spring and again during the fall. Thus a rather large deposit of yeast forms in the bottom of the container, and the flavor of these *flor*-type sherries seems to be due to both the aldehyde byproducts which are formed by the film itself and to autolysis products from the yeast deposit. The production of the cheaper *flor* sherries could probably be speeded up by keeping the casks at a constant temperature.

The darker, more tannic, often sweet, and generally lower-quality wines may be fortified to 18 or more percent alcohol shortly after the vintage, and thus do not undergo a film stage. These wines become the *oloroso* type when blended and aged.

But the film process, or the classification into *fino* and *oloroso* types, does not explain the uniformity of quality and type of the different Spanish sherries. A system of fractional blending has been used for many years in the sherry district and this, the *solera* system, accounts for the uniformity in quality and in type characteristics of wines. In the *solera* system, casks containing wine of the same type, but of various ages, are arranged on top of each other or at least near each other. Careful sensory examination to classify the wines into types is, of course, a necessary prelude to successful operation of the system. Anywhere from 5 to 30 percent of the wine from the casks in the oldest tier may be removed. This is then replenished with wine drawn and blended from casks in the next oldest tier, and so on up to the youngest. These *soleras* may be from four to as many as eight steps or stages in depth. The wine coming from the oldest barrel will, in the second year of operation, contain wine one year older than it was originally, plus the younger wine from the next oldest tier used to replace

FIG. 34. Sherry butts in a Spanish bodega.

it, which will also be one year older (Figure 34). Thus, as only a limited amount of wine is taken from the lower (older) stage each year, the average age of the wine from the lower barrel continues to rise until it reaches a constant value. If the *solera* is eight stages deep and if 25 percent is removed each year, the composition of the wine coming from the oldest container will reach an average and constant age of about eight years after ten years of operation. Therefore, the first advantage of the *solera* system is that it produces wine of a constant average age after a period of operation (Figure 35).

Another advantage of the *solera* system is that if the wine of one particular year is of lesser quality, it will not all reach the older stage at the same time and hence its lesser quality will tend to be blended out. Its lower quality will thus not have an abrupt adverse effect on the quality of the *solera*. One other advantage of the *solera* system is that, because of the periodical renewing of the wines, the alcohol content does not go up so rapidly and the *flor* yeast continues to grow on the surface. The reason for this is that under the very dry conditions of the sherry district the wines increase in alcohol, since moisture is lost through the surface of the containers faster than alcohol. The *flor* yeast will not grow above about 15.5 or 16 percent alcohol; so, unless a certain amount of renewal was taking

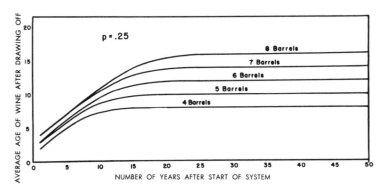

Fig. 35. Average age of the wine in the oldest container for 4-, 5-, 6-, 7-, and 8-barrel systems after operation for up to 50 years, when 25 percent of the wine is removed twice a year.

place constantly, the alcohol in the oldest container would gradually go above 16 percent and the *flor* yeast would no longer develop. Just so, it is common for the older stages to have little or no yeast growth on the surface.

Not all the *flor* sherries are of the same character; different *soleras* produce slightly different quality products, and a given firm may have two or three different dry *(fino)* types of *flor* sherries on the market at the same time. A great deal of blending of one type of wine with another takes place, which helps the winemakers to produce and maintain uniformity in different types of *fino* sherries. The older type of *finos* are called *amontillados.* The *finos* produced in the area of Sanlúcar de Barrameda are called *manzanillas.* At the time of export from Spain, most of the *fino* wines are fortified to 17 or more percent alcohol with brandy or industrial alcohol. However, in Spain *finos,* particularly the *manzanillas,* are sold at only 14 to 16 percent alcohol and may be consumed much as if they were table wines.

Very different from the dry *fino*-type sherries which are now so important are the *oloroso* type, wines of moderate quality and with less favorable prospects for forming a good *fino* wine. At no time do they have a *flor* film on the surface after they are fortified to about 18 percent alcohol. They are aged, however, by the *solera* process in the same kind of containers as the *flor* sherry wines. Many of the *oloroso soleras* are even older than those of the *flor*-type sherries. Obviously it does not make any difference whether their alcohol goes up or not, since there is no yeast-film growth. Occasionally an *oloroso solera* reaches 21 or even 22 percent alcohol. Some blending sherry is made from boiled-down grape juice and fortified juice from very ripe grapes. These are also aged in *solera* systems and used for blending. Modern sherry is a highly blended product: it is blended not only in the *soleras* from year to year but between *soleras* in order to produce wines of distinctive and uniform types, and there are shipping *soleras* for the final aging of the blended wines. This is an expensive method of aging.

The wines of the Montilla district south of Córdoba are quite similar to those of Jerez de la Frontera and are of great interest, though unfortunately they are less well known in this country. These wines are produced primarily from the Pedro Ximenes variety of grapes, but they are crushed and processed much as the Palomino variety is in the Jerez de la Frontera district. Both *flor*- and *oloroso*-type wines are produced. They are usually good buys, when one can obtain them, because they are less expensive than the traditional sherries.

The important quality factor of the drier sherries and *montillas* is that they have undergone a film stage. The careful classification of the wines and the aging and fractional blending are also important. The critical demands of the English market have had a highly important influence in raising and maintaining the quality standards for sherry.

The wines of Málaga are made from grapes which have been allowed to partially or almost completely dry (i.e., raisin) in the sun before they are crushed. The grapes are then crushed and pressed. They ferment very slowly. Some wines are fortified to about 16 percent alcohol soon after fermentation begins. Therefore some Málagas contain as much or more sugar than alcohol. They all have a very distinct raisin flavor and are usable only as dessert wines. Our grandparents' use of them in cooking was as rational as any other. Surprisingly, they are rather cheap considering the expense of producing them. The varieties of grapes used are Muscat of Alexandria and Pedro Ximenes. Of course the Muscat raisins of Málaga have been well known in commerce for many years. Málaga's strong and obvious raisin flavor and its low acidity and high sugar do not recommend it to many consumers today. However, in Málaga one may taste some complex old aged wines of notable quality.

ITALY

The wines of Italy have been known since pre-Roman times. Modern Italian wines, except for Chianti, vermouth, and

Marsala, have not achieved the international consumer recognition of French and German wines. Nevertheless, Italy is often the largest producer of wine, with over four million acres producing 1.5 billion gallons of wine. Per capita consumption is high, though not as high as in France.

Because of its population density, Italy's fertile plains are needed for the production of grains and vegetables. In most regions vines have been pushed onto the less fertile and often warmer slopes. This results in generally low yields, and in warmer regions, excessive sugar and low acid. This alone, however, would not be so objectionable were it not for the multicrop or promiscuous culture system necessitated on small and overcrowded subsistence farms. Vines are grown on or between trees and in competition with potatoes, tomatoes, olives, and other crops in the fields. It is estimated that only 10 percent of the vineyards of Italy are now of this type. Obviously, vines on trees cannot be properly pruned or sprayed for disease control. When several crops are grown on the same plot, there is always the problem of timing the proper care of each; none can receive as much attention as when a single crop is planted. There are reports that this practice is decreasing.

Winemaking procedures have frequently been rather primitive. The small size of the vineyards makes it difficult for the winemaker to receive proper training. There are more schools for training winemakers in Germany than in Italy, although Italy produces eight or more times as much wine as Germany. Many of the traditional Italian production practices are outmoded. The *governo* process of Tuscany, for example, is admittedly poor, but continues to be used. In this process one variety of grapes, Colorino, is placed on trays to dry until December or January. It is then crushed, and about 10 percent by volume of the fermenting must is added to the regular new red wine. This adds color, tannin, and alcohol, but it also may result in undesirable or incomplete fermentations. In addition, published data on the composition of Tuscan wines shows that they are exceedingly variable: 10.6 to 14.5 percent in alcohol and 0.13 to 0.36 percent in tannin.

In northern Italy, many of the red wines are *frizzante* (gassy) from continuing malo-lactic fermentations. In Calabria, table wines of 15 and 16 percent alcohol are common. Many of the white wines are amber in color and low in acidity. This lack of attention to wine quality is not only because untrained winemakers in small wineries often use outmoded processes and grapes of poor quality. It is a result also of a fundamental difference in attitude toward wine of the Italian as compared to the French. Wine is as necessary as bread or oil to the Italian, and he drinks it much as we drink milk, without thought or critical evaluation. Consequently, the small wine producers of Italy are able to sell wines which in other countries would not be acceptable. The wine found in many of the stores and restaurants, particularly in the rural districts, is often not up to commercial standards of other countries.

The Italian industry has had other handicaps. The main one is that Italy was not a national entity until the middle of the nineteenth century. Thus while there was a great deal of local pride, there was little interest in one district in the wines of another district. Hence wines received very little critical attention from connoisseurs in other parts of Italy. The wines of Naples were virtually unknown in the north of Italy, and likewise the wines of Verona were (and are) seldom found on wine lists in Rome or in southern Italy. This robbed local wine producers of an export market and of the critical attention to quality which the export market would have brought to them. It emphasizes again the great value of the English and Belgian markets in improving the quality of the wines of France, and the English influence on port and sherry. Italian table wines lacked distribution throughout Italy, and until the twentieth century had very little export trade with other countries. The main exceptions, even today, are vermouth, Marsala, and to a lesser extent the wines of Tuscany and Piedmont. Recently, many Italian wine districts (over 100) have been delimited, which is to be applauded. The best of these wines carry the appellation DOC, for *denominazione di origine controllato,* which has many of the requirements of the French appellations of origin.

Thus, in summary, many of the wines of Italy have been made from small vineyard holdings in mountainous areas in promiscuous culture, and the many untrained winemakers too óften use rather primitive techniques. The wines have not enjoyed sufficient distribution among critical consumers either inside or outside Italy to force an improvement in the quality. The average Italian consumer has not been critical of the quality of his wines. The freedom of wine trade within the European Economic Community and the increasing demands for Italian table wines on the American market are causing major changes in this situation. It appears that Italy is making relatively rapid and large-scale improvements in technology, particularly of standard quality wines.

The best-known wine districts of Italy are those of Piedmont, the Brenner Pass region near Bolzano, Lombardy, the region north of Venice, Tuscany, the hills near Rome (Castelli Romani), Naples, eastern Sicily near Etna, and western Sicily near Marsala. Sicily now has a number of DOC with many others projected.

The wines of Piedmont are usually sold with varietal labels. Some of them are gassy from malo-lactic fermentation, but when properly aged they can be among the best red table wines of Italy. Typical varietal names are Barbera, Freisa, Grignolino, and Nebbiolo. Barolo is a district wine produced from the Nebbiolo grape. A small amount of sparkling muscat is produced from Muscat blanc; known as Asti spumante, these wines are probably the best of the type available. They have an obvious and floral aroma but are usually low in alcohol and, if not too sweet or oxidized, are perhaps the best introductory wines extant. The wines of Piedmont are often of better quality than those of other Italian districts, because mixed planting is comparatively rare here. Also, several large and modern wineries have raised the standards.

The highest overall standard of quality of Italian wines is in the Brenner Pass region, where varieties such as Merlot, Walschriesling, Traminer, and Pinot noir are widely grown and made into very acceptable wines. If this district were not so small, it might develop a considerable export trade. It is significant that it is a German-speaking district which belonged to Austria before World War I, and the labels and wineries reflect German influence. They are seldom of exceptional quality, but are well-made wines.

Just to the south near Verona are the wines of Lombardy, many of which are very palatable if not exceptionally high quality dry table wines. Among the best known are Valpolicella and Bardolino, both of which are red, and Soave, which is white. Although these are not classical wines of high quality, they are among the most pleasant drinking wines of northern Italy. A great variety of wines of similar character and quality are produced in the region to the north and west of Venice.

Tuscany is perhaps the best-known wine district in Italy, because of the Chianti wines which were formerly sold in the typical raffia-covered *fiaschi*. Both red and white wines are made in Tuscany, but the reds are by far the best-known and the best in quality. The varieties used are Sangioveto and Colorino. In many cases when only the Sangioveto is planted, the *governo* process is not used. The wines are normally aged for two or three years and then bottled. The *fiasco* is not a very good bottle for aging, and Bordeaux-type bottles are now used, particularly for the wines from Montepulciano. A well-aged red Chianti can be very good. Of white Chiantis and Orvietos which are made from Saint-Émilion (here called Trebbiano) and Malvasia bianca, the less said the better. They are usually slightly oxidized and almost always too low in acid. Many of the Orvietos are made *abboccato*, which means they are sweet.

The wines of Castelli Romani are of only moderate quality. Often they are carbonated for the tourist trade of Rome and sold at exorbitant prices. The wines of Naples and of Vesuvius are also often of ordinary quality. Even the famed Lacrima Christi, produced from vines grown on the slopes of Vesuvius, will not be found memorable. These are often made into sparkling wine by bottle- or tank-fermentation processes. The wines are of moderate quality and are sometimes sweetened to cover up their normal defects. The wines of Capri and Ischia, which are well known to the tourist, perhaps should stay on the islands and be left for the tourist, as they certainly are not worthy of export. The table wines of the Etna district, in spite of their southern origin, can be quite pleasant, especially some of the red wines. They are seldom exported.

The wines of the Marsala district are the most interesting of the Sicilian wines. This district was deliberately developed by English wine merchants at the end of the eighteenth century and throughout the nineteenth century as the source of a substitute for sherry. The raw products which the wine merchants had to deal with were very unpromising: dry white wine (usually oxidized), grape juice, boiled-down grape juice, and alcohol. Later, when the production of concentrate became possible, grape concentrate was used. The dry white wines were blended with the grape juice, with a certain amount of the boiled-down grape juice to give it color and a burnt flavor, and fortified with alcohol up to 18 or 19 percent. These were made more or less sweet and rather highly colored, and were aged for some years in oak casks. The different types of Marsala were blended in a sort of fractional blending *(solera)* system so that wines of a fairly constant age and type were being produced.

The English influence began to diminish after World War I and was completely eliminated during World War II. There is a feeling in the trade that the quality of Marsala has not been as high after World War II as it was earlier. Certainly the postwar export trade of Marsala has been limited. Marsala has such a strong flavor that it takes time to acquire a taste for it. In Italy the drier and less alcoholic types are used as apéritifs, but in this country they may be too strong in flavor for this purpose. They are probably best used in cooking, and occasionally the sweeter types are served with cake. Marsala is another example of how careful attention to blending and classification of wines produces distinctive wines of uniform type and quality which have thus gained consumer acceptance.

Vermouths are produced primarily in the district near Turin in northern Italy. These are direct descendants of the flavored wines of the Greeks, but in the eighteenth and nineteenth centuries they were much improved. About fifty or sixty different herbs have been used in the production of the Italian type of vermouth. The raw material is a sweet muscat wine, originally from the Piedmont district. The herbs are macerated in the wine for shorter or longer periods of time, then are separated from the wine, and the product is aged. In the more modern process, the flavors of the herbs are extracted with alcohol solutions. These extracts are clarified and aged, and various amounts are then blended directly into the wines. Sweet vermouth is always slightly amber in color, owing to the use of caramel syrup, and is quite sweet—usually about 12 to 15 percent sugar—and contains only about 17 percent of alcohol. It is used without blending as a sweet dessert wine in Italy, but in this country is used mainly in manhattan cocktails. Dry (or French-type) vermouths are also produced in Italy—nowadays usually of very light color for the American market. Also some half-and-half blends of the two are produced. The best vermouths should not have any dominating characteristic of a single herb, but a well-blended herb flavor. The presence of too much vanilla or any other ingredient in sweet vermouths definitely lowers their quality.

YUGOSLAVIA

Many of the vineyards of Yugoslavia are subject to a Mediterranean climate, but those to the north have a typical continental climate. Grapes and wines are produced in all of the six republics of Yugoslavia: about 50 percent of the production is in Serbia, 35 percent in Croatia, 9 percent in Slovenia, 4 percent in Macedonia, 2 percent in Bosnia-Herzegovina, and a negligible amount in Montenegro.

Serbia produces table wines, more red than white, which are usually named for the regions where they are produced: Zupa, Krajina, Vlasotinci (rosés), Smederevo (white), etc. Croatia produces mainly white table wines. In the Danube basin the wines are usually made from Walschriesling, which may be a native variety. In Dalmatia (a part of Croatia) the reds are more important. The best Dalmatian wines are made from a native variety, Mali Plavac. These are often high in alcohol and tannin and are much in demand as blending wines. In Slovenia, many distinctive white table wines are made from western and northern European varieties such as Traminer, Sylvaner, or Sémillon. Merlot is widely used for reds.

Yugoslavian wines are now finding a place in the world market; 15 to 20 percent are exported—mainly to central European countries. They have one labeling feature which is almost unique and is clearly desirable: the sugar content, as well as the alcohol content, is sometimes stated on the label. (Some wine labels in the Soviet Union also indicate the sugar content.) The white table wines that have appeared on the American market seem more interesting than the reds.

GREECE

The wines of Greece go back to Homeric times, and were an important item of commerce in the pre-Roman and Roman period. During the centuries of Turkish domination the wine industry suffered, and it was not until Greece became a kingdom in the nineteenth century that winemaking began again to become important. There was considerable German influence in the winemaking industry, and many of the cellars reflect this. Some of the wines, however, still show the influence of ancient practices: e.g., many of the wines of Greece are resinated. These resinated wines, which contain 1 to 3 percent of dry resin, have a very strong turpentine-like odor and are called *retsina*.

The vineyard area of Greece covers over half a million acres, the wine industry produces over 100 million gallons per year. The soil is generally not fertile, and production per acre is low.

A limited amount of sweet muscat wine from the island of Samos is shipped to central and northern Europe for blending or bottling. The amber-red, slightly muscat-flavored wine called Mavrodaphne is a smooth tawny-port type of wine made near Patras in Peloponnesus. Other than these, there are many pleasant but rarely outstanding white and red table wines. The hot climatic conditions and lack of attention to technological details are major problems. Wines are not only produced on the mainland but also on many of the islands: Crete, Rhodes, Corfu, etc.

Although phylloxera has not infested many of the vineyards of Greece, and especially those of the southern part, phylloxera in France had an important influence on the grape industry of Greece. When there was a great shortage of grapes in the 1880s and early 1890s in France, importation of raisins was encouraged. The raisin industry of Greece was then greatly expanded, and heavy plantings of grapes for making raisins were made, particularly in Peloponnesus. These grapes became surplus when the French vineyards were replanted, and have remained so to this day. The overproduction of grapes still constitutes one of the largest single agricultural economic problems in Greece. Many of the surplus raisins have been converted to wine and distilled for brandy or industrial alcohol.

CYPRUS

The wines of Cyprus are very ancient. There was certainly a Greek colony on Cyprus in the pre-Roman period. During the long period of Turkish domination winemaking was discouraged. At present the vineyards are very subdivided, production per acre is low, the climate is hot, and the quality of the grapes and of some of the wines is often poor. Some musts are converted into concentrate for export to Great Britain for the making of "British wines." One wine of importance is produced: Commanderia, a tawny dessert wine with a slight raisin flavor, was originated by the Knights Templars when they made their headquarters on the island of Cyprus; its reputation appears to be greater than its real quality. The Cyprus government is trying to improve the quality standards of the Cyprus industry, and some progress has been made, but it remains to be seen how much they will be able to do. We have tasted an outstanding Cyprus *fino*-type sherry made by the film-yeast method.

ISRAEL

The wines of Israel are, of course, very ancient, but during the Turkish domination the wineries were almost entirely eliminated, and it was not until the late nineteenth century that one of the Rothschilds encouraged the planting of grapes. Several wineries were established and the grape acreage continued to expand, especially after Israel became a state in the 1940s. Israeli wines are of both table and dessert types, but the latter are usually the more pleasant. This is because Israel has very warm climatic conditions, closely resembling Regions IV and V in California, and its grape varieties are more adaptable for the making of dessert wines. However, the technology of both grape growing and winemaking is improving, and the quality of Israeli table wines has improved. Recently we tasted a fresh, crisp Israeli French Colombard.

Recently, Israel has agreed to subscribe to the Madrid agreements on appellations of origin; so "burgundy," "chablis," and other European-type names are no longer being used on Israeli labels. This is an important step forward on the part of the Israeli government.

Israel enjoys a large export trade for its wines because of their religious use. Wine is a part of Jewish culture and is a necessary part of the religious ceremonies at Passover and on other feast days. It seems natural that the devout Jewish family should prefer to use wines made in Israel on these occasions.

OTHER COUNTRIES

Syria has a large grape industry, over 170,000 acres, but being largely Moslem produces only half a million gallons of wine. Lebanon, with more Christians, produces a million gallons per year from its 60,000 acres. Turkey has nearly 1.9 million acres of grapes and produces about 12 million gallons of wine. Wine production was formerly under French direction. Some fair red and white table wines are produced; little has been exported. Iran has had wines for many centuries, but only recently has quality wine production been seriously undertaken. It is possible that with better varieties and improved technology, wines of interest to the serious wine consumer may be produced. Shiraz, a town in Iran, presumably was the origin of the Shiraz or Sirah grape. Malta has only 3,000 acres of grapes and produces about 1 million gallons. Use of sugar is a negative quality factor, and little of the wine is exported. Japan has a small grape and wine industry, but where *V. vinifera* varieties are used, some pleasant and an occasional good wine is produced. One negative factor is the production of blended (water, acid, and alcohol) sweet "wines" which contain only about 20 percent wine. Koshu is a native variety which appears more adapted to table use than to wine.

Grapes are planted in a number of regions on the central island. The best wines are produced near Kofu in Yamanashi prefecture. Grapes are used not only for wine but as table grapes and for grape juice. The technology has been brought to modern standards in recent years.

Summary.—The Mediterranean countries have climatic problems, but from too much heat rather than too little. The production of dessert wines is thus favored, though some areas may be too warm to produce the highest quality of dessert wine. In the Douro, for example, the best port is often produced in the coolest years.

Technologically, except possibly for Israel and some small areas and individual wineries, the winemaking practices of these countries could be improved. Italy is making rapid strides in some areas toward improving technology. The very small subdivisions of vineyards and persistence of primitive winemaking procedures in such warm countries as Italy and Cyprus do not lead to the production of high quality wine.

Legal regulatory assistance is needed to define the wine types and to set up means of improving or protecting their quality. Wines which vary too greatly in type and quality can hardly hope to achieve an export market. The great contribution of the English wine merchant (for port, sherry, and Marsala) was to emphasize the necessity of uniformity of types and quality standards.

The varietal complement of many vineyards is still too varied for production of wines of the highest quality. Planting grapes and other crops together, as in Italy, does not lead to fine wines. Nevertheless, localized regions such as the Brenner Pass area, individual companies and growers, and careful wine merchants can combine to produce and export wines of quality which have the added merit of being inexpensive. A spirit of adventure may yield pleasant results to the consumer.

Sparkling and bright in liquid light
Does the wine our goblets gleam in;
With hue as red as the rosy bed
Which a bee would choose to dream in.
—CHARLES FENNO HOFFMAN

Chapter 16

WINES OF AFRICA, AUSTRALIA, AND MEXICO AND SOUTH AMERICA

NORTHERN AFRICA

In northern Africa, grapes are grown and wine is produced in Tunisia, Algeria, Morocco, Egypt, and Libya.

Tunisian wines have been exported, mostly to France, as the Moslem religion forbids the consumption of alcohol by the orthodox. These wines are mainly table wines, 13 to 14 percent alcohol; most of them were exported for blending with the low-alcohol wines of the south of France.

The Algerian wine industry was developed by the French, particularly during the phylloxera period, to complement the low-alcohol wines of the south of France; this also helped to make up the deficit for the wines that could not be produced because of the ravages of phylloxera. Many of the vineyards were very large and planted to common varieties, such as Carignane, Alicante Bouschet, and Clairette blanche.

Most of the wineries were large, many of them cooperatively owned. The wines were stored in large concrete containers, much as they were in California before World War II.

The future of the Algerian wine industry is uncertain. Many

vineyards have been abandoned. Even if the industry were promptly brought back to its pre-1960 condition, it is questionable whether France would now accept large quantities of Algerian wines. The internal policies of the European Economic Community alone may make such large-scale importations impossible. Some Algerian wine has been exported to the Soviet Union, and production of brandy is being encouraged. The most popular wines are those of 13 and 14 percent alcohol, which were formerly shipped in tank ships or in barrels in France. There seem to be no other export markets to replace France for large quantities of ordinary wine.

Since there are both cool and warm regions in Algeria, higher-quality wines could be produced if the demand should develop. But it is difficult to see how a viable export market of quality wines can develop in Algeria, or any other Moslem country, when the winemakers are forbidden by their religion to even taste their product. Certainly no large internal market can be foreseen.

Morocco is likewise a Moslem country, and although it has a small resident French population, they can only consume a small part of the wine produced there. Hence the future of the Moroccan wine industry is likewise uncertain. The grapes are grown mainly in a valley running east from Rabat, which in many respects resembles Region IV in California. The wines produced are of the 12 to 14 percent alcohol red and white table-wine type, and formerly most of them eventually found their way into blending tanks in France.

Egypt developed vineyards near Alexandria in the last century and exported much of the wine to Europe as blending wines. The technology has been poor, and many of the wines of only passable quality. A few wines have been produced in Libya, but the future of wine production in this intensely Moslem state is very problematical.

SOUTH AFRICA

The first vines were planted in South Africa over 300 years ago by Dutch settlers, and a commercial wine industry developed there during the seventeenth and eighteenth centuries. A

Cape wine, called Constantia, became famous in Europe in the early nineteenth century; this seems to have been a tawny red muscatel, made from a red Muscat variety of grapes. Its disappearance has never been satisfactorily explained. A probable reason is that the red muscats are rather low in acid, and their high pH wines are readily subject to *Lactobacillus* spoilage. If all the wineries of the region became infected with *Lactobacilli,* eventually the wines may have become so mousy in odor that they lost their export market. This is the only specific wine of South Africa that has achieved international reputation, and the industry is now bringing it back into production on a limited scale.

Under the British, from the 1890s onward, the wine industry was again developed and expanded for the shipment of table grapes to Europe and for the production of port and red sweet wines for shipment to the English market. These were quite successful ventures, and eventually the vineyards were overplanted. Therefore the South African government in the 1920s had to organize some control over prices to forestall a disastrous economic depression for the growers and the small wineries. This was done by organizing the KWV (Afrikaans initials for the cooperative winegrowers' organization), a semigovernmental agency which controls the price of wine grapes, of fortifying alcohol, and of new wine. It also directly or indirectly controls the quality and price of wines and brandies which are exported from South Africa and the acreage that is planted. Each lot of wine proposed for export must pass a sensory panel for minimum quality and trueness to type before it can be shipped.

The KWV provides technical assistance to its own wineries as well as to others, and in general has had a salutary effect on the South African industry. It has been instrumental in developing two important types of products: a *flor* sherry resembling *amontillado* is produced by the Spanish process of growing yeast on the surface of wines in barrels, plus long aging; and the quality of South African brandies has been upgraded by improving the distilling procedures and by tasting and standardization of the blends. Pot stills are used.

The English market has tended to demand rather sweet and cheap ports and rather alcoholic and inexpensive table wines from Australia as well as South Africa. Consequently, the South African wines have not had the best reception among wine connoisseurs in England. This is an example of how wine merchants can sometimes prevent the best wines from reaching potential consumers by demanding only low-quality and cheap wines. In the cooler districts of South Africa, dry and slightly sweet white wines and lesser quantities of red table wines are produced. The shift from dessert and appetizer wines toward table wines, both within South Africa and particularly in the potential export market, has produced strains in their production. Stocks of aging dessert wines increased to more than eightfold annual exports. Large-scale shifts to table wines are hampered by sizable plantings in climatic Regions IV and V and a high percentage of Palomino (white) and Cinsaut (red) grapes unsuited for quality table wines.

Nevertheless, by experimentation and adaptation of modern technology, very creditable and inexpensive (in South Africa) white table wines are being made from South African Riesling and Steen (Chenin blanc) varieties. In the cooler areas, outstandingly drinkable light, fresh, but often slightly sweet white table wines are delightfully served as afternoon cooling drinks if you visit a wine farm, and are widely and inexpensively available in restaurants and hotels. Acreage of better red varieties is small but increasing in the face of rising demand, with Shiraz, Pinotage, and Cabernet Sauvignon producing some good and frequently well-matured wines. Table wines have been exported for some time by the KWV, but only recently have branded or estate wines been exported to the United States.

Since September 1973 South Africa has had a "Wines of Origin" regulation. Its purpose is to ensure that the wine in the bottle conforms to what is stated on the label as far as geographical origin, variety, and vintage year are concerned. A detailed system of production and stock records as well as minimum standards, sampling, sensory testing, and certification have been instituted. Fourteen geographical regions are recognized, and estate wines are authorized. To qualify as a "Wine of Origin," 80 percent of the wine must be from the defined area. For a varietal appellation, 75 percent must be from the variety and the wine must be "characteristic of the variety." However, less stringent regulations apply until 1982, when the industry can more easily comply with the percentage requirements. Stable export markets have been a problem further compounded by Britain's entry into the European Economic Community. The booming economy, appreciation of the value of technology, and the potential shift of Johannesburg-area residents from beer toward wine are favorable factors.

Because of climatic conditions, it is unlikely that a wine industry will develop in the southern part of the continent except in the Republic of South Africa. Some areas in Rhodesia might be suitable for grapes, but with the decreasing European population it is unlikely that a stable wine industry will develop there. Africa seems to be the only continent where grape acreage is not increasing at the present time.

AUSTRALIA

The Australian and the Californian wine industries started at about the same time in the late eighteenth century. Many European varieties were imported. Dessert wines formed the bulk of the wine trade until recently. Almost from the start, wines were exported to England. The industry is still somewhat dependent on this export market (though not as much as the California industry is on shipments to the eastern United States).

About 180,000 acres of grapes have been planted, mainly in South Australia, West Australia, New South Wales, and Victoria. Table and raisin grapes are also important. A quarantine has long been imposed to keep phylloxera out of South Australia; this has also prevented rapid introduction of new and better varieties and clones. This is no longer the case, as vines intended for importation may be held in quarantine until certified free of virus diseases and phylloxera. Wine production is about 80 million gallons annually, but some of it is distilling material, and about 40 million gallons of finished wine are consumed. Overall climate does not seem to be a limiting factor, although it is rather humid in the Hunter River district and irrigation is required in some areas.

A wide variety of types of wine is produced: red and white table, *flor* sherry, sweet sherry, red dessert, muscatel, sparkling, and so on. There is a lively interest in improving Australian wines, and many special bottlings and well-aged wines are available. The wineries are modern and have good technological control.

One interesting feature of the Australian industry is the number of family-owned firms which have been in existence for more than a hundred years. These take great pride in the quality of their product and have certainly been a positive factor in improving Australian wines. Some of these have recently merged into larger conglomerates.

As in California, the use of appellations of European origin is common and no doubt has had a baneful effect on quality improvement and the development of unique local types. And the large beer consumption is a factor which has repressed wine drinking.

New Zealand imports wine from Australia and has a small but growing grape and wine industry of its own. The climate is cool, but with the proper varieties and techniques quality table wines may be produced if excessive use of sugar can be controlled. Larger acreages of *V. vinifera* varieties are now in production, and there seems to be no reason why the better New Zealand wines could not compete on the international market.

MEXICO AND SOUTH AMERICA

The discovery of America was followed by the conquest of Mexico and this, in turn, by the settling of Spanish colonists in the New World. Simultaneously, missionaries came to the New World to Christianize the natives. The Catholic religion required wine for its ceremonies, and consequently one of the important items of export from Spain was wine during the colonial period. Moreover, life was not easy on the frontier, and wine was welcome to the civilian and military personnel.

Mexico. —It is not known whether vines or seeds were first brought to Mexico, but it is certain that a small grape industry was started north of Mexico City in the sixteenth century. The variety of grape which they began to develop, either from cuttings or seeds brought from Spain or by inadvertent hybridization, was eventually called Criolla. It was taken farther north in Mexico and eventually was imported into the new missions which were developing in Baja California. The cuttings were brought from Baja California into California proper some time after the establishment of the San Diego Mission in 1769. The Criolla, then, is the same as or closely related to the variety we call Mission in California.

The Mexican wine industry developed slowly, because of the very warm climate in the interior of Mexico and in Baja California. Just before and after World War I, new plantings were made in the Aguascalientes area and near Ensenada in Baja California, and these and other plantings were expanded during the 1920s and 1930s. At the present time Mexico has about 25,000 acres. The best wines produced in Mexico have been of the dessert type, which would be expected from the warm climatic conditions, and we have tasted excellent muscatels from a winery at Ensenada. One disadvantage has been the difficulty of preventing the sophistication of the wines with alcohol and sugar; these wines could be sold at a very cheap price and have tended to prevent the development of a quality wine industry. Recently this practice seems to have been stopped. The technology has been improving, both viticultural and enological, and local micro-climates and better varieties may even permit production of some premium quality table wines.

Peru. —Grapes were taken from Mexico to Peru soon after the downfall of the Inca empire. A small grape industry developed there, based upon the Criolla type of grape. Again, climatic conditions were too hot and, in Peru, far too dry for the development of a quality wine industry. It is no wonder that in the nineteenth century much of the wine was distilled and made into a colorless brandy called *pisco*. Many a miner's thirst in California during the Gold Rush days was slaked with *pisco* brandy from Peru. There was an expansion of the vineyards and some attempt to improve wine quality in the early twentieth century, but the industry tooday is still small, with only a few standard wines. Peruvian wines are seldom of exportable quality; most of them appear to be sold as a weekend beverage.

Chile.—In contrast to the climate of Peru, that of Chile ranges from Region II to Region IV conditions, and there is adequate moisture in most vineyard areas except those in the northern part of Chile. Furthermore, the background of the Chilean grape industry is entirely different. Because of large migrations from France and Great Britain, particularly at the time of phylloxera, the Chilean industry has developed on the French model rather than on the Spanish or Italian. The most important grape varieties are from France; aging procedures in the making of the white and red wines resemble those used in France.

The white wines, however, tend to be aged in the wood too long. They thus acquire a woody flavor and are too dark or amber in color, and have not been very successful on the international market. Attempts have been made to import them into the United Stats in various kinds of fancy bottles, but so far none of these attempts has been permanently successful.

On the other hand, many of the red wines are well aged and have a good barrel and bottle bouquet. A few are worthy of export. Again, some may be aged too long, but the better-quality red wines of Chile probably can now compete on the international market. Certainly the potential is great, with many vineyards in the equivalent of Regions II and III and with some planted to premium tablewine varieties.

A small amount of red sweet dessert wine and some *pisco* brandy (often with a muscat flavor) are produced in Chile. It is sad that Chile is one of the few countries where wine constitutes a major source of alcoholism. This was originally a part of life on the large haciendas, where the workers were allowed as much cheap wine as they could drink on weekends. The result has been that alcoholism from wine is a serious Chilean social problem. The development of public transportation, enabling the worker to travel to town, appears to have helped reduce alcoholism and the problem no longer appears as serious as it once did.

Argentina.—The Criolla grapes which originated in Mexico were exported to Peru, later to Chile, and were brought across the Andes to Argentina, certainly by the beginning of the seventeenth century. They are still planted there, but a large number of other varieties, both French and Italian, have also been planted. Argentina is the largest wine-producing region in the Western Hemisphere, with 853,000 acres of grapes and about 718 million gallons of wine. The average annual consumption of wine in Argentina, per capita, is also greater than that of other Western Hemisphere countries. The predominant influence on the Argentine wine industry has been that of the Italian immigrant, who demands wine daily but is not particularly interested in quality. The vineyards are extensive, often 1,000 to 2,000 or more acres, and the wineries are frequently very large. Continuous fermentation systems have not improved quality; the wines are generally of only moderate quality. Red and white table wines are shipped and sold mainly in bulk to workmen in Buenos Aires and other large cities. Some moderate quality sparkling wine is produced. Currently some wine is exported to the United States.

The most important area for the growing of grapes in Argentina is in Mendoza. Here some palatable red wines from Merlot are produced, but the emphasis is generally on very high production per acre. With few exceptions, the wines do not reach the international standard that are found in the best red wines of Chile.

Brazil.—The grape regions of Brazil are too warm and humid for the best growth of *V. vinifera* grapes. It is therefore no surprise to find many American varieties and direct producers growing in Brazil; the Isabella is a well-known grape here. In some regions *V. vinifera* grapes can be grown, and these areas are increasing.

A number of different ethnic influences have been brought to bear on the Brazilian wine industry: Portuguese, Italian, Spanish, French, and German. Quality standards of the Brazilian wine industry so far have fluctuated very widely. Export of a Brazilian Riesling to the New York market met with only moderate success, because it was not of high quality. Wines meet great competition from other alcoholic beverages in Brazil. This factor, along with the hot, humid climate, makes it difficult for a large premium wine industry to develop in that country. However, good experimental work is being done, and the amount of wine with a high volatile acidity has decreased. Recently a number of large new vineyards have been planted in new regions recommended for planting vines. The last word has obviously not been written, especially considering improved technology.

Others. —Uruguay has a very small wine industry, and some fairly good wines have been made in that country. Likewise, there are small plantings of grapes in Paraguay and Ecuador, but these are not likely to become important grape regions because of poor climatic conditions. In Venezuela, where there is a large Italian population, a considerable amount of wine is being produced from imported grape concentrate to satisfy the demand of recent immigrants for a vinous table beverage. A few table grape vineyards have been planted and some wine is being produced from surplus table grapes.

Summary. —The future of wines in northern Africa seems doubtful unless the European markets can be maintained. North African wines have seldom been of high quality. South Africa, on the other hand, has developed several quality products, particularly sherry and brandy, which could compete on world markets. Australia also has a flourishing export trade and many good table and dessert wines.

European grapes were first grown in Mexico, from where they were carried to California and to Peru, Chile, and Argentina. The original vines produced well, but the quality of the wine was poor. Better vines were later imported from Europe. The hot dry climate is the biggest handicap in Mexico and Peru, and the hot humid climate in much of Brazil. The largest vineyards are in Argentina and Chile; the aged red wines of Chile are praiseworthy. Some of the cultural factors influencing the types of wines produced in these countries have also been discussed here.

Very good in its way
Is the Verzenay,
Or the Sillery soft and creamy;
But Catawba wine
Has a taste more divine,
More dulcet, delicious, and dreamy.
—HENRY WADSWORTH LONGFELLOW

Chapter 17

THE WINES OF THE EASTERN UNITED STATES, CANADA, AND RELATED AREAS

One of the world's richest floras of the genus *Vitis* is found in the Mississippi Valley, in the eastern United States, and in parts of Canada. Although many native species of vines were growing in the eastern United States, and elsewhere east of the Rocky Mountains, none of these appeared very useful to the early settlers for eating or winemaking. One reason for this was that most of the vines were growing in trees and the clusters and berries were very small and seedy. The grapes had low sugar, high acidity, and distinctive and strange new flavors, the predominant one of which eventually became known as "foxy." It is not surprising, therefore, that many varieties of grapes were brought from Europe to the New World by the early settlers. All these early ventures into the growing of *Vitis vinifera* varieties in the Western Hemisphere failed. There were, and still are, several reasons for their failure to do well in the eastern United States. The most important was (and is) the extremely low winter temperatures in certain years. Another reason was the high humidity of the summer months, which led to infection of the *V. vinifera* vines with mildew, oïdium, black rot, and other fungus diseases and insect pests. Moreover, the root-infesting insect phylloxera was present in this country but not in Europe. It was not immediately recognized that phylloxera was one of the causes of the early failure of *V. vinifera* in the United States, for the causal organism was not identified until the middle of the nineteenth century. Probably virus diseases were also a problem for varieties of *V. vinifera* under the climatic conditions of the eastern and southeastern United States.

Attempts to bring in *V. vinifera* continued in spite of the failures. There are even reports of importations of soil from Europe! A large number of European grape growers and winemakers came to this country with the idea of establishing a wine industry based on the use of varieties of *V. vinifera*. These attempts succeeded for a few years, and a fair quantity of wine was made. But finally each vineyard succumbed to one or another of the causes listed above, and the experiments failed.

The colonists turned to three different methods of acquiring an alcoholic beverage. One was the importation of wines from Europe, especially from the Madeira Islands. Madeiras became the most important wines in colonial America, and the most appreciated. Moreover, many French and German wines were also imported.

Second, large amounts of hard cider were made from apple juice, and eventually applejack, or distilled cider. This became one of the most important alcoholic beverages of the New World. Apples were grown in the New England states and farther south, and there were numerous apple distilleries, particularly in Massachusetts. Wines were made also from peaches and distilled into peach brandy, and New England imported molasses from the West Indies and made rum.

The third type of endeavor to supply alcoholic beverages was the development of the whiskey industry. This is related to the American frontier and its particular demand for easily transportable alcoholic beverages. Whiskey supplied this need better than any other alcoholic beverage except brandy and rum, and it became the most used alcoholic beverage on the American frontier.

Because the attempts to establish *V. vinifera* failed, interest in grapes of the native species gradually increased. Between 1800 and 1852 many attempts were made to domesticate varieties from the native species, such as *V. labrusca* and *V. rotundifolia*. It was found that a rich supply of native grapes could be developed, of different colors, ripening at different periods, and with a sugar content somewhat better than that of varieties which the colonists had first used.

Among the varieties which came from this period were Isabella, Ives Seedling, Delaware, Niagara, Catawba, and the well-known Concord. The Isabella is a red variety with a very strong foxy flavor but of very attractive appearance. Catawba has a tawny red color, again with a rather strong foxy flavor, but not too high total acidity. Ives Seedling is a red variety, one of the most important for the production of red wines in the eastern United States before Prohibition. Delaware is perhaps the least foxy of the older group. It has a pink color and is the main eastern variety which can be made into wine without the use of sugar.

However, the Concord variety finally dominated, and still dominates plantings in viticultural regions of the eastern United States. The Concord is a vigorous grower with good production. Although it is not high in sugar, usually about 16 percent, and has a strong foxy flavor, it appealed to the grower because of its regularity of production and its freedom from fungus and other diseases. It also produces a tasty grape juice and grape jelly which have become the standard in the United States.

Whether all these varieties are pure American species or represent accidental hybrids with *V. vinifera* is not known. A large number of grape breeders and nurserymen were at work in the eastern United States in the early nineteenth century. Some of the new varieties developed during the nineteenth century may have been chance hybrids between *V. vinifera* varieties growing in the nursery and the newly domesticated varieties of American species growing near them. Use of seedlings was common at that time, and makes this more probable. Especially for the Delaware, there seems to be evidence that crossing with *V. vinifera* may have occurred. The new varieties were not the same as those to which the original immigrants had been accustomed in Europe. However, several generations had been born in this country and had forgotten much of the settlers' taste for European wines. The nineteenth century saw the development of a native American wine industry throughout the eastern United States. Wineries were established in almost every state except the northernmost New England states; even the Niagara Peninsula in Canada became an important viticultural region. Wineries were small and sold their wines to a local clientele. There were a large number of these local wineries, and they produced a very wide range of wines from American varieties of grapes. Some of these varieties have unique flavors, and their future on the American market does not seem to have been adequately tested.

From the time of the introduction of the Concord, however, interest in native varieties gradually slackened. The areas devoted to growing grapes in the eastern United States began to decline about the turn of the century. The Prohibition period eventually caused restrictions in grape planting in the eastern United States, although transitory increases occurred after Repeal. Grape plantings in the eastern United States are now mainly confined to five areas and cover less acreage than before Prohibition, although there has been a recent renewal of interest and new plantings.

The most important vineyards for wine-grape production in the eastern states are in the Finger Lakes district of New York state. These narrow and deep lakes ameliorate the winter as well as the spring and summer temperatures. Large areas are planted to vineyards on the lower slopes around the lakes. A few vineyards survive in the Hudson River area, but are not as important. The Finger Lakes region is not only the center of an important grape-producing area but also the center of the eastern wine industry. While most of the grapes are *V. labrusca* varieties, some direct producers and *V. vinifera* varieties have been planted. The direct producers seem well adapted to the region, but the economic status of the *V. vinifera* industry is not yet clear in spite of the enthusiasm of local protagonists. Only time will reveal the final answer, hopefully favorably.

French hybridizers attempted to develop a direct producer which would incorporate the resistance to phylloxera, winter cold, and fungus of American species with the flavor qualities of varieties of *V. vinifera*. This attempt was carried to great extremes in France, and many thousands of hybrids were produced. Many are still planted in France, and a few have achieved recognition for production of quality wines.

The resistance to phylloxera has been lost in many of the hybrids, but some seem to be good producers with a fair degree of cold- and mildew-resistance. Unfortunately, few of them have entirely lost their wild or foxy flavors. Most of the older direct-producer varieties were given the name of the hybridizer and a serial number. In order to have a more salable varietal name, some of these have recently been renamed by the Eastern producers, particularly in New York. Ravat 51 has become Vignoles, Seibel 7053 is now called Chancellor, and Seibel 13053 is now Cascade, for example.

Virtually all the sparkling wines made in the eastern United States come from this region. The sparkling wines made from eastern grapes have achieved a recognition which their non-sparkling counterparts lack. Apparently a foxy flavor in a sparkling wine is not as objectionable or as strange as it can be in a table wine. This region has also developed a process for treating fortified wines with oxygen to remove the foxy flavor. This old French treatment, which was originally proposed for table wines, leads to aldehyde formation and darkening of the color in white table wines (or browning in red table wines), as well as reduction of the foxy flavor. However, it is very well adapted to the production of sherry, since the formation of aldehyde is a desirable part of this process.

In western Pennsylvania and along the shores of Lake Erie in Ohio, a large Concord grape industry has grown up, primarily for the production of grapes for juice purposes. Some of the grapes are used in the local markets as table grapes. Concord grapes do not need to become very sweet for the production of grape juice or jelly, and a stable industry has developed in this region. Recently a number of wineries have been established in Pennsylvania, and a liberalization of state laws has given them considerable local advantage. Some good direct producers and suitable varieties of *V. vinifera* have been planted.

In Ohio, Nicholas Longworth was one of the first to plant vines and was their greatest protagonist. He was especially fond of the Catawba variety, which had been introduced into Ohio about 1826. It is preferred for producing sparkling wines, and although it is tawny in color it is used primarily for white wine.

Along the Lake Erie shore near Sandusky, a wine-producing area was formerly very important. A number of islands just off the coast near Sandusky were planted to wine grapes, and there were several wineries in this area. Only a few of these remain today, and the region is now of much less consequence than it was. The significant factor was the moderating effect of the lake climate on the growing of grapes. This had to do with less winterkilling, as well as warmer conditions during the autumn ripening season. It is not impossible that a quality wine-producing industry could develop in these areas of moderate winter temperatures if the proper varieties were planted. Both direct producers and *V. vinifera* varieties are being tested.

Also because of the ameliorating effect of the Great Lakes, a vineyard area in southern Michigan produces a number of wines from Concord and related varieties, but none have yet achieved marked recognition for quality. Wines were, and still are, produced in Missouri and Arkansas, largely from native varieties. Illinois and other states also have small vineyard areas and produce some wine. Recently varieties of *V. vinifera* have been planted in these areas, and some promising wines have been produced.

In Canada, on the Niagara Peninsula, there are several large wineries and an extensive area is planted to grapes. Not only Concord but a number of other eastern varieties, direct producers, and a few *V. vinifera* varieties are grown.

There is a small vineyard area near Baltimore, Maryland,

where direct producers are grown. One winery in this region converts them into very palatable wines. It would be a grave error to assume that direct producers capable of producing high quality wines cannot be developed. Their use will expand the potential vineyard area available in the United States.

The wines of Canada, as well as those of all the eastern United States, enjoy the privilege of diluting the must with as much as 35 percent by volume of a sugar-water mixture. This dilution reduces the acid content and also dilutes the foxy flavor. It gives these winemakers an economic advantage which California producers do not enjoy.

There was formerly a grape and wine industry based on grapes of *V. rotundifolia* in Virginia and North and South Carolina. These grapes look more like cherries than grapes. They have a distinctive strong flavor, quite different from that of the Concord type of grape. There are still a number of small wineries in this region, but the quality of the wines is ordinary at best, and the industry does not seem to have much future unless the wines can be improved and standardized. However, new plantings in North Carolina and nearby states suggest renewed efforts in this direction.

The long series of experiments in the eastern states to acclimate *V. vinifera* varieties to that area has generally been a failure. Recent experiments in New York state and elsewhere appear to be more successful, but still chancy. The contention that use of cold-resistant rootstocks would permit growing *V. vinifera* scions without winterkilling is not clearly established as a long-range venture. The wines produced, however, have often been good, especially the whites, and one can still hope that *V. vinifera* grapes will be permanently and successfully grown east of the Rockies.

Hence the future of the wine industry in the eastern states seems to be: (1) to produce wine with more or less of the foxy flavor of the *V. labrusca* type of grapes or with the strong flavor of the *V. rotundifolia* type of grapes; (2) to produce blends of foxy-flavored eastern wines and California wines; (3) to produce wines from direct producers; and (4) possibly to make wines from *V. vinifera* varieties. Plant breeders may eventually develop a variety with all the good flavor qualities of *V. vinifera* and the desirable cold- and mildew-resistance of the native species of *Vitis*. This is certainly still in the future.

In the meantime, California wine is shipped to eastern states for blending with native varieties, primarily to dilute their foxy flavor. California grapes are less expensive than those produced in the east, and consequently there is an economic advantage for eastern producers in blending of this kind. One can always determine whether the wine is 75 percent or more from New York state or Ohio, because that is the minimum amount of native wine which is required before it can be labeled with the geographical appellation of the state. Wines bottled in the eastern states which are labeled "American" wines almost certainly contain more than 25 percent California wine. Otherwise they would have the geographical appellation of New York, Ohio, or wherever.

Washington state has a large acreage of Concords, and some *V. vinifera* and direct-producer varieties have been planted. Some of the *V. vinifera* wines have proven promising. Fall frosts may be a hazard for *V. vinifera* in Washington. In Oregon, fall rains pose a problem, as they reduce ripening and favor mold growth. However, a number of new vineyards of *V. vinifera* varieties and wineries have been established and some creditable wines produced.

Summary. —Canada and the eastern United States generally have cool climatic conditions for growing grapes. Most areas are unsuitable for varieties of *Vitis vinifera* because of winter-killing, high humidity, lack of fungus resistance, and susceptibility to virus diseases. European grapes cannot be grown unless grafted on phylloxera-resistant stocks. The strong foxy (methyl anthranilate) odor of many eastern wines, particularly those made from Concord and related varieties, makes them less acceptable to wine tasters who have a preference for wines made from European grapes. Although equally strong and obvious, the unique flavor of the muscadine grapes and their ability to thrive in the humid southeast entitle them to a place in the world of wine.

However, the possibility of acclimating *V. vinifera* varieties and direct producers to conditions in the eastern and northwestern United States and in Canada is still under active study, and one hopes for their success.

"What is the best California wine?" Now it is impossible to answer that question as phrased. The range of wines is wide and the list of different types and their makers is long. . . . —LINDLEY BYNUM

Chapter 18

THE WINES OF CALIFORNIA

The first missionaries from Baja California arrived at San Diego in 1769, and within one or two years vines had been transferred from the missions of Baja California to San Diego. The variety which they brought with them was one of the Criolla type which had originated in Mexico; it was later called the Mission variety in California. The missions had an abundance of very cheap labor and needed wine not only for sacramental purposes but also for the use of the clergy at meals and as an article of commerce. The largest vineyards in southern California seem to have been at Mission San Gabriel Archangel, but all the missions in the southern and central coast counties developed vineyards. The first vineyard failures were at Santa Cruz and San Francisco, and later at Santa Clara. So far as we know, few vines were grown to production at these missions, and the reason is now obvious—the Mission grape would not ripen properly in these very cool localities.

At San Gabriel, wine was produced and a number of brandy stills were introduced in the early nineteenth century. The brandy was used as an article of exchange with ships visiting the Los Angeles harbor, as well as for sale to local settlers. This mission also apparently began the development of a new type of wine, containing three parts of grape juice and one part of brandy, which we now believe to be the origin of the type known as angelica.

The most important enological contribution of the Mission period was to show that vines could be grown in many regions of the state and that the Mission variety was well adapted to the warmer regions. The development of the angelica wine type was also a notable achievement. However, the Mission vine proved to be a late ripener, with inadequate color for the production of red wines and insufficient acidity for the production of table wines. It is possible that angelica was developed because table wines made from Mission grapes often spoiled because of their low acidity.

The secularization of the missions occurred during the Mexican period in 1833, and thereafter the vineyards at the missions gradually deteriorated, though some of the vines at San Gabriel were preserved for a longer period of time. The Mission period was important because it introduced grape growing to the state and showed how widespread was the area suitable for grapes. The idea of producing brandy may also be attributed to this era.

Prior to the Gold Rush in 1848, a number of settlers from Europe and the eastern United States settled in the Los Angeles area. One of them, Jean Louis Vignes, a Frenchman, imported *Vitis vinifera* directly from France in the early 1830s. This is probably the first direct importation of *V. vinifera* into California from Europe. Although we are not certain of any varieties still growing which he introduced, this began a long series of importing varieties directly from Europe, a practice which still continues. Although now subject to quarantine control, the original introductions were uncontrolled and probably served also to introduce to California *from Europe* phylloxera and other pests of grapes not native to areas west of the Rocky Mountains.

Vignes was one of the first large-scale commercial wine producers. The vineyards around and near Los Angeles were used not only for the production of wine but also for table grapes. Even before the Gold Rush, grapes, wines, and brandy were shipped from Los Angeles to San Francisco. A Kentuckian, William Wolfskill, was Vignes' chief competitor in wine production in Los Angeles in the 1840s.

An important viticulturist in the 1850s and 1860s was Agoston Haraszthy, who settled at San Diego in 1849. Haraszthy, a Hungarian, had apparently had some experience with grapes in Europe. At any rate, he was an enthusiastic grape grower and a fascinating, flamboyant figure in western history. He began to develop a vineyard near San Diego and imported vines from Europe in 1851. Before he had progressed very far, he moved to northern California. There he established a vineyard in the region near Crystal Springs, not far from San Mateo. In 1857 he established the Buena Vista vineyard in Sonoma County, one of the largest, if not the largest, of the vineyards established in the state in the late 1850s. His most important contribution, however, was a pamphlet in 1858 on grape growing and winemaking which led directly to his appointment to a committee to study grape production. As a member of this committee, he convinced Governor Downey that a trip to Europe to collect grape cuttings was necessary.

Haraszthy's importation in 1862 of about 200,000 cuttings, as well as his earlier importations of European varieties, was undoubtedly of prime importance for the future industry. Unfortunately, the political temper of the legislature had changed by the time of his return from Europe, and when Haraszthy presented the bill for his trip he was on the wrong side of the political fence. He was never paid for the cuttings. Many were sold and obviously helped improve the varietal complement of California vineyards. There is some evidence that the Zinfandel variety was here before Haraszthy's 1862 importation—from where and by whom is not known. Haraszthy wrote a book about his trip to Europe in which he gave advice on the growing of grapes and the making of wine. He had one of his sons trained in France in the production of sparkling wines. The development of sparkling wines at Buena Vista, while not the earliest in California history, was one of the most important.

The vineyard area increased rapidly in all parts of the state in the period 1860 to 1900. Among the early vineyardists were General Vallejo, near the present town of Sonoma; Sutter, of

Sutter's Fort (now Sacramento) fame, who was of Swiss origin; Drummond, in the Sonoma County Valley of the Moon, of English origin; Wilson, at Los Angeles, from Ireland. The Wentes in Livermore Valley came from Germany, as did Krug in the Napa Valley, and Kohler, the pioneer wine merchant of San Francisco. Captain Gustave Niebaum, who developed Inglenook (in the Napa Valley), was a Finn. The huge German colony at Anaheim, started in 1857, planted one of the largest vineyards in the state. This vineyard was destroyed by Pierce's disease in 1888.

Some of the best white varieties of the Livermore Valley were imported directly from Bordeaux, and some of the original Sauvignon blanc vines survived until after World War II. The immigrants brought with them European methods of growing grapes, making wines, and labeling them according to European nomenclature; the use of European appellations for American wines has plagued the industry ever since.

During the period 1860 to 1900, grape growing expanded rapidly in all parts of the state—from Escondido near San Diego to Vina, Senator Stanford's huge vineyard in northern Sacramento Valley. Heavy plantings were made in Sonoma and Napa counties, near Livermore, and in Fresno County. The Zinfandel was especially popular and became the most widely planted red wine variety by 1900.

However, the industry soon suffered from overproduction and a period of reduced prices. This up-and-down economic curve has been the picture of the California industry from about 1870 to the present, and may cloud the foreseeable future. The early industry suffered from planting the wrong varieties, from failure to harvest early enough, and from poor control of fermentation, particularly of the temperature. The predominance of the Mission variety was partially responsible for the poor wines. In 1862 the California Wine Growers' Association was founded to deal with these problems. It was particularly concerned with reducing the tax on California wines and increasing the tax on imported wines; these have been consistent objectives of the California wine industry since that date. Haraszthy made two trips to Washington to lobby for the industry, with some success.

Still, from time to time overplanting inevitably occurred. The wine quality was often poor, not only because of the Mission variety but because of the inexperience of the new winemakers. The first depression lasted from 1876 to 1878: wine sold at 10 to 15 cents a gallon, and many vineyards were abandoned.

In 1880 two progressive steps were taken: the California legislature provided funds for research in viticulture and enology at the University of California, and established a Board of State Viticultural Commissioners.

The University's research was under the direction of Professor Eugene Waldemar Hilgard. Hilgard recognized at once two of the critical problems: the adaptation of varieties to the different climatic regions of the state, and the much warmer conditions in California compared to Europe. It was these warm climatic conditions which led to the harvesting of grapes after full maturity. Musts of the high-sugar, low-acid grapes would not ferment completely dry, and these slightly sweet, flat wines spoiled easily and rapidly. As late as 1900 salicylic acid was widely used to prevent spoilage, and the practice ceased only after the passage of the Pure Food and Drug Act of 1906.

Between 1880 and 1892, Hilgard attacked the varietal problem in a masterful study of the composition and quality of the musts, and their wines, of the major varieties of grapes growing in different regions. These studies established the importance of grape variety to the quality of the wine produced, and no doubt had a salutary effect on the generally high quality of the grape varieties in the vineyards of the state before Prohibition. Hilgard was also known as a determined protagonist of high quality wines and of better winemaking practices. He was, accordingly, not popular with some of the commercially oriented wineries.

The Board of State Viticultural Commissioners began at once to try to change the public attitude toward California wines. They carried on educational activities, sponsored conventions, published translations of important European enological treatises, and wrote reports on industry statistics and problems. Although the legislature abolished the Board in

1894, its work was important. The Wine Institute, and formerly the Wine Advisory Board, performs some of the services of this original Board.

This Board also led the fight against phylloxera, which had appeared in Sonoma vineyards in the 1870s. The legislature specifically delegated the Board to establish quarantines to prevent spread of the pest. The present California plant quarantine regulations date from this legislation. The second depression in wine prices occurred in 1886 and lasted until 1892; this too was partially due to the sale of poor quality wine.

The depression of the 1890s led to the formation of the California Wine Association, financed by San Francisco businessmen. A very large and modern aging and bottling plant was constructed at Richmond, in Contra Costa County. They purchased wine from wineries throughout the state, often at prices more or less of their own choosing, and sold them under their own label throughout the United States. It has been said that the California Wine Association never sold a bad bottle of wine or a great bottle of wine. However, they certainly had the highest standards of any of the bulk distributors of wine, and in Henry Lachman they had one of the finest tasters of wine which the California wine industry has produced. Lachman's legendary abilities were supposed to include infallibility in identifying wines of different varieties and from different districts.

The California Wine Association had one of the first chemical laboratories and analyzed the sugar content of the new wines. Charles Ash, as the chief chemist of the Association, became a recognized authority in the industry. Since residual sugar was one of the most important causes of spoilage of wines in the state, work on this problem was a great help in preventing spoilage and improving quality. A winery was constructed in the Fresno area for the production of dessert wines. The Association was supposedly ruthless in controlling the market and did not favor competition.

Two other large wineries were established around the turn of the century. One in northern California, north of Santa Rosa at a town called Asti, was established by San Francisco philanthropists for Italian-Swiss colonists who were unable to find work in the San Francisco area. They planted vineyards and built a large winery; both prospered. They became well known, especially for their Tipo chianti, in the pre-Prohibition period. Later, apparently at the suggestion of the Italian government, this became simply Tipo red and Tipo white. Immediately after Repeal they were probably the best-known American wines.

In southern California a large vineyard and winery under Italian philanthropists was developed near Ontario. The Italian Vineyard Company at one time had about 4,000 acres of grapes. Because of sandy soil and lack of water, the vineyards had a low yield. The company planted a large number of good varieties of grapes and made many different types of wines.

Many small wineries with high standards made and bottled wines which were widely distributed in the immediate pre-Prohibition era. In fact, the demand for California wines seems to have been good between 1895 and 1918. Some of this demand was probably due to the 6,000,000 wine-drinking southern European immigrants who entered the United States between 1901 and 1915.

However, with the approach of Prohibition these wineries began to go out of business, and during Prohibition only a few were still in existence. Most of the wineries were dismantled, although some kept their cooperage. A few, perhaps six or seven wineries, continued in limited business for the production of wines for sacramental and medicinal purposes.

Prohibition did not have the effect which had been predicted. Instead of the price of grapes dropping, it went up. The reason for this increase was the unexpected and very large demand for California grapes on the eastern markets. These grapes were intended for the production of wines at home, which was still legal at that time. Unfortunately, most of the premium-quality thin-skinned red wine grape varieties were unsuited for shipment to the eastern seaboard, and there was a rapid change-over in varietal plantings to meet the demand for red wine grapes in the eastern United States. The most sought-after variety was the Alicante Bouschet, which had a skin thick enough to stand shipment and an intense color so that, after the juice was drawn off, sugar and water could be added and a second wine could be made which would still be red. It is estimated that some eastern winemakers were able to make as much as 600 and even 700 gallons of "wine" from a ton of grapes by this method. Unfortunately, the wine of Alicante Bouschet lacked quality (poor flavor and unstable color). This replanting had the unfortunate effect on the industry of reducing the acreage of the finer wine grape varieties, especially of the better whites, as they were grafted over to red varieties which shipped well but produced ordinary quality wines.

Prohibition had other influences: there was a gradual decrease in drinking of wines with meals at home and, of course, no wine was legally served in restaurants. The winemakers, having lost their profession, moved into other fields; so at the time of Repeal, although it was only fourteen years after Prohibition, there was a serious shortage of trained winemakers. The distribution system of wines had completely broken down. When Prohibition was repealed, a new type of distributor appeared in the wholesale business in many areas: the converted bootlegger. Bathtub gin had reduced the taste of Americans for wines, and homemade wine often did little to reverse the trend. Consequently, at the time of Repeal in 1933 the industry found itself with vineyards planted to varieties of grapes which would produce only ordinary qualities of wine, without an adequate amount of cooperage in which to ferment the wine, without enough well trained winemakers to make the wine, without a distributing system in the hands of trained personnel, without retail stores and wine waiters in hotels and restaurants to sell and serve the wine, and, most important, without a clientele familiar with California wines or any other wines of quality.

Repeal, therefore, did not bring the expected boom to the California wine industry. During the great flurry of winemaking in 1933 and 1934, nearly 800 wineries were established in California, many by men with little experience in producing wines and few with experience in producing wines which could be aged. The standards of the new industry were frankly low, partly dictated by the poor quality of the available grapes, but mostly because of the poor methods used to produce the wine. Some of this wine was rushed onto the market, and naturally the consumers found it unpalatable. Then the price of wines fell and the price of grapes declined to uneconomic levels: the new industry was suddenly in the throes of another economic crisis.

To solve these problems, the industry established the Wine Institute, a nonprofit organization composed of most of the wineries of California. The Wine Institute continues to exist, with its main office in San Francisco. Its first and most important activity was to deal with the multitudinous problems which the Twenty-first Amendment to the United States Constitution brought to the alcoholic beverage industry. Under this Amendment, much of the control of alcoholic beverages reverted to the individual states. Each state set up a little trade kingdom of its own and established new and often different and difficult rules for the importation of wines and other alcoholic beverages into the state. Many of these rules had to do with the percentage of alcohol, putting a special tax stamp on the bottle, and irrational and excessive taxes on wines. To protect the supposedly important local grape and wine industries, a number of states, especially Washington and Michigan, established high import duties on wines from other states.

The Wine Institute's legal department was active throughout this period in trying to reduce these inequalities. The Institute also set up a wide program for the improvement of standards in California wineries, and now has a technical staff to deal with sanitation problems and the evaluation of new methods and equipment. The Wine Institute was also responsible for the advertising of California wines in general, through its public relations program, and has done much educational work and published many pamphlets on the use of wine. A correspondence course on wine and wine appreciation has been especially successful.

The California Department of Public Health, through its Food and Drug Inspection Division, was also active during this period. It established standards for California wines aimed primarily at preventing the dilution of wines with water and the sale of wines of high volatile acidity or vinegary character. Enforcement was fairly strict, but as the wineries improved their practices, enforcement gradually became less necessary. This agency later sponsored better sanitation practices in California wineries; the federal Food and Drug Administration also participated in establishing the winery sanitation program.

The University of California, primarily through its Department (then Division) of Fruit Products at Berkeley, instituted a wide range of training programs and conferences for raising the standards of the California wine industry. Professor W. V. Cruess and his staff organized classes for potential winemakers. These had a salutary influence, but many small wineries remained outside the scope of the program and continued to produce poor wines. In trying to improve the quality of California grapes, the Department (then Division) of Viticulture at Davis was active in the same conferences, and instituted a long-range program of research aimed at showing the growers the importance of planting better varieties of grapes for making high quality wines. These activities continue. Most of the research and training in this field are now in the Department of Viticulture and Enology, which is part of the College of Agriculture and Environmental Science at the University of California, Davis. Research and teaching are also conducted at California State University, Fresno, in the Department of Agricultural Industry and Education. Enological and viticultural research in California now covers a wide range of fundamental and applied projects and serve as the major American source of technical information in these fields. Enological experiments on grape pigments, polyphenolic compounds, and aroma-producing compounds, factors influencing color extraction and stability, controlled fermentation and aging, submerged culture of *flor* sherry, use of *Botrytis* mold for sweet table wine production, fractional blending, malo-lactic fermentation, variety evaluation, new antiseptics and clarification agents, brandy production, waste disposal, use of concentrate, automation of winery operations, and sensory examination of wines have been or are under way. Viticultural research on acid formation, effect of mold attack, maturity, development and evaluation of new varieties, and the influence of rootstocks, fertilizers, irrigation, pruning, and other practices on grape maturity and wine quality and on automation of vineyard operations, is in progress.

When the surplus of grapes was most acute in 1938, the Bank of America and the federal government organized a prorate program which was aimed at distilling wine and removing it from the market. This program was pursued energetically during that year, and millions of gallons of wine were converted into brandy. Had it not been for this program, many wineries could not have operated during the 1938 season, so tenuous was the financial position of the industry at that time. In the normal course of events this prorate brandy would not have been easy to dispose of, since surpluses each year would have had to be converted into brandy. However, World War II created a market for almost any alcoholic beverage, and all the prorate brandy was gradually moved into the channels of trade and disposed of before the end of the war.

The men of the industry felt at this time that they were not getting adequate advertising. Under a law which permitted a small tax on all California wines prepared for market, the Wine Advisory Board was established under the Director of Agriculture of the State of California. Over two million dollars of tax per year was collected in this program, most of which was used for trade promotion, public relations, and advertising. However, under the terms of the State Marketing Act some of the funds were used for research to improve the quality of California wines, and the Wine Advisory Board sponsored an important research program for this purpose. Much of this research was on the medical aspects of wine— some of it to counter the attacks on the wine industry by those who claimed that wines cause disease, and the rest on constructive research on the beneficial effects of wine in certain kinds of medication (see also Chapter 20). The Wine Advisory Board ceased to exist on July 1, 1975.

The prosperity which World War II brought to the California wine industry ended abruptly in 1947 when the price of wine dropped very rapidly throughout the state. The activities of the Wine Advisory Board continued throughout the nation, but the industry was far from prosperous from 1947 to 1960. However, the consumption of wine increased slightly, and there were no extreme years of very low or very high prices. By 1960 surpluses of grapes were again developing, and the federal government established the so-called set-aside program of 1961, which was continued into the 1962 season. This program called for setting aside a certain percentage of the wines or brandy or concentrate from the San Joaquin Valley, the main surplus area of grapes, and later disposing of these products into other channels of trade. Most of the surplus was disposed of in the form of alcohol for industrial purposes. It is not certain what the future of this type of program will be, but the likelihood of developing methods of removing such surpluses to profitable channels of trade outside the wine industry does not seem very favorable.

The most important tendency of the California wine industry since World War II has been the trend toward centralization. A few wineries have gradually absorbed the middle-sized wineries, so that five or six companies now control about 75 percent of the total production of California wine. Recently several of these large winery companies have been purchased by national or international companies with broad food and beverage interests. The centralization trend for ordinary wines has definite economic advantages. Larger equipment can be used and the cost per gallon can be markedly reduced. This gives the larger winery an economic advantage over the smaller winery, and gradually the latter finds it impossible to continue in business for standard wines.

The logical development, then, is for the smaller winery to turn its attention to the production of high quality wines which are unsuited to the processes used by the larger wineries, and this seems to be what is happening in the industry at the present time. There are perhaps thirty to forty wineries producing wines on a rather large scale; another fifty to one hundred wineries produce high quality wines primarily for bottling and selling at good prices. A number of small family wineries and wineries for local trade (Figures 36 and 37) still continue, and will probably survive. The future of the industry seems to lie with a few highly industrialized wineries producing wines at competitive prices, some wineries producing higher quality but widely distributed wines, and a number of wineries specializing in premium quality wines.

The California wine industry today includes a number of large firms with national distribution and advertising which sell bottled wines of sound character at less than $2 per bottle. These are labeled with generic names—burgundy, chablis, rhine, sherry, or port—or with varietal names, and provide a good value for the money.

Several wineries with national distribution market wines in the $2 to $3 range. They sell both generic and varietal wines. These wines are considerably better values than most

Fig. 36. Vineyard in the Santa Cruz Mountains. (Source: The Wine Institute.)

FIG. 37. Barrels and oak ovals for aging table wines in an underground cellar. (Source: The Wine Institute.)

of the imported wines in the same price range. Recently some have carried a vintage date.

Some small wineries in the state may sell a special wine locally and sell the rest of their produce in gallon containers. Occasionally these special wines are high quality products. We remember a Zinfandel of a small winery which was as fruity and characteristic as one could wish. Formerly these wineries sold most of their wine in bulk to larger wineries and sold only a small amount locally under their own label. Now they bottle a greater percentage of their wine for direct sale.

There are many California wineries whose main efforts are directed toward the production of the finest quality varietal wines, often labelled with geographical origin and the vintage date; these may be priced at $3 to $8 or more per bottle. They may also simultaneously market generic and nonvintage wines of lesser quality in the $1.50 to $3 range. We do not mean to imply that every $5 vintage wine is great and every $1.50 nonvintage wine less fine. In individual cases the opposite may be true; but in general, one gets about what one pays for.

Because of the favorable climatic conditions for growing grapes to produce high quality table wines, the best California wines are produced in the cooler coastal counties: Mendocino, Sonoma, Napa, Alameda, Santa Clara, San Benito, Monterey, and Santa Cruz. Recently, especially large plantings have been made in Monterey County. Currently, new plantings in Lake, San Luis Obispo, Santa Barbara, and San Diego counties are believed capable of producing quality table wines. Vineyards with varietal grapes have also been planted in areas where the climatic conditions are too warm for production of high quality table wine.

The best California table wines, for reasons already outlined in Chapter 3, are labeled with the variety from which they are produced. The best dessert wines are produced from grapes grown in the warmer districts. A renewed interest in premium dessert and appetizer wines would be a favorable development and seems to be starting to gather momentum.

Summary.—The California wine industry was established during the Mission period. The variety planted, the Mission, was a poor one for table wine production but was suited to the production of angelica, a fortified dessert wine. Many European vines were imported between 1830 and 1862. Haraszthy was an important figure in popularizing the planting of new varieties after about 1860.

The center of the first commercial industry was Los Angeles, but this gradually shifted to northern California in the 1860s. Vineyards were planted throughout the state at an increased rate between 1850 and 1880.

The industry suffered a severe depression in 1876 and again in 1886, because of overplanting and wines of poor quality. However, aided by the efforts of the Board of State Viticultural Commissioners and the University of California's College of Agriculture, the quality gradually improved.

The early winemakers brought European winemaking practices and nomenclature with them. Use of foreign names for California wines still plagues the California industry.

Prohibition had a severe effect on the industry, because the vineyards of fine varieties were gradually grafted to varieties which could be shipped to distant markets without spoilage. It also drove trained winemakers into other professions, allowed the cooperage to deteriorate, disrupted distribution channels, and interrupted consumers' acquaintance with California wines.

Repeal, however, showed the industry to have much resilience. A severe depression in prices in 1937-38 required federal assistance. The Wine Institute (and Wine Advisory Board) have had important influences in solving the industry's legal, economic, technical, and public relations problems. The University of California's College of Agriculture has supplied scientific information and trained personnel.

Recently the industry's production has become more centralized. A few wineries now produce and distribute most of the standard competitive wines, and a number of smaller wineries produce the higher quality, more expensive wines. Many of these wines have gained a worldwide reputation for quality. Both types of wineries produce wines which represent some of the best buys for the American wine consumer. Increased demand raised prices very rapidly in the early 1970s, but increased supply from new wineries and expanded vineyards (150,000 acres of wine grapes too young to bear in 1973) should return excellent wines to relatively reasonable prices in the next decade. Continued emphasis by consumers on appreciation of high quality should aid the California industry in its efforts to raise both the average and the ultimate wine quality level.

It is hoped that California sherries and dessert wines will regain some of their former popularity. The potential diversity and high quality in this large group of wines deserve some recognition, even as one applauds the popularity of table wines. The recently authorized shift from 20 percent to 18 percent (17 percent for sherries) alcohol is a step in the right direction, making the wines lighter, less heady, and hopefully more attractive to the connoisseur as well as the ordinary consumer.

When the wines were good they pleased my sense, cheered my spirits, improved my moral and intellectual powers, besides enabling me to confer the same benefits on other people.   —GEORGE SAINTSBURY

Chapter 19

WINE APPRECIATION, EVALUATION, AND SERVICE

The most important requirement of any wine is that it give pleasure. However, appreciation of wines is dependent on two factors. It involves not only the composition of the wine itself but also the attitude and experience of the consumer. Those who drink wines or other alcoholic beverages to excess can have little or no real appreciation of quality. It is also true that the newly initiated wine taster has a very limited range of appreciation; he or she may like only one or two wines, or may change preferences from one tasting to another.

In the appreciation of quality in wines, as in the appreciation of any aesthetic creation, a learning curve is involved. At first we like products which are easily recognized and understood. Later, with more experience, we demand greater complexity in foods, music, or art for aesthetic appreciation.

Just so with wines: at first the simple, white (low tannin), slightly sweet, low-alcohol type of wine seems to be the easiest for the new consumer to appreciate. This is probably one reason why the German Liebfraumilch has been so popular in this country; it is low in alcohol and rather highly sugared. Of all the German wines, it is among the least complex. With time, however, the drier, more flowery, and more distinctive varietal California white table wines (or those of the Moselle, Rhine, Alsace, Loire, Chablis, Graves, etc.) are preferred.

And from whites there seems to be a progression in the learning curve to reds, and specifically to older reds. The consumer who has never tasted a red wine which has been aged in the bottle for ten or fifteen years can have very little concept of the additional quality gained by such aging. But to the connoisseur, an old bottle of California Cabernet Sauvignon wine, one that has been in the bottle for ten or fifteen years, has an incredibly richer and more complex aroma and has assumed a very different character from that of the wine when it was younger. With such complex wines, repeated tasting does not bring satiation but reveals new aspects of quality.

To summarize, then; quality in wines is associated with complexity, and this is not easily achieved without special techniques, as in the production of the *Auslese* wines of Germany or the Sauternes of France; or the use of very great varieties, such as the Chardonnay for the white Burgundies; or the use of great varieties and aging, as in the red Burgundies and red Bordeaux, or in a California Pinot noir or Cabernet Sauvignon.

But it would be foolish to say that quality was altogether in the wine. The appreciation of quality is in the consumer, and one's experience with wines will determine his or her appreciation of them. Some people appreciate one type of wine more than another. Many people in England do not care for the richer, more alcoholic wines of Burgundy; and many people in the Burgundy region or in Belgium do not care for the harder, drier, more acid and tannic wines of Bordeaux. These preferences are due primarily to differences in experience, but some of them seem to depend also on differences in individual temperament.

The eclectic taster, however, is one who has had experience with many wines and has learned to appreciate different types. The claim of some Europeans that the wines of California or of South Africa or of Australia are not of high quality is based largely on the fact that they have had very limited experience in tasting these wines, and particularly the better wines of these regions. It would be the same if an American went to France and formed an opinion of all French wines on the basis of a single tasting of an ordinary red in some small restaurant in Cette or Bezier in the wine district of the Midi, the *vin ordinaire* district.

Wine appreciation demands quality in the wine and critical experience and evaluation from the consumer.

The problem of wine classification is simple compared to the problems of wine appreciation and evaluation. We receive impressions from the world about us through our senses. As far as wines are concerned, our impressions are based upon visual, olfactory, gustatory, and tactile sensations, and from our mental synthesis of these sensations comes appreciation. The visual appreciation of wines is one of the important aspects of wine evaluation. Not only is there an aesthetic appreciation when the wine is an appropriate and beautiful color, but our subsequent evaluation of quality will be based partly upon what we see. Visually, we are aware of two aspects of wines: appearance or clarity—that is, freedom from suspended material—and color. The clarity of wine is frequently a good indication of its condition.

Wines should be brilliantly clear when served. Most commercial wines are now filtered before shipment and normally reach the consumer in brilliant condition. Occasionally a white wine becomes cloudy, particularly slightly sweet wines such as Graves. This is usually due to growth of yeasts in the wine. If it is pronounced enough to give the wine a yeasty odor or to make the wine gassy, it is a negative quality factor.

Wines may have a slight haze if they were not processed under cool enough conditions to remove the excess cream of tartar which young wines contain. In some wines, tartrate crystals may be found in the bottom of the bottle. Such wines may be decanted and served free of the crystals. Even though the tartrate crystals have no harmful effect on the flavor, they are aesthetically unappealing.

Red wines after some years in the bottle will develop a precipitate of coloring matter. This is unavoidable and is almost a guarantee of the age of the wine. In old wines it is thus not considered a negative quality factor. However, if the deposit is disturbed and clouds the wine, it detracts from the appreciation of the wine. By proper decanting it is usually possible to serve a brilliant wine.

Color is one of the most attractive aesthetic features of wines. Wines come in many different colors, and the different types of wines have their appropriate color range. An acceptable California rosé is neither too light nor too dark in red color. If it is on the light side and has a brown or orange tint, we can be sure that it has become somewhat oxidized or been aged too long. And if it is on the purple side, that is, too dark, it is probably rather bitter for a rosé (owing to having been left on the skins too long); or it may be very young, have been made from certain red-purple varieties, or be too high in pH. One learns only by experience the appropriate color for each type, but in general the white table wines should be free of brown color, since browning usually indicates excess oxidation and the development of vapid or aldehyde-like odors. The young red table wines should certainly have a full red color, but a slight browning (shift toward orange) of the color is expected in old red wines.

Dessert wines come in an even wider range of colors, all the way from the very light yellows of a young *fino* sherry to the very dark-amber colors of some Marsalas. Among the reds are wines with a very slight amber red, as in the California tokay, to the very deep purple-red of a young vintage port. In the older red wines, a certain amount of browning of the color is permissible.

The accompanying tabulation indicates the desirable ranges in color and preferred usage of different types of wines.

There are many acceptable variations which such a list cannot show. Old reds—Cabernet Sauvignons, for example—have a definite amber tint. The tint must be appropriate not only to the type but to the age of the wine. Within the sweet baked sherry group there are wines almost pure gold in color and others very amber.

	Preferred color	Preferred usage
WHITE TABLE		
White Riesling	greenish yellow to yellow	with fish and entrée, with meats; apéritif
Chablis	light yellow	
Chardonnay	yellow to light gold	
Sauvignon blanc	yellow to light gold	
SWEET TABLE		
Auslese types	light gold to gold	with cheeses, fruits, desserts
Sauternes	light gold to gold	with fruits, desserts
Tokay (Hungarian)	light gold to amber gold	
Rosé	pink (no amber or purple)	with fish and entrée, with meats; apéritif
RED TABLE		
Pinot noir	low to medium red	with meats and cheese
Cabernet Sauvignon	medium red	
Zinfandel	medium red	
SHERRY		
Fino (flor)	light amber yellow	apéritif
Oloroso	brownish gold to amber	desserts or after meals
Dry baked	light amber	apéritif
Sweet baked	medium amber	with desserts or after meals

The "made" wine types, such as Marsala, *flor* sherry, Madeira, baked sherry, and dessert wines in general, thus may have a color appropriate to the standards of the producer. Even within a single type, say port, the winemaker may produce a variety of subtypes, each with a distinctive color.

As beautiful and appropriate as color is, it is an external matter. The most important quality factor is the odor—more important than taste because of the almost infinite variety of

	Preferred color		Preferred usage
RED DESSERT			
Tawny port	amber-red	⎤	with cheese, fruits,
Ruby Port	ruby red	⎦	desserts, or after meals
WHITE DESSERT			
Muscatel	light amber-gold to gold	⎫	
Tokay (California)	pink-amber	⎬	with fruits, desserts, or after meals
White port or angelica	medium yellow	⎭	
Madiera	medium amber	⎤	apéritif or dessert
Malaga	dark amber	⎬	with desserts or
Marsala	dark amber	⎦	after meals
VERMOUTH			
Dry	light yellow		apéritif or in cocktails
Sweet	medium to dark amber		with desserts or after meals; in cakes
CHAMPAGNE			
Red (Rouge, sparkling burgundy, or Cold Duck)	red		with meats, cheese
Rosé	pink	⎫	apéritif, with fish and entrée, with meats and cheese, fruits, desserts
White	light yellow	⎭	

delicate, subtle differences which are possible. Odor consists of inappropriate or undesirable odors and natural and appropriate odors. The olfactory sense can distinguish around 4,000 or even more different odors! Connoisseurs who have studied the wines of a given district for many years are able to detect differences in odors between wines of different vintages and wines from different vineyards. The amateur, even the educated amateur, who does not study the wines of a given district thoroughly and carefully, rarely acquires such an appreciation of the differences between vintages and vineyards. Although a good deal can be learned about the differences among wines from their color, certainly among different types but also between wines of the same type, difference in odor is the critical factor in evaluating or differentiating wines. Since the sensitivity to odor of the amateur is generally as good as that of the professional, there is no reason why the interested wine drinker cannot learn to identify a wide variety of vinous odors if he or she acquires sufficient experience. One cannot identify an odor one has not experienced.

The good or desirable odors of wines come from the variety of grape from which they are produced, from the byproducts of alcoholic fermentation, and from treatments given during aging or by the aging process itself. The odors originating in the grape we call aromas; those from processing or aging, bouquet. The varietal aromas we expect are particularly important in wines named after the variety of grape from which they are produced. Thus we expect muscatels to have a muscat aroma, Cabernets to have a Cabernet aroma, Rieslings to have a Riesling aroma, and so on. In many regions of the world, all the wine of the region is made from a single variety of grape and thus, even though the bottle may not have a varietal label, we expect it to have a varietal aroma. This is true, for example, of the Burgundy region of France, where Pinot noir is the predominant red variety planted: thus we expect the red wines of Burgundy to have a Pinot noir aroma. The same thing is true of the wines of the Bordeaux district, where the variety designation is omitted, except for some wines for export. A Cabernet aroma is to be expected, since Cabernet-type varieties of grapes predominate in this region.

Fermentation odors are the background odors that we find in all wines. They are apparently due to ethyl alcohol, higher alcohols, and small amounts of a large number (about 250 odorous, volatile substances have been identified from wines) of compounds, particularly esters. These compounds give the wine its grapy and winy (vinous) character. Further reactions among the grape aromas, the fermentation byproducts, and compounds extracted from the wood change and develop new odors, i.e., give the aging changes.

The odors which are due to treatments given during aging or to the aging process itself are often of great importance. Among such odors are those due to baking of Madeiras or California sherries, the odors resulting from the addition of boiled-down grape juice, as in the Marsalas, and the odors arising from the activities of a *flor* yeast, as in Spanish sherries and *montillas* and California, South African, Soviet, or Australian *flor*-type wines. For odors due to aging, we have the gradual disappearance of fermentation odors during short periods of aging. The characteristic odors of red table and dessert wines continue to develop during long aging. One effect of aging seems to be due to the dissolving of a slight amount of the flavors from the wood, especially important in red table and dessert wines and in brandies. There also seem to be special odor constituents, possibly from amino acids and esterification, which are slowly formed during aging. Wine in the bottle develops special odors called bottle bouquet. These odors are much desired, particularly in old red table wines and vintage ports, and they are also to be looked for in fine, white Burgundies, California Chardonnay or Sauvignon blanc, most Sauternes, and the sweeter German wines.

The most common off-odors found in wines are fermentation or yeast off-odors which often involve hydrogen sulfide and mercaptans. These usually disappear owing to oxidation and aeration during the early aging of the wine. Occasionally, however, a wine retains more than a threshold amount of the fermentation off-odors. We sometimes object to too much higher alcohol in fortified wines; however, a recognizable amount seems to be favored by producers of Portuguese ports. This emphasizes the difference in standards. The consumer who is willing to appreciate a variety of wines obviously will find more wines to enjoy.

Off-odors resulting from excessively warm fermentations, called pomace odors, are usually found only in red table wines. Off-odors can arise from the use of moldy grapes or containers. The most common off-odors are due to excessive oxidation in table wines or to the use of too much sulfur dioxide as an antiseptic agent. Many German, most Graves, and some other white wines, particularly of the cheaper competitive domestic types, contain excessive sulfur dioxide. The newer antiseptic agent, sorbic acid, has a slight off-odor and produces an undesirable geranium-like odor when attacked by bacteria in the wine. Formerly a good deal of acetic acid was present in table wines, but since Pasteur, particularly since 1900, it is rather rare to find a bottled wine which has an acescent or vinegary smell. However, in countries where wine is still produced on small farms or distributed in bulk, some wines may have a vinegary odor. Actually this odor in wine is due more to excessive ethyl acetate than to acetic acid, but it is easily recognized as being a vinegary type of odor.

At present few wine disorders are permitted to develop to the stage where an off-odor develops. Yeastiness has been mentioned as one possible odor if sufficient yeast growth occurs (or if wines are bottled very soon after fermentation). Off-odors from lactic acid bacteria are occasionally found in wines from Burgundy and from Italy. There seem to be, however, some desirable odorous byproducts from a properly conducted malolactic fermentation of a red wine by a desirable strain of lactic acid bacteria.

If the grapes are not picked soon enough in California and in regions of similar climate, a raisin-like odor may occur. Also, very late-harvested grapes of low total acidity and high pH have an undesirable odor.

Occasionally, particularly in red table wines that have been bottled for a number of years, the cork may communicate an off-odor to the wine. Corkiness is a very undesirable odor, reminiscent of moldiness, and when unmistakably present is sufficient excuse for refusing the wine in a restaurant. On the other hand, we have found it to be extremely rare.

Excessive aeration of table wines, particularly of white table wines, leads to an oxidized or aerated odor. While this may be desirable in some dessert wines, it is not in table wines. With whites it is accompanied by a brownish tint.

Table wines occasionally have excessive woodiness from over-aging in small cooperage. A slight woodiness is desirable in some red table wines, in brandies, and in many dessert wines, but not if excessive, especially in white table wines, not even in a flavorful wine such as Chardonnay.

In contrast to the multiple nuances of odor which we are able to distinguish, we seem to be limited to four taste characteristics: sour or acid, sweet, bitter, and salty. Wines rarely have a salty taste, although wines from the Colares district, on the Atlantic seaboard near Lisbon, may have a salty taste. It has been reported in certain wines from the south of France, from Italy, and in highly plastered wines (those to which gypsum has been added to lower the pH).

The sour or tart taste, despite the frequent opinion of the amateur, is a very necessary and desirable part of the taste of the wine. The amateur's negative reaction is less likely to occur if the wine is consumed with food. Without acidity the wines would be exceedingly flat, would be subject to bacterial spoilage, would not ferment as well, and would not have the lovely yellow and red colors which give so much pleasure. However, the acidity must be appropriate for the type. In some wines we expect more acidity than we do in other types of wines. Rieslings taste fresher and fruitier if they have a rather high total acidity. All dry white table wines require a recognizable degree of acidity to give them interest. In red table wines we wish a moderate acidity, but they should not be too tart, since their tannin may accentuate tartness. Excessively high acidity in sweet table wines or in dessert wines is not desired, since a distinct sweet-sour taste tends to be unpleasant. However, some individual variation in reaction to the sweet-sour taste does occur. Furthermore, the sweetness is usually sufficient to add a dominant note of interest to the wine, and acid is more likely to be too low than too high in dessert wines, for climatic reasons. Where the sugar content is low, as in dry sherries or dry vermouths, the processing and herb flavors provide a focus of interest. This does not mean, however, that sweet table wines and dessert wines should not have reasonable acidity. Many dessert wines are too low in acidity—some Málagas and California tokays, for example—and thus taste flat and uninteresting or cloying.

The sweet taste in wines is due primarily to the presence of two sugars, glucose and fructose, as well as to the higher alcohol glycerol. Fructose is considerably sweeter than glucose, but in most sweet wines they are present in about equal proportions. The sugar threshold (minimum delectable concentration) for the sweet taste in wines is somewhere between 0.75 and 1.5 percent, depending on the sensitivity of the individual. Wines with less than 1 percent sugar are usually noted by the wine judge as being without sweetness. This sweet taste is partially masked by acids, and vice versa.

The sugar content of different wines should be appropriate for the type. It is customary for most ports to have 10 to 14 percent sugar. The Soviet Union, however, produces a number of dessert wines with over 20 percent sugar, and the wines of Málaga are often equally sweet. The wines of Sauternes may range from 5 percent to as much as 15 percent sugar. In sparkling wines, the driest kinds have only about 1 percent sugar and are labeled *brut*. The *sec* (or dry) types may have as much as 3 percent sugar, and some even sweeter types of sparkling wines are occasionally produced. The driest sherries are actually somewhat sweet, usually with 1 to 2 percent sugar. The same is true of most of the dry vermouths, which have as much as 4 percent sugar.

Table wine connoisseurs tend to "look down their noses" at sweet wines. It is true that defects in wine are easily masked by raising the sugar content, particularly in sparkling wines. Thus the connoisseur has the assurance that when a table wine is dry and very good, it is also very honest. This is not entirely a fair comparison, however, because sweetness is not an undesirable taste and it is not out of place in certain kinds of wines. Sugar is inappropriate in wines which are intended to be drunk with foods. Here the presence of sugar tends to appease the appetite and thus reduce the enjoyment of food. Certainly with our meals we need wines which are quite dry, just as we normally eat foods before dessert which are not sweet. A number of

California red wines contain 1.5 percent of sugar; this low amount of sugar probably does not have a major effect on appetite. Unfortunately, however, the tendency seems to be to sugar content of over 1.5 percent in table wines, as in many German, South African, and European white table wines and in standard California white, rosé, and red table wines.

Though it is not normally appreciated by new wine drinkers, with experience consumers do develop an appreciation for a moderately bitter taste. The bitter taste in wines is due to some tannins, flavonoids, and probably other compounds. Since white wines have a very low tannin content, they are also generally nearly free of a bitter taste. Even in rosé wines the tannin content is so low the wines have only a slightly bitter taste. Only in red wines, particularly young red wines, is the tannin content high enough to be noticeable to the taste. Modern technology can reduce the tannin content of young wines so that it will not be objectionably high. However, the tannins act as antioxidants in the wine and help protect it against overoxidation during aging in the bottle. In addition, the side products of the oxidation of tannins may lead to the development of desirable flavors in red wines after they have been bottled. However, even a well-aged red wine retains a slightly bitter taste which is not objectionable to the connoisseur.

A related but separate sensory response is to astringency, which relates to the "feel" of the wine rather than to the bitter taste. A "smooth" wine is one lacking in astringency and a "rough" one is too high in this character. Red wines may be made very astringent, resembling a green banana or persimmon in their "puckeriness," but such wines should not reach the consumer and may be corrected by shorter fermentations with the skins, by proper fining, or by longer aging.

A great deal has been written about the *body* of wines. Often this seems to have been based on the feel or texture of the wine. It is difficult semantically to define body. We prefer to think of it as a measure of the alcoholicity of the wine, which is expressed in the degree of "wateriness" or the viscosity of the wine. A wine of low alcohol would then be said to have a low body or have a "thin" feel. Wines of higher alcohol content would not be thin. It is almost impossible to react to this alcoholicity, within limits, if the wines are very sweet. High sweetness makes it difficult for the palate to distinguish the body, (or alcoholicity) of the wine. Nevertheless, the term "body" is useful if it is restricted to the meaning we have indicated. Certainly its use as a measure of the glycerol content is not correct. The amount of glycerol in wines is only slightly above the glycerol threshold, and in the presence of sugar the sweetness of the glycerol is completely covered. The total of the non-sugar solids is related to the body, since this is higher the greater the alcohol content.

The trigeminal or free nerve endings in the nose may be stimulated by excess sulfur dioxide, causing sneezing. Some other constituents of special wines may stimulate the pain receptors, e.g., in wines of high aldehyde content.

Theoretically, if wine tasting has been properly done, the visual, olfactory, gustatory, and tactile impressions should comprise all the sensory characteristics of a wine. However, *flavor* is a useful term for the synthesis of taste and in-mouth odor. A number of odorous characteristics do not come to the attention of the wine taster until the wine has been placed in the mouth and its temperature raised; among the most important is the fruitiness of the wine. While this is measured somewhat by the degree of acid taste, it may be related also to the presence of a small amount of leaf aldehyde or other fruity aromatic constituents.

When we say that a wine has a hot taste, this may refer to excessively high ethanol or to a flavor characteristic of aldehydes or other compounds. The earthy character of wine is rarely perceived until the wine has been in the mouth several seconds. While this is apparently an odor, it is usually perceived along with other mixed sensations and can properly be spoken of as a flavor. The earthy flavor is found in wines made from grapes grown on certain types of soil. Wines which have been left on the yeast too long (so that there has been excessive yeast autolysis) will sometimes get a rotten type of flavor which is perceived with difficulty when present at threshold concentrations. The "corked" characteristic of many wines should be noted early in the tasting under the "off-odors," but sometimes it is not perceived until the wine has been tasted. This is true also of the moldy taste of wines which have been made from moldy grapes. If the examination has been properly done, the sensory impressions should summate to give the quality of the wine. However, this does not seem to be true, for when scorecards are used the wine does not seem to be quite the sum of the individual sensory impressions. This implies that there is a sensory summation which may be called "general quality." This has also been demonstrated by a mathematical technique known as factor analysis; hence the characteristic known as general quality, although not precise, does seem to have some justification. The aftertaste or finish of the wine is also important, although we do not know its precise parameters. Lack of extreme bitterness is the most obvious. As a first approximation, "general quality" can be thought of as the sum of the aftertaste and the "overall" impression of the wine.

The amateur wine taster will not wish to bother with the elaborate scorecards used in the sensory examination of foods. However, he may wish to use a simple scorecard when attending wine tastings, visiting wineries, or for comparative home tastings. Scorecards have another advantage in that they force the taster to examine the wine systematically and not to forget any of its characteristics. We suggest a simple scorecard with twenty points; European wine scorecards also have twenty points.

The visual aspects, appearance and color, are rated at two points, or 10 percent each, for a total of 20 percent. The visual aspects are more important to some tasters, and especially with some white wines may be worth more than 20 percent. The olfactory characteristics of aroma and bouquet and the vinegary smell add up to six points, or 30 percent of the total. The two points for flavor and the two points for general quality are partially based on olfactory sensations; so, of the total score, at least 40 to 50 percent is probably due to olfactory sensations. The gustatory characteristics are rated under acidity, sweetness, and bitterness for five points, or 25 percent of the total.

Again, a certain amount of the flavor and general quality is based on gustatory sensation; hence taste is approximately 30 percent of the total. The texture or feel sensations get only one point, or 5 percent of the total.

SCORECARD FOR WINE

APPEARANCE	2
Cloudy 0, clear 1, brilliant 2	
COLOR	2
Distinctly off 0, slightly off 1, correct 2	
AROMA AND BOUQUET	4
Vinous 1, distinct but not varietal 2, varietal 3 or 4	
Subtract 1 or 2 for off-odors, add 1 for bottle bouquet	
VINEGARY	2
Obvious 0, slight 1, none 2	
TOTAL ACIDITY	2
Distinctly too low or too high for the type 0, slightly high or low 1, normal 2	
SWEETNESS	1
Too high or low for the type 0, normal 1	
BODY	1
Too high or low for the type 0, normal 1	
FLAVOR	2
Distinctly abnormal 0, slightly abnormal or deficient 1, desirable for the type 2	
BITTERNESS AND ASTRINGENCY	2
Distinctly high 0, slightly high 1, normal 2	
GENERAL QUALITY	2
Lacking 0, slight 1, impressive 2	

As a guide to the consumer, we suggest that wines of outstanding characteristics should score seventeen to twenty points. Sound commercial wines with no outstanding defect or merit will normally score thirteen to sixteen points. It is not likely that many commercial bottled wines for sale in this country will have less than thirteen points; however, wines of nine to twelve points are of commercial acceptability, but with a noticeable defect. Obviously the effective scoring range for most commercial wines falls within a range of no more than ten points. This is probably about the maximum quality range which can be categorized.

Sometimes the consumer (and often the producer) will wish

to know whether there is a really noticeable difference in some identifiable characteristic between two specific wines. Since the odds are 50 percent that one or the other wine may be correctly identified in a single blind trial by guessing, it is necessary to repeat the test in order to make sure that there is a statistically significant difference between them. In a test with two wines where they are presented together, both wines must be correctly identified in nine out of ten tests to be significant at the 5 percent level. Significance at the 5 percent level means that only once in twenty times would such a result be due to chance. Other methods of determining differences between two samples to standardize blends, etc., are outlined by Amerine and Roessler, (1976).

If more than two wines of the same type are to be judged for quality on a single occasion, it may be desired to rank them in the order of their merit. The difficulty in a ranking procedure is that not all the judges may have the same quality standard in mind for the wines. If one judge considers the appearance and color to be exceedingly important aspects of the quality, he may rank the wines on the basis of their freedom from sediment and their conformity to the proper color for the type of wine. Another judge may feel that appearance and color are of minor importance and may judge the wines primarily on odor or on taste. It is unlikely that the rankings of the two judges will conform well. The averaging of their ranks will certainly not give a good measure of the relative merits of the wines. The judge who ranks mainly on visual aspects may rank the wines BCDAE, while the judge who ranks on odor or flavor may rank the wines EADCB. The average rank is then the same for all the wines! Therefore, all the judges should clearly understand the basis of the ranking. We suggest that only experienced judges will get meaningful results in ranking.

Even after the ranking has been done, however, we have no information on how much difference there is between the wines. For example, there might be two very good wines and one exceedingly bad wine. In the rankings these would rank "one," "two," and "three," and we would think that the difference between rank two and rank three was the same as the difference between rank one and rank two, but of course it is not.

Evaluation of wine quality is not an easily acquired art. A good deal of practice and comparisons of various wines are necessary for the taster to gain confidence in his opinions. The best way to acquire this experience is in the company of an experienced person who knows the difference between the qualities of different wines and can explain the reasons for his evaluations. This can sometimes be obtained from the personnel at wineries. However, since winery tastings are an adjunct of the winery's public relations program, the relative quality of the wines is rarely explained. In some wineries, both foreign and domestic, all the wines of the particular winery are said to be of the highest quality, which may be patently untrue.

There are occasional reliable evaluations of wine quality in the literature. However, many of these are out of date almost before they have been published, since the wines are now too old or no longer available. Also, the evaluations of wines in the popular journals are frequently written, or ghostwritten at least, by writers who are working for one or another part of the industry and might be somewhat biased.

When the wine judgings at fairs and expositions have been made on a true quality basis and not on a ranking basis, they are sometimes a good indication of quality. Many wine judgings lack validity, for they are not made by experts and the representation of wines of a district or country is far from complete. The methodology formerly used at the California State Fair was probably as good as any. It involved an elimination step for each type, then a ranking step. The average rank was then placed on the wines, and in a third test the appropriate medal was awarded: gold, silver, etc. The system is described in an article by Amerine and Ough (1964). The professional judgings in Australia, Hungary, Yugoslavia, and South Africa also seem to be well done, although in some cases too many were judged each day or the judges were overly generous in awarding medals.

However, in the final analysis, quality is an individual matter and must be determined by each consumer. Thus, some consumers may like the Pinot noir better than Cabernet Sauvignon. Others may prefer well-aged tawny ports to the more fruity ruby ports; some may find the more flowery German white wines better than the French white wines. Actually, an appreciation of the differences among wines is worthwhile since it increases one's range of enjoyment. To refuse to taste Pinot noir because one prefers Cabernet Sauvignon deprives one of the very real merits of Pinot noir.

One can often obtain useful insight into the producer's opinion of the style and quality level of his wine by the packaging he uses. For example, bottles made slightly misshapen and splattered with paint to suggest great age have generally contained very disappointing wines. Most of the great wines of the world depend on the wine itself for their reputation, and except for ensuring protection and authenticity, the bottle-stopper-label combination is not unusual. Characteristic bottle shapes are shown in Figures 38 and 39. Other bottle styles such as the traditional straw-bottomed fiasco of Chianti are disappearing, owing to higher costs of the bottle and its use. The cylindrical shape of the Bordeaux-style bottle (Figure 38) is very utilitarian for stacking during aging, etc., and is widely used. It is especially appropriate for Cabernet Sauvignon, Sauvignon blanc, and other wines of the Bordeaux type. The shape originating in Burgundy is slightly more bulbous (Figure 38) and is especially appropriate for burgundy, Pinot noir, and Chardonnay wines. Except for stronger glass and a different crown or cork finish of the neck, the typical champagne bottle (Figure 39) is similar to the bottles for burgundy. White wines from the varieties originating in Germany, such as White Riesling, are usually placed in the elongated rhine-type bottle (Figure 38). Appetizer and dessert wine bottles (Figure 39) usually are similar to the Bordeaux shape except they frequently have a more bulging neck and are commonly closed with a wood-topped, replaceable cork or screw top.

The traditional bottle sizes in English-speaking countries have been splits (6.4 oz.), half bottles (12.8 oz.), fifths (or 1/5 gallon, 25.6 oz.), magnums (2/5 gallon, 51.2 oz.), and jeroboams (4/5 gallon, 102.4 oz.). These are being replaced, the wine industry leading United States industries in "going

Fig. 38. Bottles and glasses for different types of wines. From left
to right: rhine, Bordeaux (tenth, fifth, and magnum),
burgundy.

metric," by seven metric sizes: 100 ml. (3.4 oz.), 187 ml. (6.3
oz.), 375 ml. (12.7 oz.), 750 ml. (the standard bottle, 25.4 oz.),
1 liter (33.8 oz.), 1.5 liters (50.7 oz.), and 3 liters (101 oz.). How
much wine should be served with a meal varies with the guests,
the length of the meal, etc. Usually half to one bottle (a "fifth")
per person of all the wines served is sufficient. For tastings involving several wines, no more than 30 or 40 ml. per serving
will be required; thus a 750 ml. bottle should serve 20 to 25
people.

Some wines, especially well-aged red wines, are often
spoiled between the cellar and the table. The reason for this is
that the wines gradually throw a small deposit as they are aged
in the bottle, and if care is not taken, the deposit will be stirred
up in moving the wine from the cellar to the table. The wine
then appears on the table in a cloudy condition. The other
aspect of poor wine service is the fact that wines are often
served too cold or too warm.

Bottles of wine with no sediment can be stood on end and
brought directly to the table. They can be poured directly

FIG. 39. Bottles and glasses. From left to right: dessert wine, sparkling wine with crown cap finish, brandy.

from the opened bottle. Wine coasters on which the bottle can sit are desirable to prevent staining of the table linen.

But for wine that has any sediment at all, special care must be taken in bringing it to the table. In white wines the amount of sediment is normally small; it is usually crystalline and very heavy. If the bottle is placed on end a couple of hours before opening, the sediment usually drops to the bottom. Only the last glass may get a few tartrate crystals. It is with old red wines that we have to worry about service. The types of deposit in red wines are of many kinds. They may be fairly granular or adhere well to the sides of the bottle. Or the deposits may be very light, finely divided, and easily disturbed: these latter require the most care. An old bottle should be lifted up and viewed over a candle or a small electric bulb (preferably unfrosted and with filaments) to inspect any deposit present. If there is deposit, the bottle should be laid on a table without having been turned to the right or left from its original position. It can be placed in a basket; but usually this does not help, for the bottle has to be tipped up to get it into the basket, and this disturbs the sediment. Generally it is best to simply lay the bottle on a table and put an object on each side to prevent it from turning. The neck end of the bottle should then be raised about an inch from the horizontal so that a slight air-space develops under the cork. The corkscrew is inserted and the cork removed carefully, without turning or shaking the bottle. The bottle is then raised, still nearly horizontal, and a candle or small electric light bulb (again not frosted and with naked filaments) is placed under the neck. The wine is then slowly decanted into a clean dry decanter or bottle. As soon as the sediment reaches the neck of the bottle, the decanting is stopped.

Decanting is always necessary with old wines which contain sediment. The decanting should not be done more than one hour before the wine is to be served. Very old wines should be decanted immediately before serving, as the wine rapidly loses its bouquet.

Some wines—such as many young whites, rosés, Beaujolais, and red Italian—profit by decanting, particularly if they are gassy or contain a slight residual fermentation odor. The advantage of decanting is that they lose the gassiness and fermentation odor.

Some of the many different types of corkscrews are illustrated in Figure 40. We personally prefer those which have a secondary-lever action. It is most important that the screw on the corkscrew be fairly wide and that the screw be long enough to reach entirely through the cork. This is particularly important where the corks are 2 to 2¼ inches long. The open spiral corkscrew without a center rod is also usually more satisfactory. Recently a simple apparatus (Figure 40, lower left) using carbon dioxide under pressure has been developed. A hollow needle is inserted through the cork and a little carbon dioxide released between the wine and the cork, thus pushing the cork out of the bottle. Because of the danger of the bottle exploding, we prefer corkscrews. However, a small hand air-pump attached to a hollow needle is also available, without the danger of the high pressure from compressed carbon dioxide. A double-prong type of cork remover that allows one to both remove and replace corks is now on the market.

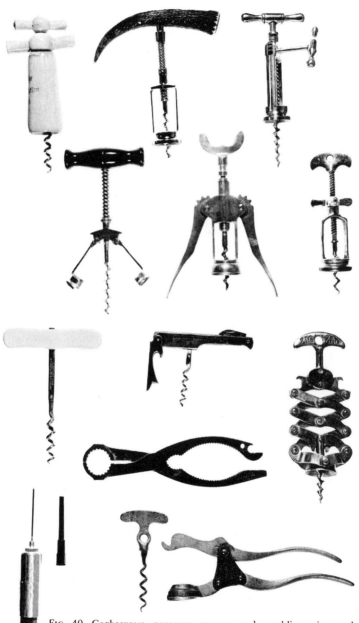

FIG. 40. Corkscrews, pressure opener, and sparkling wine cork opener.

ıble wines should be chilled to about 55° F. (12.8°
serving. Sparkling wines are best served at about
0° C.). Rosé wines and most dessert wines require
v... ight chilling to about 60° F. (15.6° C.). Red table and
old port wines should be served at a cool room temperature,
65° to 68° F. (18.3–20° C.).

Wine glasses are of many shapes and colors. The more
common types are shown in Figures 38 and 39. For everyday use, a clear tulip-shaped glass holding six to eight ounces
(180 to 240 ml.) is satisfactory for all wines. For more formal
occasions when several types are served, a variety of glasses
may be used. For dessert wines, four-ounce glasses (such as
in Figure 39, left), may be used; for white table wines, four-
to six-ounce glasses (Figure 38, left pair); for red table wines,
eight- to ten-ounce glasses (Figure 38, right pair); for champagne, tulip-shaped or hollow-stem glasses (Figure 39, center).
The brandy snifter (Figure 39, right), is useful for critical
evaluation of wines or brandies, but the all-purpose glass is
better for drinking. Colored glasses should never be used, for
they prevent proper appreciation of the wine's color.

Wine glasses should be washed with detergent in hot water,
thoroughly rinsed in soft hot water, and allowed to drain dry.
If a wiping cloth is used, it should be lint-free and thoroughly
rinsed and dried. No water stains should remain on the glass.
The sturdier types of glasses can be washed in dishwashers.

Most of our best red wines, particularly California Cabernets, Bordeaux, Burgundies, and Rhones, are being consumed too soon. They would greatly appreciate in value by
longer aging. White table wines, on the contrary, are sometimes kept too long. We prefer to err on the side of drinking
white wines too young rather than too old. By this we mean
within one to five years of bottling; some heavier-bodied and
sweeter types may profit by longer aging. It should be kept
in mind that in both white and red table wines there are two
extreme styles: the fresh, fruity picnic wines and the complex,
mature dinner wines. The picnic style is intended to be consumed young and may change without improvement if aged
too long. The dinner style may, however, be harsher and dis-

appointing if consumed too young. Many wines are intermediate and can be consumed satisfactorily early or late, but some attention should be paid to the winemaker's recommendations. Cellars for wine storage should have an even temperature throughout the year, preferably 55° to 60° F. (12.8–15.6° C.), with coolest storage for white table wines, cool for red table wines, and the warmest of the range for dessert wines or wines you wish to hasten in aging. The bottles should be laid on the side with no air bubble next to the cork.

The climatic conditions under which the grapes are grown influence the composition of the grape and hence the quality of the wine. Under the cool conditions of northern Europe, this is particularly important. In the cooler years the grapes fail to ripen, have excess acidity, and are deficient in flavor. Hence the warm years produce the best wines. For Germany the last great years were 1969, 1970, 1971, and 1975; however, good wines were produced in 1966 and 1973. The last poor years were 1965, 1967, 1968, 1972, and 1974. For France in Bordeaux, Burgundy, and Champagne, the best recent vintages were 1966, 1969 (except in Bordeaux), 1970, 1971, and 1975 (except in Burgundy). Some good wines were produced in 1967; the vintages of 1965, 1968, 1972, and 1973 were generally poor. For the Rhone, about the same holds true: 1966 and 1967 were generally very good; 1969 to 1972, good; 1968, 1974, and 1975 were ordinary. While differences in table wines produced in different years occur in Spain, Italy, Switzerland, Portugal, Austria, and other countries, these are not so well documented and the buyer must establish the quality by tasting or by consulting a knowledgeable wine merchant. Blended wines, such as sherry, Madeira, Málaga, and Marsala, cannot be vintaged. Vintage port is, however, important. Generally the best ports are from the cooler years. For example, 1969 was a failure in the Douro, but good elsewhere in Europe. The best recent vintage port years were 1960, 1963, 1966, 1967, and 1970.

Even in the best years, not all the wines are superior, and in the poorest years some fine wine may be produced. No one should be a slave to vintage labeling, but one can get some guidance from the above list of vintage years.

In California many wineries do no vintage labeling. The producers say that restaurants do not understand why a certain vintage wine cannot be kept in stock. Also, changing the vintage means that the wine list must be reprinted. Salesmen and wholesalers object because they must carry more wines in stock. The producers claim that the legal restrictions in labeling vintage wines are a nuisance and not worth the trouble (records, etc.). They also prefer to maintain a uniform quality from year to year.

However, the vintage is very important from the consumer's point of view, and we believe there should be more use of the vintage on the better California wines, particularly on varietal wines from the cooler climates. The vintage date is a guarantee of the age of a wine. It also enables the consumer to reorder and get the same wine. It is, therefore, important in building brand loyalty.

It is true that spectacular differences do not occur between years in California. However, 1948, 1962, 1967, and 1969 seem generally to have been less satisfactory, and 1951, 1958, 1968, and 1970 more satisfactory than average years. Also, wineries differ in their success with a given vintage. One winemaker may pick too early and produce a less satisfactory wine than his neighbor who waited; or, vice versa, the winemaker who waited to harvest may have been caught by prolonged rains and his wines may be poor. Thus even in years when most wines were fine, as, for example, 1959 in Europe and 1958 in the Napa Valley, some poor wines were produced. Even in poor years, some are more successful than others. We remember, for example, a 1948 Cabernet Sauvignon of Napa Valley which was excellent, while many neighboring wines were of ordinary quality.

Summary. —The factors influencing wine appreciation have been outlined in this chapter, particularly the importance of experience. The actual evaluation depends on color, appearance, olfactory properties, taste, and other sensations.

Simple scorecards, difference tests, and ranking are recommended; for best utilization they require experience.

Simple rules for the service of wines have been presented, particularly with respect to decanting, temperature of serving, and storage. Although a summary of the quality of recent vintages has been given, this is not to be taken too seriously. The proof of the quality of a wine is in the bottle, not on the label.

> *The Persians are accustomed to deliberate on matters of the highest moment when warm with wine. . . . Whatever also they discuss when sober, is always a second time examined after they have been drinking.* —HERODOTUS

Chapter 20

WINE AS ALCOHOL

Physiological, psychological, and social ills can result from the excessive consumption of alcoholic beverages, wine not excluded. There are two main types of excessive drinking; the acute episode—drunkenness—and the longer-term chronic condition—alcoholism. The problems associated with excessive drinking, particularly alcoholism, are complex, and informed opinions differ as to causes, prevention, or cure. Yet, products do not survive in commerce unless consumers consider them useful and desirable. A large segment of the adult population values alcoholic beverages, as shown by their long-continued and wide popularity in spite of a very long history of legal or religious prohibitions, exorbitant taxation, and many other restrictions. Part of this value attaches to their flavor and attractiveness as beverages, and part to their content of alcohol. In this chapter we are concerned with the latter, the effects on the drinker of beverage "alcohol"—that is, ethanol or ethyl alcohol.

Some critics have questioned the inclusion of this subject in a book celebrating wine. For several reasons we think it very appropriate. Many people use alcoholic beverages successfully, pleasurably, wisely, and healthfully. We want us all to remain in that group, and we believe wine has particular advantages toward that aim when it is consumed in the recommended ways. It is only in recent years that the voices of reasoned "permissivists" have been widely heard over the clamor of the restrictionists and prohibitionists. Surely it is healthful to understand the dangers and benefits of alcoholic beverages so that one can avoid the one and enjoy the other. Research upon both benefits of moderate and risks from excessive alcohol consumption has now given a much clearer picture, although more information is certainly needed.

Ethanol produces physiological and behavioral effects in normal individuals. This has been known since beverages containing alcohol were discovered. The term "spirits" and the German term "Weingeist" (brandy) hark back to the ancient belief that the spirit, ghost, or "soul" in wine enabled the consumer to communicate with the heavenly and/or nether worlds. Even in recent times, primitive cultures—some not so primitive—often reserved alcoholic beverages for priests. If they were available to the populace, their consumption was as a rule on infrequent special occasions, usually a communal "religious" orgy in which drunkenness prevailed, sometimes for important cultural as well as economic reasons.

Ethanol acts as an irregularly descending depressant of the nervous system—irregular in the sense that there is no simple linear relationship between the size of the dose consumed and its effect, and descending in the sense that the effects of alcohol tend to appear as a reversal of evolutionary processes. The higher levels of cortical control are inhibited first. This helps to account for the fact that a physiological depressant has been considered a stimulant. Alcohol is often a social stimulant because inhibitions on social behavior may be suppressed. Something one wishes to do, but ordinarily would repress, may be done more easily after consumption of a certain amount of alcohol. Imagine the stimulation of the social climate if everybody at a cocktail party lost their inhibitions to the point of speaking frankly about everybody else. In a more serious vein, this effect may be used deliberately or unconsciously by criminals to allow them to commit acts that they would otherwise be afraid to do. If so, many jurists believe, the legal intent to commit the act was there, and the man, not the ethanol, should be blamed.

Let us consider first the short-term effects of consuming ethanol. The symptoms of the influence of alcohol on the human system, and of intoxication, depend upon the amount, kind, timing, and rate of alcoholic beverage consumption. The common symptoms of intoxication are an alcoholic breath, flushed face, dilated pupils, obvious changes in gait, noticeable abnormality in speech, and a significant level of alcohol in the blood—which is the single best indicator of the state of sobriety or intoxication, and probably of behavior. It would, of course, take a larger amount of ethanol (or any other agent) to produce a given blood level, and therefore a given effect, in a larger person. A petite young lady matching drink for drink with a football-player will regret it sooner than he, if the indulgence is intemperate.

The blood level is expressed in grams of alcohol per 100 milliliters of blood, or percentage (v/v). A rough guide to probable condition of the drinker at different blood levels of ethanol is:

0 −0.03 g./100 ml.		Dull and dignified
0.05−0.10 g./100 ml.		Dashing and debonair, or delightful and desirable
0.15	g./100 ml.	Daring and devilish
0.20	g./100 ml.	Dangerous and disheveled (obviously intoxicated)
0.30	g./100 ml.	Delirious and disgusting (reeling stupor)
0.40	g./100 ml.	Dead drunk (coma)
0.45 + g./100 ml.		Dead

(Note the rather narrow margin between an unconscious drunk and death.)

If the level of alcohol in the blood is less than 0.10 g./100 ml., the person is unlikely to be intoxicated. At 0.20 g./100 ml., he is unlikely to be sober.

Most American states have adopted similar laws regarding automobile driving and alcohol. The driver with 0.05 g./100 ml. or less ethanol in the blood (or other body fluid) is automatically presumed not to be under the influence of alcohol. At 0.10 g./100 ml. the person is automatically considered to be under the influence of alcohol and an illegal driver. Between the two levels, behavior and circumstances will be considered. The traffic court may decide either way, but no presumption is made. Utah and Idaho have an upper limit for legal driving of 0.08 g./100 ml., and some countries use 0.05 g./100 ml. American statistics indicate that at 0.05 g./100 ml. the probability of being responsible for a fatal automobile accident. is essentially the same as for control (nondrinking) drivers, but at 0.10 g./100 ml. it is 7 times, and at 0.15 g. of alcohol per 100 ml. of blood 25 times, as likely that the drinking driver will be responsible for a fatal accident as the nondrinking driver. The fatality is often his own.

It is interesting and probably not happenstance that the amount of alcoholic beverage that is considered a usual portion or serving contains about the same amount of alcohol regardless of the beverage. One gulping swallow is about 30 ml. (or about one fluid ounce). The usual serving is about 12 oz. for beer, 1.5 oz. for distilled beverages, 4 oz. for table wine, and 2.5 oz. for dessert wine. Considering their usual ethanol content, these would contain about 13, 15, 12, and 11 g. of alcohol, respectively. The average-sized person should not therefore consume more than one "drink" on an empty stomach to be certain of legal driving (0.05 g./100 ml.) soon thereafter. On the other hand, to reach the 0.10 g./100 ml. blood level, a 170-lb. (77 kg.) man would need to consume at least 70 percent of a standard bottle of table wine (750 ml.), or four beers, or 6 oz. of 80 proof whiskey, rather rapidly and on an empty stomach. It would seem that such consumption would not be accidental.

Individuals differ in their response to the same level of alcohol in the blood, and the same individual may react differently at different times. Although 0.15 g./100 ml. in the blood is considered the limit for reasonable normal behavior, about 10 percent of a large group of people behave as if drunk before reaching this level. Impairment with respect to some activities can be demonstrated at lower blood levels (0.03 to 0.10 g./100 ml.). A few cases have been reported of clinical sobriety at 0.4 in the blood and survival after blood levels in excess of 0.5 g./100 ml. Regular heavy drinkers *may* develop some tolerance, but their general debility often leads to lower tolerance to alcohol. The performance of some tasks (such as timed solving of arithmetic) *may* by improved by *small* amounts of alcohol. Probably this is due to decreased tension and nervousness, and increased confidence.

Consumed ethanol is absorbed very quickly and efficiently. About 20 percent of the dose may be absorbed from the stomach, which is an unusually high percentage compared to other foods. The remainder of the alcohol consumed is absorbed in the small intestine, with none excreted in the feces. The entire amount consumed is ordinarily in the bloodstream within about two hours, and peak blood level is likely to be reached within 30-45 minutes if the stomach is empty. Ethanol is rapidly distributed in all body liquids. Body fluids total about 30 liters, or nearly 8 gallons per 100 pounds (45.4 kg.) of body weight, and this figure will enable one to estimate the blood level and effect of given doses of alcohol. For example, if a 150-lb. man (68 kg. body weight, 45,000 ml. of body fluid) drank a bottle of table wine (750 ml. at 12 percent v/v), he would have consumed 90 ml. of ethanol. The density of alcohol at room temperature is about 0.8 g./ml., therefore 72 g. of alcohol were consumed. When uniformly distributed in his body fluids, the maximum blood level would be $72 \div 450 = 0.16$ g./100 ml. He would be obviously intoxicated. Again we note that individuals differ. And, of course, weight is a factor.

The form and manner of consumption of alcohol affect its absorption. Presence of food in the stomach delays absorption. Ethanol in the range of 10 to 35 percent solutions is most rapidly absorbed. Lower concentrations delay absorption, owing to dilution; higher concentrations produce pylorospasm and prevent passage from the stomach. If consumption is continued, regurgitation results. Carbonated mixtures are more rapidly absorbed because the pylorus, the stomach exit valve, is relaxed by carbon dioxide solutions, and rapid passage into the intestine hastens absorption. Such nostrums as cream before drinking to increase safe capacity have little value except as they serve as diluents or affect the pylorus. Solid foods and fats are retained in the stomach longer than watery fluids. Maximum delay in complete absorption and, therefore, lowest peak blood levels of alcohol for a given consumption are obtained by a combination of solid foods plus a reasonable volume of diluents—that is, a meal. The alcohol absorbed into the body is only 2 to 10 percent excreted via the lungs and kidneys. The remaining 90 to 98 percent is completely metabolized to carbon dioxide and water. Combustion of ethanol to carbon dioxide and water produces about 7 "large," nutritional, or kg.-calories of energy per gram, whether by metabolism or by burning. A 3-ounce serving of dry table wine or champagne supplies about 60 calories; of sherry or dessert wines (depending on sugar content) about 120–170 calories; and one ounce of brandy about 80 calories. In contrast, a 6-ounce serving of cola beverage contributes about 85 calories, a 1.5-ounce jigger of whiskey about 120 calories, mixed drinks about 110 to 320 calories per serving, and a 12-ounce bottle of beer about 170 calories. A convenient rule of thumb is that 1° proof, or 0.5 percent of alcohol, yields, on the average, about 1 nutritional calorie per one-ounce serving.

The liver contains an enzyme, alcohol dehydrogenase, which produces acetaldehyde from alcohol. This product can be noticed in the odor of the breath of intoxicated persons (ketosis). The acetaldehyde is converted enzymatically to acetyl co-enzyme A, an acetic acid derivative. This substance is also a major product in the catabolism of fat, sugars, and some other dietary constituents, and is part of the normal metabolism of the body. The first step in the liver is the limiting one in clearing the alcohol from the system. The rate of this reaction is only about 0.1 g. of ethanol per kg. of body weight per hour, or about 7 g./hr. in the average man. Coffee and most other "sobering-up" treatments help little or none in speeding up the rate. This rate is approximately equivalent to two-thirds of a bottle of 80 proof whiskey in 24 hours. This amount of alcohol supplies about 1,200 calories—near the normal dietary need for energy. It is no coincidence that the terminal alcoholic often consumes about one bottle of strong spirits per day and eats little food.

Let us now turn to the regular consumption of alcoholic

beverages. In moderate doses, repeated only at reasonable intervals, the effects of alcohol appear to be completely reversible with no known detrimental effects. In fact, a number of studies of large numbers of people have shown that abstainers tend to die slightly younger than moderate but regular consumers of alcoholic beverages. Of course, regular heavy drinkers as well as sporadic heavy "spree" drinkers had a detectably higher early mortality rate than abstainers. Clearly, there are ways of drinking that do not result in alcohol problems and in fact can enhance health and longevity. Moderation appears to be the key, and excessive, high-blood-level drinking should be avoided. What constitutes moderate drinking? Still one of the best criteria seems to be Anstie's "safe limit" proposed in 1864: a daily limit of 1.5 oz. or about 35 g. of ethanol (3 oz. of whiskey, 3 bottles of beer, or half a bottle of table wine), to be taken only with meals, and the whiskey is to be well diluted. Among U.S. adults, 42 percent drank less than once a month or not at all, 49 percent drank under 1 oz. of ethanol per day (considered light to moderate), and only 9 percent drank more, according to 1972-74 surveys. Thus, about one out of five frequent drinkers is approaching or exceeding a safe limit, but 91 percent of the population does not normally approach this limit.

Alcoholic beverages and wines in particular have a long and honorable history of usefulness in both lay and formal medical therapy. With the development of modern, more specific, and more potent drugs, use of alcohol in medicine has declined but has not disappeared. Alcohol has been said to be the most thoroughly studied, most valuable, and safest tranquilizer. It helps reduce pain, anxiety, and tension. In a palatable form such as wine, it can serve as a tonic. Use of wine, especially for the aged or convalescent, can lend interest and flavor to the diet as well as a psychological and social lift. The appetite and feeling of well-being can be stimulated. Dry wine can be a source of nonsugar (mainly from alcohol) calories as well as dietary variety for diabetics and others on restricted diets. Wine is normally low in sodium and high in potassium (unless excessively stabilized by sodium ion-exchange). This, and alcohol's effect in dilation of peripheral blood vessels, make wine worthy of consideration for persons with arteriosclerosis and hypertensive vascular conditions. Alcoholic beverages, moderately used, may help induce sleep, stimulate gastric secretion, and produce mild diuresis. Properly handled and with consideration for contraindications (e.g., stimulation of gastric secretion is highly undesirable in the gastric ulcer patient, and alcohol puts an extra load on a damaged liver), alcoholic beverages and particularly wines have medical utility. Of course, when alcoholic beverages are to be used by an ill person the advice of a physician should be sought.

Alcoholism is a very serious problem. Reliable statistics are few, but it has been estimated that about two-thirds of the adults are regular consumers of alcoholic beverages in the United States. Of these, about 9 million are considered problem drinkers or alcoholics. The costs of misuse of alcohol, including public support of dependents of alcoholics, clinics, prisons, lost production, and accidents have been estimated to total $25.4 billion annually in the United States.

Alcoholism is not easy to define, but it implies a compulsion to drink alcoholic beverages that is so strong and so frequent that it leads to serious and continuing undesirable personal and social consequences. There is good reason to believe that many of the people who become alcoholics are compulsive—needing escape or gratification—before they take a drop. The feelings of well-being, the apparently diminished pressure of circumstances, and perhaps the complete oblivion eventually achieved during drinking episodes seem to afford means of escape from their problems. The pain and shame of returning to normal may add to their need for escape and reinforce the pattern. The self-administration of alcohol with the objective of blunting reality seems to be a dangerous practice, compared to familial use as a mild euphoriant and social lubricant. In the incipient stages, the origin of alcoholism seems to lie in the realm of personality defects. However, if alcohol becomes the major part of the caloric intake, as it often does, nutritional deficiencies contribute to metabolic breakdown and further psychological or neurological lesions.

They may also contribute in the form of "cravings" misinterpreted by the afflicted person and driving him to further drunkenness instead of the needed food.

Since the liver is the key organ in metabolism of alcohol, and alcohol metabolism may make up nearly all of the liver's activity in a heavy drinker, it is not surprising that the liver can be damaged by heavy drinking. Many alcoholics show reversible fatty liver conditions, some develop alcoholic hepatitis, and a few after five to twenty years of heavy alcohol intake develop cirrhosis. In one statistical study, only 3 percent of chronic alcoholics were found to have cirrhosis at autopsy. Even where liver damage is associated with alcoholism, it may be partly the result of the associated nutritional deficiencies rather than primarily a result of the alcohol, although recent data apparently do show that direct liver damage can result from excessive intake of ethanol in the absence of nutritional deficiency. Delirium tremens and the so-called withdrawal symptoms of alcoholism are best treated with thiamine and other B vitamins, and sleep. Thiamine deficiency produces nerve involvement and polyneuritis—and again, the consumption of alcohol may be only an indirect cause.

What conditions predispose or oppose an individual's becoming an alcoholic? There are some suggestive clues. Italians as a group consume a considerable amount of alcohol in the form of wine. They have about the same incidence of general neuroses as Americans, and yet have a much lower incidence of alcoholism. This apparent advantage is progressively lost in the families of Italians who have immigrated to the United States. It therefore seems to be related to cultural patterns, and probably lies in the differing attitudes toward the use of alcohol in the two countries. Studies comparing these factors not only between the United States and Italy but also in France, England, and other cultural and ethnic groups have produced a general picture of conditions favoring and opposing alcoholism.

In the typical case, the individual who avoids alcoholism contacts alcohol, particularly wine, early in life. Wine is a part of the daily diet, and the child may receive diluted wine along with the adults. He sees it in a family environment as a part of the meal, and no particular importance, positive or negative, is attached to it. By the time the child reaches adolescence he probably has consumed too much on some occasion. This might happen when the family has left the table and the child proceeds to consume the remainder of the wine. The obvious results follow: sickness and remorse. The parents take the recuperating child aside and tell him that any food can be consumed to the point of illness, and he has learned a lesson: overindulgence and drunkenness are childish, and as he becomes an adult he will learn not to do these foolish things. They also impress upon him that he must not drink to excess or he will disgrace the family. Similar patterns of early contact in the family circle, close family ties, use of wine as the common cultural or religious beverage, drinking of beverages of lower alcohol content primarily with meals, and drunkenness being shameful rather than amusing or condoned, seem to be common to groups such as the Italians, Chinese, and Jews,. who have a low incidence of alcoholism and yet consume alcoholic beverages.

Conditions favoring alcoholism include first experiences with alcohol later in life and viewing ability to "handle" large amounts of it as proof of adulthood or virility. Parental attitudes strongly against or strongly in favor of alcohol seem to favor alcoholism in the children. Drinking of strong spirits, and according to a recent study beer, rather than wine, favors alcoholism.

Wine has an undeservedly bad name as being the culprit for the lowest form of American alcoholic, the "wino." It has been determined that the "wino" drinks wine because it is the least expensive beverage for the amount of alcohol. In countries where other alcoholic beverages are cheaper, the drunk who is limited in cash does not turn to wine but to the cheapest form of alcohol. When the price is not limiting—that is, at the beginning of drinking bouts, or drinking by relatively well-to-do alcoholics—stronger spirits are commonly desired by the excessive, compulsive drinker.

Wine, and particularly table wine, seems to be much less likely to produce alcoholism than are most other alcoholic beverages. Table wines are a rather dilute source of alcohol.

Alcoholism has been defined as the daily consumption of a minimum of 135 milliliters of alcohol. Based upon this modest and perhaps questionable definition, an alcoholic would have to consume about a dozen 12-ounce cans of American beer every day. This would seem to be a rather uncomfortable and time-consuming method of maintaining status as an alcoholic. On the same basis, 135 milliliters of alcohol per day, the consumption of about one and a half bottles of table wine or one bottle of dessert wine every day would be required, as compared to just over half a pint of 100 proof spirits. Of course, the ethyl alcohol consumption of many heavy drinkers and alcoholics may be much higher than this minimum figure.

Most wines are properly consumed in association with a meal. The presence of other foods in the stomach delays absorption and lowers the level of alcohol in the blood attained with a given amount of alcohol. And of course, consumption with meals combats the additional effects of poor nutrition and resists alcoholism. The alcohol in wine is absorbed more slowly than alcohol in water alone at the same concentration.

The connoisseur's approach to wine is a strong deterrent to alcoholism. Fine wine provides a truly aesthetic experience to the connoisseur. He or she samples, evaluates, and enjoys the color, the odor, and the flavor. It is savored and not gulped down just for the alcoholic effect, but is valued as an adjunct to pleasant, sophisticated, adult dining and entertaining. The connoisseur enjoys wine's flavors and searches for the best quality, not the most alcoholic. A simple, well-made wine may be pleasing, but a harsh, coarse one will not be, regardless of their respective alcohol contents.

Summary. —Alcohol produces an inevitable sequence of effects on the human body and on behavior as its level increases in the blood stream. As with any physiologically active agent, the size and condition of the individual and the manner of administration of the dose affect the height and duration of the alcohol level in the blood. The effects of alcohol can be medically useful, and wine is often an especially advantageous form for such use.

Temperate consumers of alcoholic beverages tend to have greater longevity than abstainers, although heavy drinkers have the highest early mortality rate. Serious individual and social problems can result from excessive, compulsive, or addictive drinking of alcoholic beverages. Population groups with high levels of wine consumption tend to have a lower incidence of alcoholism than those who primarily consume other alcoholic beverages, for a number of reasons. Consumption of table wine of modest alcohol content along with food in family settings seems particularly healthful.

A quote from Julian Street's book *Wines* expresses our attitude: "Never let a drunkard choose your wine. You may be sure that he knows nothing about it. It is only sober people who know how to drink." And, from Fitzgerald's Rubaiyat of Omar Khayyam:

> Why, be this Juice the growth of God,
> Who dare
> Blaspheme the twisted tendril as a
> Snare?
> A blessing, we should use it, should
> We not?
> And if a curse—why, then, Who set
> It there?

SUPPLEMENTARY READING

This list has been selected, as far as possible, from books in print. Inclusion of a book does not indicate the authors' approval of its contents.

For current information in English, see as examples the following journals:

American Journal of Enology and Viticulture (Davis, California)
Australian Wine, Brewing and Spirit Review (Kensington, Victoria, Australia)
California Grape Grower (Fresno, California)
Harpers Wine and Spirit Gazette (London)
Vintage (New York)
Wine & Food (London)
Wine Institute Bulletin (San Francisco)
Wine, Spirit & Malt (Stellenbosch, South Africa)
Wine World (Van Nuys, California)
Wines & Vines (San Francisco)
Chapters of this book particularly supplemented are listed after each citation:

ADAMS, L. D.
   1960   The commonsense book of drinking. New York: McKay. xiv +210 pp.   *Chapters 19 and 20*
   1973   The wines of America. Boston: Houghton Mifflin. 465 pp.   *Chapters 17 and 18*

1975   The commonsense book of wine, 3rd ed. New York: McKay.   228 pp.   *Chapters 18 and 19*

ALLEN, H. W.

1932   The romance of wine. New York: Dutton.   264 pp.
    Chapters 1, 11, 13

1951   Natural red wines. London: Constable.   viii + 320 pp.
    Chapter 13

1952*a*   Sherry and port. London: Constable.   214 pp.
    Chapters 10 and 15

1952*b*   White wines and cognac. London: Constable.   278 pp.
    Chapters 11 and 13

1957   Good wine from Portugal. London: Sylvan Press.   59 + 4 pp.   *Chapter 15*

1961   A history of wine. London: Faber and Faber.   304 pp.
    Chapters 1, 13, 15

1964   The wines of Portugal. New York: McGraw-Hill. 192 pp.   *Chapter 15*

AMBROSI, H.

1976   Where the great German wines grow: A guide to the leading vineyards. New York: Hastings House.   xvi + 240 pp.
    Chapter 14

AMERINE, M. A.

1948   An application of "triangular" taste testing to wines. Wine Rev. 16(5):10-12.   *Chapter 19*

1954   Composition of wines: I. Organic constituents. Advances in Food Research 5:353–510.   *Chapter 7*

1955   The well-tempered wine bibber; 1955 Vintage Tour of the Los Angeles and San Francisco Branches of the Wine and Food Society, pp. 5-19. San Francisco: Grabhorn.
    Chapter 19

1958   Composition of wines: II. Inorganic constituents. Advances in Food Research 8:133–224.   *Chapter 7*

1959*a*   Chemists and the California wine industry. Am. J. Enol. Viticult. 10:124–159.   *Chapter 18*

1959*b*   The romance of Pan-American wines. Pan-American Med. Assn., San Francisco Chapter, Annual Bull. 1959: 24–27.
    Chapter 16

1962   Hilgard and California viticulture. Hilgardia 33(1):1–23.
    Chapter 18

1964*a*   Der Weinbau in Japan. Wein-Wissenschaft 19(5):225–231.   *Chapters 7 and 19*

1964*b*   Wine. Scientific American 211(2):46–56.   *Chapter 16*

AMERINE, M. A., H. W. BERG, AND W. V. CRUESS
  1973 The technology of wine making, 3rd ed. Westport, Conn.:
        Avi Pub. Co.   ix + 802 pp.   *Chapters 6–19*

AMERINE, M. A., AND M. A. JOSLYN
  1972 Table wines: The technology of their production, 2nd ed.,
        Berkeley and Los Angeles: University of California Press.
        xxi + 997 pp.   *Chapters 6, 8, 9, 18*

AMERINE, M. A., AND R. E. KUNKEE
  1968 Microbiology of wine making. Ann. Rev. Microbiol. 22:
        323–358.   *Chapter 4*

AMERINE, M. A., AND G. L. MARSH
  1962 Wine making at home. San Francisco: Wine Publications.
        31 pp.   *Chapter 7*

AMERINE, M. A., AND C. S. OUGH
  1964 The sensory evaluation of California wines. Lab. Practices
        13:712–716, 738.   *Chapter 19*
  1974 Wine and must analysis. New York: Wiley.   viii +
        121 pp.   *Chapter 7*

AMERINE, M. A., AND E. B. ROESSLER
  1952 Techniques and problems in the organoleptic examination
        of wines. Proc. Am. Soc. Enol. 1952:97–115.   *Chapter 19*
  1958 Field testing of grape maturity. Hilgardia 28(4):93–114.
                                                Chapter 3
  1976 Wines: their sensory evaluation. San Francisco: Freeman.
        xiv + 230 pp.   *Chapters 6 and 19*

AMERINE, M. A., E. B. ROESSLER, AND F. FILIPELLO
  1959 Modern sensory methods of evaluating wine. Hilgardia
        28:477–567.   *Chapters 6, 18, 19*

AMERINE, M. A., AND V. L. SINGLETON
  1971 A list of bibliographies and a selected list of publications
        that contain bibliographies on grapes, wines, and related
        subjects. Berkeley: Div. Agricultural Sciences, University
        of California.   39 pp.   *Chapters 1–20*

AMERINE, M. A., AND A. J. WINKLER
  1938 Angelica. Wines & Vines (19(9): 5, 24.   *Chapter 18*
  1944 Composition and quality of musts and wines of California
        grapes. Hilgardia 15:493–673.   *Chapters 3 and 18*
  1963a California wine grapes: Composition and quality of their
        musts and wines. Calif. Agri. Exp. Sta. Bull. 794.   83 pp.
                                            Chapters 2 and 18

1963*b* Grape varieties for wine production. Calif. Agri. Ext. Service Leaflet 154. 2 pp. *Chapter 18*

ANDRES, S. P.

1960 Die grossen Weine Deutschlands. Berlin: Im Verlag Ullstein. 199 pp. *Chapter 14*

ANONYMOUS PUBLICATIONS:

1947 Cognac et sa région, ses grandes eaux-de-vie. Bordeaux: Bordeaux et la Sud-Oeste. Éditions Delmas. 101 pp. *Chapter 11*

1958*a* Grape and wine industry of Mexico. Am. J. Enol. 9:92–93. *Chapter 16*

1958*b* Flavor research and food acceptance. New York: Reinhold. 391 pp. *Chapter 19*

1959 Produce better grapes for better wines. Calif. Agri. Ext. Service. 16 pp. *Chapter 3*

1961 Wine-producing in Yugoslavia. Belgrade: Federal Chamber of Foreign Trade. 64 pp. *Chapter 15*

1973 A survey of wine growing in South Africa 1972–73. Paarl: Public Relations Dept. of KWV. 56 pp. *Chapter 16*

1974 Alcohol and health, new knowledge; 2nd special report to the U.S. Congress. Rockville, Md.: National Institute on Alcohol Abuse and Alcoholism. xxii + 219 pp. *Chapter 20*

ANTONIO DE VEGA, L.

1958 Guía vinícola de España. Madrid: Editora Nacional. 3 + 318 pp. *Chapter 15*

ASH, C.

1952 Reminiscences of pre-Prohibition days. Proc. Am. Soc. Enol. 1952:39–44. *Chapter 18*

BAILEY, L. H.

1906 Sketch of the evolution of our native fruits, 2nd ed. New York: Macmillan. 472 pp. *Chapter 2*

BAKER, G. A.

1954 Organoleptic ratings and analytical data for wines analyzed into orthogonal factors. Food Research 19:575–580. *Chapter 19*

BAKER, G. A., AND M. A. AMERINE

1953 Organoleptic ratings of wines estimated from analytical data. Food Research 18:381–389. *Chapter 19*

BAKER, G. A., M. A. AMERINE, AND E. B. ROESSLER
1952 Theory and application of fractional blending systems. Hilgardia 21:383–409. *Chapters 10, 15, 18*

BALZER, R. L.
1964 The pleasures of wine. Indianapolis: Bobbs-Merrill. xiv + 329 pp. *Chapter 18*

BECK, F.
1964 The Fred Beck wine book. New York: Hill and Wang. xiii + 242 pp. *Chapters 17 and 18*

BENSON, C. T.
1959 The Canadian wine industry. Wines & Vines 40(9):23. *Chapter 17*

BENVEGNIN, L., E. CAPT, AND G. PIGUET
1951 Traité de vinification, 2nd ed. Lausanne: Librairie Payot. 583 pp. *Chapter 14*

BENWELL, W. S.
1961 Journey to wine in Victoria. Melbourne: Sir Isaac Pitman and Sons. 120 pp. *Chapter 16*

BERG, H. W.
1968 The South African wine industry: an evaluation. Wines & Vines 49(4):51–54. *Chapter 16*

BERG, H. W., F. FILIPELLO, E. HINREINER, AND A. D. WEBB
1955 Evaluation of thresholds and minimum difference concentrations for various constituents of wines: I. Water solutions of pure substances; II. Sweetness: The effect of ethyl alcohol, organic acids and tannin. Food Technol. 9:23–26, 138–140. *Chapter 19*

BERG, H. W., AND A. D. WEBB
1955 Terms used in tasting. Wines and Vines 36(7):25–28. *Chapter 6*

BERIDZE, G. I.
1965 Vino i kon'iake Gruzii. Tbilisi; Izdatel'stvo "Sahchota Sakartvelo." 360 pp. *Chapter 14*

BESPALOFF, A.
1975 Guide to inexpensive wines. New York: Simon and Schuster. 159 pp. *Chapter 19*

BIERMANN, B.
1971 Red wine in South Africa. Capetown: Buren. 158 pp. *Chapter 16*

BLAHA, J.
1952 Československá ampelografia. Bratislava: "Oráč." 361 pp.
Chapter 14

BOBADILLA, G. F. DE
1956 Viníferas jerezanas y de Andalucía Occidental. Madrid: Instituto Nacional de Investigaciones Agronómicas. 272 pp. *Chapter 15*

BODE, C.
1956 Wines of Italy. New York: McBride. 135 pp.
Chapter 15

BOSDARI, C. DE
1966 Wines of the Cape, 3rd ed. Capetown and Amsterdam: A. A. Balkema. 95 pp. *Chapter 16*

BROADBENT, J. M.
1973 Wine tasting: A practical handbook on tasting and tastings. London: Christie Wine Publications. viii + 60 pp.
Chapter 19

BRUNET, R.
1946 Dictionnaire d'oenologie et de viticulture. Paris: Éditions M. Ponsot. 534 pp. *Chapters 13–19*

BRUNI, B.
1964 Vini italiani portanti una denominazione di origine. Bologna: Edizioni Calderini. 255 pp. *Chapter 15*

BUNKER, H. J.
1961 Recent research on the yeasts. *In* D. J. D. Hockenhull (ed.), Progress in industrial microbiology 3:1–41. New York: Interscience. *Chapter 4*

CAROSSO, V. P.
1951 The California wine industry, 1830–1895: A study of the formative years. Berkeley and Los Angeles: University of California Press. 241 pp. *Chapter 18*

CHAFETZ, M. E., AND H. W. DEMONE, JR.
1962 Alcoholism and society. New York: Oxford University Press. 319 pp. *Chapter 20*

CHAMINADE, R.
1930 La production et le commerce des eaux-de-vie de vin. Paris: Librarie J.-B. Ballière et Fils. 157 pp. *Chapter 11*

CHAPPAZ, G.
1951 Le vignoble et le vin de Champagne. Paris: Louis Larmat. xvii + 414 pp. *Chapter 13*

CHARLEY, V. L. S.
1949   Principles and practices of cider making. London: Leonard
        Hill.   367 pp.   *Chapter 12*
CHEDEVILLE, C.
1945   Manuel d'oenologie. Tunis: Bascone et Muscat.   137 pp.
                                                  Chapter 16
CHROMAN, N.
1973   The treasury of American wines. New York: Rutledge/
        Crown.   256 pp.   *Chapters 17–18*
CHURCH, R. E.
1963   The American guide to wines. Chicago: Quadrangle Books.
        272 pp.   *Chapters 13–18*
CHURCHILL, C.
1961   A notebook for the wines of France. New York: Knopf.
        xv + 387 + xxviii pp.   *Chapter 13*
1964   The world of wines. New York: Macmillan.   xii +
        271 pp.   *Chapters 13–18*
COCKS, C., AND E. FERET
1969   Bordeaux et ses vins, classés par ordre de mérite, 12th ed.
        Bordeaux: Féret et Fils.   xviii + 1744 pp.
CONN, E. E., AND P. K. STUMPF
1972   Outlines of Biochemistry, 3rd ed. New York: Wiley.
        xii + 535 pp.   *Chapter 5*
CONSTANTINESCU, G.
1958   Raionarea viticulturii. Bucharest: Accademiei Republicii
        Populare Romîne.   153 pp.   *Chapter 14*
COOK, A. H.
1958   The chemistry and biology of yeast. New York: Academic
        Press.   763 pp.   *Chapter 4*
COOK, J. A.
1960   Vineyard fertilizers and cover crops. Calif. Agr. Ext. Ser-
        vice Leaflet 128.   2 pp.   *Chapter 3*
CORNELSSEN, F. A.
1970   Die deutschen Weine; ein Kursbuch für Geniesser. Stutt-
        gart-Degerloch: Seewald Verlag.   228 pp.   *Chapter 14*
COSMO, I.
1966   Guida viticola d'Italia. Treviso: Longo e Zoppelli.   244
        pp.   *Chapter 15*
COX, H.
1967   The wines of Australia. London: Hodder and Staughton.
        192 pp.   *Chapter 16*

CROFT-COOKE, R.
1956 Sherry. New York: Knopf.   210 pp.   *Chapter 15*
1957 Port. London: Putnam.   219 pp.   *Chapter 15*
1961 Madeira. London: Putnam.   224 pp.   *Chapter 15*

CSEPREGI, P.
1955 Szölöfajlárnk; ampelográfia. Budapest: Mezögazdasági
      Kiado.   386 pp.   *Chapter 14*

DALMASSO, G., AND V. TYNDALO
1957 Viticoltura e ampelografia dell'U.R.S.S. Atti Accad. Ital.
      Vite e Vino 9:446–548.   *Chapter 14*

DAVISON, A. E.
1971 Wine Institute sanitation guide for wineries, rev. ed. San
      Francisco: Wine Institute.   94 pp.   *Chapter 6*

DELAMAIN, R.
1935 Histoire de Cognac. Paris: Librairie Stock.   140 pp.
      Chapter 11

DETTORI, R. G.
1953 Italian wines and liqueurs. Rome: Federazione Italiana
      Produttori ed Esportatori di Vini, Liquori ed Affini.
      158 pp.   *Chapter 15*

DION, R.
1959 Histoire de la vigne et du vin en France des origines au
      XIX e siécle. Paris: (Author)   xii + 768 pp.
      Chapters 1 and 13

DUBOS, R. J.
1950 Louis Pasteur, free lance of science. Boston: Little, Brown.
      418 pp.   *Chapters 1 and 5*

1960 Pasteur and modern science. New York: Doubleday.
      195 pp.   *Chapters 1 and 5*

EAKIN, J. H., JR., AND D. L. ACE
1970 Winemaking as a hobby. State College, Pa.: Pennsylvania
      State University.   63 pp.   *Chapters 7 and 8*

EVANS, L. (compiler)
1973 Australia and New Zealand complete book of wine. Sydney:
      Paul Hamlyn.   528 pp.   *Chapter 16*

FERRÉ, L.
1958 Traité d'oenologie bourguignonne. Paris: Institut Nation-
      al des Appellations d'Origine des Vins et Eaux-de-Vie.
      viii + 303 pp.   *Chapters 7, 8, 13*

FORBES, P.
1967   Champagne: the wine, the land and the people. London: Victor Gollancz.   492 pp.   *Chapter 13*

FORNACHON, J. C. M.
1943   Bacterial spoilage of fortified wines. Adelaide: Australian Wine Board.   126 pp. Reprinted 1969.   *Chapter 4*

FREDERICKSEN, P.
1947   The authentic Haraszthy story. Wines & Vines 28(6): 25–26, 42: (7):15–16, 30; (8):17–18, 37–38; (9):17–18, 34; (11):21–22, 41–42.   *Chapter 18*

FROLOV-BAGREEV, A. M.
1946–1965 Ampelografia S.S.S.R. Moscow: Gos. Pishchepromizdat.   8 vols.   *Chapter 14*

GALHANO, A. B.
1951   A região dos vinhos verdes. Porto: Comissão de Viticultura da Região dos Vinhos Verdes. (Also published in French as Le vin "verde.")   37 pp.   *Chapter 15*

GALLAY, R., AND L. BENVEGNIN
1950   Les enseignements d'une dégustation. Rev. Romande d'Agric., Vitic. Arbor. 6:38–39.   *Chapter 19*

GAUBERT, I.
1946   Armagnac, terre Gasconne. Paris: Édition Havas.   82 pp.   *Chapter 11*

GEORGIEV, I.
1949   Vinarstvo. Sofia: Zemizdat.   xvi + 456 pp.   *Chapters 7, 8, 13*

GOLDSCHMIDT, E.
1951   Deutschlands Weinbauorte und Weinbergslagen. 6th ed. Mainz: Verlag der Deutschen Wein-Zeitung.   263 pp.   *Chapter 14*

GONZALES GORDON, M. M.
1972   Sherry: the noble wine. London: Cassell.   xv + 237 pp.   *Chapters 10 and 15*

GOT, N.
1953   La dégustation des vins. Beziers: Sodiep.   157 pp.   *Chapter 19*

1963   Le livre de l'amateur de vins. Perpignan: En Vente Chez l'Auteur.   357 pp.   *Chapters 14, 15, 19*

GROSSMAN, H. J.
1974   Grossman's guide to wines, spirits and beers, 5th ed. New York: Scribner.   viii + 564 pp.   *Chapters 11–18*

HALASZ, Z.
1962 Hungarian wine through the ages. Budapest: Corvina Press. 186 pp. *Chapter 14*

HALLGARTEN, S. F.
1965 Rhineland, wineland. Manchester: Withy Grove Press. xiv + 210 pp. *Chapter 14*
1970 Alsace and its wine gardens, 2nd ed. London: Wine and Spirit Publications. 183 pp. *Chapter 13*

HANNUM, H., AND R. S. BLUMBERG
1971 The fine wines of California. New York: Doubleday. 311 pp. *Chapters 18 and 19*

HARASZTHY, A.
1862 Grape culture, wines and wine-making, with notes upon horticulture. New York: Harper; reprinted 1973. xxx + 420 pp. *Chapter 18*

HARTMANN, G.
1955 Cognac, Armagnac, Weinbrand. Berlin: Carl Knoppke Grüner Verlag and Vertrieb. 124 pp. *Chapter 11*

HEALY, M.
1963 Stay me with flagons. London: Michael Joseph. 262 pp. *Chapter 13*

HEDRICK, U. P.
1908 The grapes of New York; 15th Annual Report, New York State Dept. of Agriculture, part II. Albany: State Printer J. B. Lyon. 564 pp. *Chapters 2 and 17*
1945 Grapes and wines from home vineyards. New York: Oxford University Press. 326 pp. *Chapters 2, 3, 7, 12, 17*

HELIODORO VALLE, R.
1958 The history of wine in Mexico. Am. J. Enol. 9:146–154. *Chapter 16*

HINREINER, E., F. FILIPELLO, H. W. BERG, AND A. D. WEBB
1955 Evaluation of thresholds and minimum difference concentrations for various constituents of wines: IV. Detectable differences in wines. Food Technol. 9:489–490. *Chapter 19*

HINREINER, E., F. FILIPELLO, A. D. WEBB, AND H. W. BERG
1955 Evaluation of thresholds and minimum difference concentrations for various constituents of wines. III. Ethyl alcohol, glycerol and acidity in aqueous solution. Food Technol. 9: 351–353. *Chapter 19*

HYAMS, E. S.
1965   Dionysus: a social history of the wine vine. New York: Macmillan.   381 pp.   *Chapters 1, 13, 15*

INGRAM, M.
1955   An introduction to the biology of yeast. New York: Pitman. 273 pp.   *Chapter 4*

ISNARD, H.
1951–1954 La vigne en Algérie. Gap: Ophrys.   2 vols.   *Chapter 16*

JACKSON, G. H.
1928   The medicinal value of French brandy. Montreal: Thérien Frères.   315 pp.   *Chapter 11*

JACOBY, O. F.
1948   Developing the vermouth formula. Wines & Vines 29 (4):73–75.   *Chapter 12*

JACQUELIN, L., AND R. POULAIN
1962   The wines and vineyards of France. New York: Putnam. 416 pp.   *Chapter 13*

JAMES, W.
1966   Wine in Australia, 4th ed. Melbourne: Georgian House. 6 + 148 pp.   *Chapter 16*

JEFFS, J.
1970   Sherry, 2nd ed. London: Faber and Faber.   283 pp.   *Chapter 15*
1971   The wines of Europe. London: Faber and Faber.   524 pp.   *Chapters 13–15*

JOHNSON, H.
1968   Wine. London: Sphere.   347 pp.   *Chapters 13, 14, 15*
1971   The world atlas of wine. New York: Simon and Schuster. 272 pp.   *Chapters 13–18*

JOSLYN, M. A., AND M. A. AMERINE
1941a Commercial production of dessert wines. Calif. Agi. Exp. Sta. Bull. 651.   186 pp.   *Chapters 10, 12, 15, 18*
1941b Commercial production of brandies. Calif. Agr. Exp. Sta. Bull. 652.   80 pp.   *Chapters 11 and 18*
1964   Dessert, appetizer and related flavored wines; the technology of their production. Berkeley: Division of Agricultural Sciences.   xii + 483 pp.
    Chapters 6, 7, 10, 12, 18, 19

KASIMATIS, A. N., AND L. A. LIDER
1962   Grape rootstock varieties. Davis: Calif. Agr. Ext. Service, AXT 47.   25 pp.   *Chapter 2*

KELLER, D. J.
1953 Pfalzwein Almanach. Neustadt a.d. Weinstrasse: Neustadter Druckerei. xvi + 448 pp. *Chapter 14*

KITTEL, J. B., AND BREIDER, H.
1958 Das Buch vom Frankenweine, Würzburg: Universitätsdruckerei H. Stürz. 207 pp. *Chapter 14*

KLENK, E.
1960 Die Weinbeurteilung nach Farbe, Klarheit, Geruch und Geschmack des Weines. Stuttgart: Eugen Ulmer. 95 pp. *Chapter 19*

KRAEMER, A.
1961 Im Lande des Bocksbeutels. 3rd ed. Würzburg: Pius Halbig. 232 pp. *Chapter 14*

KUNKEE, R. E., AND M. A. AMERINE
1970 Yeasts in winemaking. *In* A. H. Rose and J. S. Harrison, The yeasts 3:5–71. New York: Academic Press. *Chapter 4*

LACHMAN, H.
1903 A monograph on the manufacture of wines in California. U.S. Dept. Agr. Bur. Chem. Bull. 72:25–40. *Chapter 18*

LAFFORGUE, G.
1947 Le vignoble Girondin. Paris: Louis Larmat. xi + 319 pp. *Chapter 13*

LAFON, R., J. LAFON, AND P. COUILLAUD
1973 Le Cognac: sa distillation, 5th ed. Paris: J.-B. Baillière et Fils. 285 pp. *Chapter 11*

LANGENBACH, A.
1962 German wines and vines. London: Vista Books. 190 pp. *Chapter 14*

LARREA REDONDO, A.
1957 Arte y ciencia de los vinos españoles. Madrid: Siler. 135 + 2 pp. *Chapter 15*

LAYTON, T. A.
1961 Wines of Italy. London: Harper Trade Journals. xi + 221 pp. *Chapter 15*

LEAKE, C. E., AND M. SILVERMAN
1966 Alcoholic beverages in clinical medicine. Chicago: Year Book Medical Publishers. 160 pp. *Chapter 20*

LEGGETT, H. B.
1939 The early history of the wine industry in California. M.A. thesis, University of California, Berkeley. 124 pp. *Chapter 18*

LEIPOLDT, C. L.
1974 Three hundred years of Cape wine, 2nd ed. Capetown: Tafelberg. 218 pp. *Chapter 16*
LEÓN, V. E.
1947 Uvas y vinos de Chile. Santiago: Sindicato Nacional Vitivinícola. 340 pp. *Chapter 16*
LEONHARDT, G.
1962 Das Weinbuch. Leipzig: Fachbuchverlag. 418 pp. *Chapter 14*
LICHINE, A.
1974 New encyclopedia of wines and spirits, 2nd ed. New York: Knopf. xii + 716 pp. *Chapters 1–19*
1969 The wines of France, 7th ed. New York: Knopf. x + 310 pp. *Chapter 13*
LIDER, L.A.
1958 Phylloxera-resistant grape rootstocks for the coastal valleys of California. Hilgardia 27:287–318. *Chapter 2*
1960 Vineyard trials in California with nematode-resistant grape rootstocks. Hilgardia 30:123–152. *Chapter 2*
1963 Field budding and care of the budded grapevine. Calif. Agr. Ext. Service Leaflet 153. 2 pp. *Chapter 3*
LODDER, J.
1970 The yeasts. Amsterdam: North-Holland. 1385 pp. *Chapter 4*
LOLLI, G.
1960 Social drinking. Cleveland: World. 317 pp. *Chapter 20*
LOOMIS, N. H.
1963 Growing American bunch grapes. U.S. Dept. Agr. Farmers' Bull. 2123. 22 pp. *Chapter 3*
LUCIA, S. P.
1954 Wine as food and medicine. New York: Blakiston. 149 pp. *Chapter 20*
1963a Alcohol and civilization. New York: McGraw-Hill. 416 pp. *Chapter 20*
1963b A history of wine as therapy. Philadelphia: Lippincott. xiii + 234 pp. *Chapters 1 and 20*
MAGISTOCCHI, G.
1955 Tratado de enología adaptado a la República Argentina. Buenos Aires: Ed. El Ateneo. 765 pp. *Chapter 16*

MARESCALCHI, A.
1974 La degustazione e l'apprezzamento dei vini, 5th ed. Casale Monferrato: Case Editrice Fratelli Marescalchi. 200 pp.
Chapter 19

MARESCALCHI, C.
1965 Manuale dell'enologo, 13th ed. Casale Monferrato: Casa Editrice Fratelli Marescalchi. 700 pp.
Chapters 8, 12, 15

MARRISON, L. W.
1973 Wines and spirits. 3rd ed. London: Penguin. xii + 335 pp.
Chapter 17

MARTEAU, G.
1953 Recherche de la qualité par l'examen organoleptique des vins. Prog. Agr. Vitic. 140:281–289, 310–313. *Chapter 19*

MASSEE, W. E.
1961a Massee's wine handbook. New York: Doubleday. 217 pp.
Chapters 13–18
1961b Wines and spirits: A complete buying guide. New York: McGraw-Hill. 427 pp.
Chapters 11, 13–18

MAVEROFF PIAGGIO, A.
1949 Enología. Mendoza: J. Best. 511 pp. *Chapter 16*

McCARTHY, R. G.
1959 Drinking and intoxication: Selected readings in social attitudes and controls. New Haven: Yale Center of Alcohol Studies. 455 pp. *Chapter 20*

McCARTHY, R. G., AND E. M. DOUGLASS
1949 Alcohol and social responsibility: A new educational approach. New York: Crowell. 304 pp. *Chapter 20*

McCORD, W., AND J. McCORD
1960 Origins of alcoholism. Stanford, Calif.: Stanford University Press. 193 pp. *Chapter 20*

MELVILLE, I.
1976 Guide to California wines. (revised by Jefferson Morgan). 5th ed. San Carlos, Calif.: Nourse Publishing Co. xiv + 237 pp. *Chapter 18*

MENSIO, G.
1957 Manuale sull'assaggio e l'apprezzamento dei vini. Asti: Ordine Nazionale degli Assaggiatori di Vino. 55 pp.
Chapter 19

MORGAN, J.
  1976   Adventures in the wine country. San Francisco: Chronicle
         Books.   128 pp.   *Chapter 18*
MUNSON, T. V.
  1909   Foundations of American grape culture. New York:
         Orange Judd.   252 pp.   *Chapters 15 and 17*
NAVAS ROMANO, E.
  1950   La bodega moderna, 2nd ed. Barcelona: Editorial Gustavo
         Gili.   399 pp.   *Chapter 15*
NEILANDS, J. B., AND P. K. STUMPF
  1958   Outlines of enzyme chemistry. 2d ed. New York: Wiley.
         411 pp.   *Chapter 5*
NELSON, K. E., AND M. A. AMERINE
  1957   The use of *Botrytis cinerea* Pers. in the production of sweet
         table wines. Hilgardia 26(12):521–563.
                                     Chapters 3, 13, 15, 18
OLMO, H. P.
  1948   Ruby Cabernet and Emerald Riesling, two new table-wine
         grape varieties. Calif. Agr. Exp. Sta. Bull. 704.   12 pp.
                                         Chapters 2 and 18
OLMO, H. P., AND A. KOYAMA
  1962a Niabell and Early Niabell, new tetraploid varieties of the
         Concord type. Calif. Agr. Exp. St. Bull. 790.   10 pp.
                                                  Chapter 2
  1962b Rubired and Royalty, new grape varieties for color, con-
         centrate, and port wine. Calif. Agr. Exp. Sta. Bull. 789.
         13 pp.   *Chapters 2 and 18*
OPPERMAN, D. J. (ed.)
  1968   Spirit of the vine. Capetown: Human and Rousseau.
         360 pp.   *Chapter 16*
ORDISH, G.
  1972   The great wine blight. New York: Scribner.   237 pp.
                                          Chapters 1 and 3
OUGH, C. S., AND M. A. AMERINE
  1963   Regional, varietal, and type influences on the degree Brix
         and alcohol relationship of grape musts and wines. Hil-
         gardia 34(14):585–600.   *Chapters 2 and 3*
  1966   Effects of temperature on wine making. Calif. Agr. Exp.
         Sta. Bull. 827.   36 pp.   *Chapters 5–8*
PACOTTET, P., AND L. GUITTONNEAU
  1926   Eaux-de-vie et vinaigres. Paris: Librairie J.-B. Baillière et
         Fils.   480 pp.   *Chapter 11*

1930 Vins de Champagne et vins mousseux. Paris: Librairie J.-B. Baillière et Fils.   412 pp.   *Chapters 9, 13, 18*

PENINOU, E., AND S. GREENLEAF
1954*a* Wine making in California: I. How wine is made: II. From the Missions to 1894. San Francisco: Peregrine Press.   35 pp.   *Chapter 18*
1954*b* Wine making in California. III. The California Wine Association. San Francisco: The Porpoise Bookshop.   36 + 6 pp.   *Chapter 18*
1967 A directory of California wine growers and wine makers in 1860. Berkeley: Tamalpais Press.   vii + 84 pp.   *Chapter 18*

PENNING-ROWSELL, E.
1973 The wines of Bordeaux, 3rd ed. London: Penguin.   573 pp.   *Chapter 13*

PESQUIDOUX, J. DE, E. JANNEAU, C. SAMARAN, L. MAZARET, J. LASCOURREGES, AND DE RAQUINE
1937 L'Armagnac. Condom, France: A Bosquet et Fils.   101 pp.   *Chapter 11*

PESTEL, H.
1959 Les vins et eaux-de-vie à appellations d'origine contrôlées en France. Mâcon: Imprimerie Buguet-Comptour.   44 pp.   *Chapter 11*

PEYER, E, AND W. EGGENBERGER
1965 Weinbuch. 5th ed. Zurich: Verlag Schweizerischer Wirteverein.   235 pp.   *Chapter 14*

PEYRONNET, F. R.
1950 Le vignoble nord-africain. Paris: J. Peyronnet.   357 pp.   *Chapter 16*

PILONE, F. J.
1954 Production of vermouth. Am. J. Enol. 5:30–46.   *Chapter 12*

PITTMAN, D. J., AND C. R. SNYDER
1962 Society, culture and drinking patterns. New York: Wiley.   616 pp.   *Chapter 20*

PRESCOTT, S. C., AND C. G. DUNN
1959 Industrial microbiology. New York: McGraw-Hill.   945 pp.   *Chapter 5*

PUISAIS, J., AND R. L. CHABANON
1974 Initiation into the art of wine tasting. Madison, Wisc.: Interpublish.   95 pp.   *Chapter 19*

PULS, E.
1939 Die Weinkostprobe. Prufung und Beurteilung von Wein. Neustadt a. d. Weinstrasse: D. Meininger. 24 pp.
Chapter 19
RAINBIRD, G. M.
1966 Sherry and the wines of Spain. New York: McGraw-Hill. 224 + 6 pp. *Chapter 15*
RAINBOW, C.
1961 The biochemistry of the Acetobacters. *In* D. J. D. Hockenhull (ed.), Progress in industrial microbiology 3: 45–70. New York: Interscience. *Chapter 4*
RAY, C.
1966 The wines of Italy. New York: McGraw-Hill. 192 pp.
Chapter 15
RIBÉREAU-GAYON, J., AND E. PEYNAUD
1960–1961 Traité de oenologie. Paris: Librairie Polytechnique Ch. Béranger. Vol. I. Maturation du raisin, fermentation alcoolique, vinification. xl + 756 pp.
Vol. II. Composition, transformations et traitements des vins. xxviii + 1065 pp. *Chapters 4, 7–9, 19*
ROBINSON, W. B.
1963 Homemade wine. Cornell University Extension Bulletin 1119. 11 pp. *Chapters 7 and 8*
RODIER, C.
1948 Le vin de Bourgogne, 3rd ed. Dijon: Louis Damidot. xv + 350 pp. *Chapter 13*
ROGER, J.-R.
1960 The wines of Bordeaux. New York: Dutton. 166 pp.
Chapter 13
ROSE, A. H.
1961 Industrial microbiology. Washington, D.C.: Butterworth. 286 pp. *Chapter 5*
ROUECHE, B.
1960 The neutral spirit: A portrait of alcohol. Boston: Little, Brown. 151 pp. *Chapter 20*
SCHELLENBERG, A., AND E. PEYER
1951 Weinbuch für die schweizer Wirte. 3rd ed. Zürich: Schweizerischen Wirteverein. 204 pp. *Chapter 14*
SCHOONMAKER, F.
1956 The wines of Germany. New York: Hastings House. 152 pp. *Chapter 14*

1973   Encyclopedia of wine, 5th ed. New York: Hastings House.
       vi + 454 pp.   *Chapter 1–19*

SCHOONMAKER, F., AND T. MARVEL
1941   American wines. New York: Duell, Sloan and Pearce.
       312 pp.   *Chapters 17 and 18*

SCHULTZ, H. B., A. J. WINKLER, AND R. J. WEAVER
1962   Preventing spring frost damage in vineyards. Calif. Agr.
       Ext. Service Leaflet 139.   7 pp.   *Chapter 3*

SELTMAN, C.
1957   Wine in the ancient world. London: Routledge & Kegan
       Paul.   xvi + 196 pp.   *Chapter 1*

SHAND, P. M.
1929   A book of other wines than French. New York: Knopf.
       162 pp.   *Chapters 14–16*
1964   A book of French wines (rev. and ed. by Cyril Ray).
       London: Penguin.   306 pp.   *Chapter 13*

SIMON, A. L.
1934   Champagne. London: Constable.   140 pp.   *Chapter 9*
1957   The noble grapes and the great wines of France. New York:
       McGraw-Hill.   xi + 180 + 8 pp.   *Chapter 13*
1961   Wines and Spirits: the connoisseur's textbook. London:
       Charles Skilton.   194 + 6 pp.   *Chapters 7–10, 13–15*
1962   Champagne. New York: McGraw-Hill.   224 pp.
                                                 Chapter 13
1963   A dictionary of wines, spirits and liqueurs. New York:
       Citadel Press.   190 pp.   *Chapters 6, 11, 13–19*
1967   The wines, vineyards and vignerons of Australia. London:
       Paul Hamlyn.   xiii + 194 pp.   *Chapter 16*

SIMON, A. L., AND S. F. HALLGARTEN
1963   The great wines of Germany and its famed vineyards.
       New York: McGraw-Hill.   191 pp.   *Chapter 14*

SINGLETON, V. L.
1962   Aging of wines and other spiritous products: Acceleration
       by physical treatments. Hilgardia 32:319–392.
                                          Chapters 7 and 10
1972   Effects on red wine quality of removing juice before fer-
       mentation to simulate variation in berry size. Amer. J.
       Enol. Viticult. 23:106–113.   *Chapters 3, 7, 8*
1974   Some aspects of the wooden container as a factor in wine
       maturation. Adv. Chem. 137:254–277. *Chapters 7 and 11*

SINGLETON, V. L., AND D. E. DRAPER
1961   Wood chips and wine treatment: The nature of aqueous
       alcohol extracts. Am. J. Enol. Viticult. 12:152–158.
                                                   Chapter 10
SINGLETON, V. L., AND P. ESAU
1969   Phenolic substances in grapes and wine, and their signifi-
       cance. New York: Academic Press.   282 pp.
                                              Chapters 2–10
SMITH, L. M., AND E. M. STAFFORD
1955   Grape pests in California. Calif. Agr. Exp. Sta. Circular
       445.   63 pp.   *Chapter 3*
SONNEMAN, H. O.
1952   Ohio State wines: their history and production. Proc. Am.
       Soc. Enol. 1952:17–22.   *Chapter 17*
STILLMAN, J. S.
1955   Fruit and berry wine production in California. Am. J. Enol.
       6:32–35.   *Chapter 12*
STORM, J.
1962   An invitation to wines. New York: Simon and Schuster.
       xii + 201 pp.   *Chapters 13–18*
STREET, J.
1961   Wines, 3rd ed. New York: Knopf.   243 pp.
                                         Chapters 13–18, 20
THERON, C. J., AND NIEHAUS, C. J. G.
1948   Wine making, 3rd ed. Union South Africa Dept. Agr. Bull.
       191.   98 pp.   *Chapter 16*
THOMPSON, B. (ed.)
1973   California wine. Menlo Park, Calif.: Lane.   244 pp.
                                                Chapter 18
THUDICHUM, J. L. W., AND A. DUPRÉ
1872   A treatise on the origin, nature, and varieties of wine.
       London: Macmillan.   xvi + 760 pp. *Chapters 6, 13–15*
TROOST, G.
1961   Die Technologie des Weines. 3rd ed. Stuttgart: Eugen
       Ulmer.   702 pp.   *Chapter 14*
TROOST, G., AND E. WANNER
1955   Weinprobe. Weinansprache. 3rd ed. Frankfurt-Main:
       Verlag Sigurd Horn.   63 pp.   *Chapter 19*
UNDERKOFLER, L. A., AND R. J. HICKEN
1954   Industrial fermentations, vol. I. New York: Chemical
       Publishing Co.   565 pp.   *Chapter 5*
U.S. INTERNAL REVENUE SERVICE
1954   Rectification of spirits and wines; Part 235 of Title 26

(1954), Code of Federal Regulations, IRS Publ. 167. Washington, D.C.: U.S. Govt. Printing Office. 70 pp.
Chapter 11

1961 Regulations under the Federal Alcohol Administration Act; Title 27 (1954), Code of Federal Regulations, IRS Publ. 449. Washington, D.C.: U.S. Govt. Printing Office. 70 pp. *Chapter 6*

1962 Wine, Part 240 of Title 26 (1961), Code of Federal Regulations, IRS Publ. 146. Washington, D.C.: U.S. Govt. Printing Office. 114 pp. *Chapters 6–12*

VALAER, P.
1950 The wines of the world. New York: Abelard Press. 576 pp. *Chapter 12*

VAUGHN, R. H.
1955 Bacterial spoilage of wines with special reference to California conditions. Advances Food Research 6:67–108. New York: Academic Press. *Chapter 4*

WAGNER, P. M.
1937 Wine grapes: their selection, cultivation, and enjoyment. New York: Harcourt, Brace. 298 pp. *Chapter 2*

1956 American wines and wine-making. New York: Knopf. 246 pp. *Chapters 7–9, 12, 17*

1965 A wine-grower's guide, rev. ed. New York: Knopf. xii + 224 pp. *Chapters 2, 3, 17*

1976 Grapes into wine; a guide to winemaking in America. New York: Knopf. 320 pp. *Chapters 1, 17, 18*

WAIT, F. E.
1889 Wines and vines of California. San Francisco: Bancroft; reprinted 1974. 215 pp. *Chapters 1 and 18*

WASHBURNE, C.
1961 Primitive drinking. New York: College and University Press. 282 pp. *Chapter 20*

WAUGH, A.
1959 In praise of wine and certain noble spirits. New York: William Sloane Associates. 304 pp.
Chapters 11, 13–16, 19

WEAVER, R. J., AND S. B. McCUNE
1961 Effect of gibberellin on vine behavior and crop production in seeded and seedless *Vitis vinifera*. Hilgardia 30(15): 425–444. *Chapter 3*

WEBB, A. D.
1959 The Australian wine industry. Wines & Vines 40(7)29–30. *Chapter 16*

1974 Chemistry of winemaking. Advances in Chemistry 137. Washington, D.C.: American Chemical Society. viii + 311 pp. *Chapter 2–12*

WILHELM, C. F.
1956 In- und Auslandsweine; ABC der internationalen Weinkarte. Berlin: C. Knoppke Gruner Verlag. 188 pp.
Chapters 13–15

WILLIAMS, R. J.
1959 Alcoholism: The nutritional approach. Austin: University of Texas Press. 118 pp. *Chapter 20*

WINKLER, A. J.
1959a Pruning grapevines. Calif. Agr. Exp. Sta. Circular 477. 11 pp. *Chapter 3*
1959b Spacing and training grapevines. Calif. Agr. Ext. Service Leaflet 111. 2 pp. *chapter 3*

WINKLER, A. J., AND M. A. AMERINE
1937 What climate does. Wine rev. 5(6):9–11; (7):9–11, 16.
Chapters 3 and 18

WINKLER, A. J., J. A. COOK, W. M. KLIEWER, AND L. A. LIDER
1974 General viticulture, 2nd ed. Berkeley and Los Angeles: University of California Press. 710 pp.
Chapters 2, 3, 18

WINKLER, A. J., AND A. N. KASIMATIS
1959 Supports for grapevines. Calif. Agr. Ext. Service Leaflet 119. 2 pp. *Chapter 3*

WOSCHEK, H.-G.
1970 Der deutsche Weinführer. Munich: Moderne Verlag. 302 pp. *Chapter 14*

YANG, H. Y.
1953 Fruit wines: Requisites for successful fermentation. J. Agr. Food Chem. 1:331–333. *Chapter 12*

YOKOTSUKA, I.
1955 The grape growing and wine industry of Japan. Am. J. Enol. 6:16–22. *Chapter 16*

YOUNGER, W. A.
1966 Gods, men, and wine. Cleveland: World. 516 pp.
Chapter 1

YOXALL, H. W.
1970 The International Wine and Food Society's guide to the wines of Burgundy. New York: Stein and Day. 191 pp.
Chapter 13

INDEX

abboccato, 255
accessory products, 191, 199. *See also*
  byproducts
acetaldehyde, 70–71, 91, 99–100,
  168, 170, 175, 176, 177, 181, 247,
  277, 301, 329; acetal, 175; content
  of sherry, 170, 310
acetic acid (acetification, vinegar, volatile acidity), 16, 22, 60–61, 71, 91,
  106, 127, 175, 177, 191, 244, 247,
  272, 290, 306, 311, 312. See also
  Acetobacter; bacteria; vinegar; volatile acidity
Acetobacter (acetic acid bacteria, acetic
  spoilage), 23, 60, 61, 106, 165, 170,
  191. *See also* acetic acid
acidity: determination of, 91; in
  grapes, 40–41, 48–51, 72, 73, 121,
  125, 126, 167, 213, 224, 226, 233,
  240, 245, 251, 252, 253, 255, 265,
  137, 138, 167, 233; lack of, 62, 160,
  240, 245, 252, 252, 253, 255, 265,
  282, 285, 306, 307, 308; reduction
  of, 48–51, 72–73, 197, 199, 204,
  224, 240, 279; taste (sourness, tartness), 62, 205, 233, 307–308, 310,
  311. *See also* amelioration; malo-
  lactic; pH; various acids and wine
  types; weather

acreage, 38, 283; of other countries,
  214, 234, 236, 245, 252, 258, 260–
  261, 267; United States, 38, 44
  (fig.), 297
aeration, 61, 68, 69, 104, 114, 131,
  140, 147, 148, 305, 306. *See also*
  acetaldehyde; oxidation; oxygen
aesthetics, 14, 74, 200, 298–300, 301,
  334
Africa, 39, 48, 263–267, 272
Agawan, 31
aging, 20, 105–110, 116, 130–131,
  133, 207, 210, 214, 244, 249, 255,
  289, 299, 300, 301, 307; brandy,
  181–182, 185, 187; cellars, 123,
  141 (fig.), 152, 169 (fig.), changes
  during, 108, 111, 249–250, 304,
  305; dessert wines, 86, 152, 158–
  159, 161, 165, 168, 169 (fig.), 241;
  effect of humidity, 108, 171; home,
  110, 116, 123, 131, 163; quick, 159,
  161, 164, 166; rosé, 125; sherry,
  168, 169 (fig.), 170, 247, 248 (fig.),
  249–250; sparkling wine, 140, 141
  (fig.), 143, 144, 146, 147; table
  wine, 122–124, 125, 130–131, 211,
  245, 268, 316; temperature for,
  123; vermouth, 195; wood, 122,
  130–131, 211. *See also* bottle,

357